The Development of Language and Reading in Young Children

Second Edition

Merrill Comprehensive Reading Program

The Development of Language and Reading in Young Children
Second Edition

Susanna Pflaum-Connor

*The University of Illinois
at Chicago Circle*

Charles E. Merrill Publishing Company
A Bell & Howell Company
Columbus, Ohio 43216

Published by Charles E. Merrill Publishing Company
A Bell and Howell Company
Columbus, Ohio 43216

This book was set in English and Windsor.
The production editor was Jan Hall.
The cover was prepared by Will Chenoweth.

Photographs: *Julie Estadt,* cover; *Celia Drake,* pages 1, 23; *Joan Bergstrom,* pages 3, 45, 71, 109, 111, 167, 195; *Bill Stoll,* page 131.

Library of Congress Catalog Card Number: 77-93194

International Standard Book Number: 0-675-08392-3

Printed in the United States of America

1 2 3 4 5 6 7 8 9 10 /85 84 83 82 81 80 79 78

Other titles in *Merrill Comprehensive Reading Program*
ARTHUR HEILMAN, *Consulting Editor*

Preface

Teachers of children between the ages of three and seven need to understand how language is acquired and how language is used as literacy begins. This volume is concerned with language acquisition, its development, pre-reading experiences, and the beginning of reading instruction. Language acquisition and the development of reading and writing skills are important objectives in the schooling of young children. With both preservice and inservice teachers in mind, the discussion of language does not require previous linguistic study. Theory of language and reading and critical research findings provide important background information for teachers to plan and execute instruction sensibly. This volume suggests directions for the application of research and theory by including techniques for teaching that are intended to serve as models for instruction.

The first part of the book is about language. The four chapters within this part (1) introduce the theory of language development and how adult language influences the child's acquisition; (2) describe what child language is like at various points during acquisition and development from the beginnings in infancy into the early school years; (3) discuss questions on language of minority groups in the United States—both linguistic and racial minority groups; and (4) apply content from previous chapters to programmatic design in preschool education.

The second part of the book is about reading. The four chapters here (1) describe the reading process and relate language development to the requirements reading makes on young children; (2) report on the preparation of children for reading during the preschool years; (3) describe extant reading programs for beginning literacy; and (4) apply findings from previous chapters to programmatic design in the teaching of reading. Thus, there are two parallel "little books" within this volume. However, the parallel structure masks the underlying integration of language with reading on which the entire volume is based.

Changes from the first edition of the book are extensive. Retained material has been updated, and major additions have been made to discussion of language acquisition and development (chapter 2), in reports on attitudes toward nonstandard dialect (chapter 3), on bilingualism (chapter 3), on the reading process (chapter 5), on the question of dialect interference in learning to read (chapter 5) and in the assessment of read-ind readiness (chapter 6). Some of the changes were made at the sugges-tions of other students and colleagues, while others were due to recent development in the field and the author's classroom observations. Furthermore, there have been innumerable attempts to clarify organiza-tion in the rearrangement of material. All chapters conclude with selected activities which, for the most part, are designed to encourage the reader to apply concepts to new situations not discussed directly in the chapters.

In a small book of this nature, it is not possible to pursue important and complex matters as thoroughly as one might wish. It is hoped that the content and the bibliographies will lead the reader to further study and to enrich, exploratory classroom practice. Definitive statements on difficult educational subjects are seldom achieved, and I make no claim that this book provides any. Instead, I hope that the book will serve as a stimulator for future endeavor by those who teach young children.

I am appreciative of the suggestions from the Charles Merrill staff, from colleagues, and especially from student readers of the first edition. We wish to say a special thanks to Professor Harland Merriam, Dr. Jane L. Thorn, Dr. Eldon Ekwall and Dr. Art Heilman for their detailed comments concerning the first edition and reactions to the revised manu-script. Judith Soltis' critical reading of some of the chapters was most helpful.

Susanna Pflaum-Connor

Contents

PART I

Language Growth
During the Preschool Years

1

Language Beginnings: Different Viewpoints

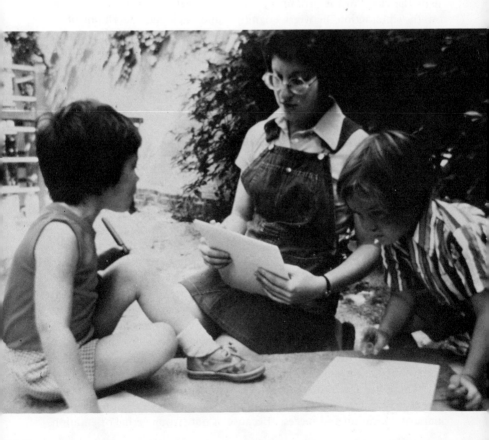

The first part of this book is concerned with language development. Chapter 1 presents viewpoints on the interaction of language and thinking and some theory about the initial motivation for language learning. Chapter 2 describes specific characteristics of language growth: how words are acquired, sentences lengthened, sounds learned, and meanings attached to words. Chapter 3 broadens the view of language development by its discussion of the language of children who speak a variant form or another language. Chapter 4 brings together the material of the first three chapters and makes recommendations about language development in schools.

This first chapter describes how language growth and thinking intersect in the young child's development. Different scholars have different views on the relationship between language and cognitive growth. Discussion of these views is meant to increase understanding and clarify concepts developed later in the book. The first section of the chapter presents the views of the prominent scholars Piaget, Vygotsky, and Bruner on the interaction between cognitive and language development. A second section is a discussion of what motivates the start and continual growth of language during the preschool years. Included in the discussion is assessment of the role that adults play in the development of children's language.

Language and Cognitive Development

We should try to examine thought and language separately. By so doing, we will make clearer the role of language in human life and will be able to outline the boundaries of the following discussion. But it is extremely difficult, if not hazardous, to try to separate language from thought. Since most adult Western thought is verbal in orientation, it is difficult to imagine nonverbal thinking; nonetheless, even adults have nonverbal thoughts. Fleeting, unremembered dreams are nonverbal. The reaction to speeded-up visual displays seen on television may be nonverbal. Certainly our affective reaction to many of our perceptions is nonverbal. Even some types of complex thought are nonverbal. Many artists, for example, find it difficult (and unnecessary) to try to verbalize their thinking, for they "think" directly onto their canvasses, into their musical scores, through their choreography, or in their sculptures without the need of mediating language.

There are few other examples of complex thinking which are not verbal in Western society; indeed, our society prizes verbal ability as a mark of education and success. Because of our strong verbal orientation, it is difficult to recognize nonverbal characteristics which, as we will see in the following discussion, probably mark many children's early cognitive activities. However, we should try to abandon for the time being our predilection for verbal translation of thought so that we can begin discussion of the tremendous insights into the intersection of thought and language in young children that various scholars offer us.

Piaget

A strong influence in educational circles today is from Piaget's study of human development. While not intended by Piaget as an approach to education, many educators, particularly in the fields of science education, early childhood education, and art education, have found important implications of the Piaget theory in application to curriculum building and even instruction. Piaget's major study is of how infants, children, and adolescents build logical thought. However, he has also been interested in language, at least in early publications *(21)*. Close colleagues of Piaget, such as Sinclair-deZwart *(24),* have worked more directly with developmental language within the Piaget framework of logical, cognitive development.

We will review a few major Piagetian concepts of children's cognitive development before analyzing his position on language. For Piaget, cognitive development, from the very beginnings of life through adolescence, is marked by individuals' active and unconscious structuring of the input they perceive in the environment. That is, children deal only with those aspects of their world out of which they can make sense. In Piaget's terminology, children *assimilate* environmental input into their present cognitive structure. If the input is new and adds a new dimension to their thinking, their thought patterns are modified or changed by *accommodation.* Assimilation and accommodation are the basic processes by which individuals learn.

During the first year of life, even before language is acquired (the *sensori-motor stage*), children begin to figure out their own reality for themselves. Infants' thoughts during this stage are tied to actions or specific sensory qualities of stimuli. Children's first words also are tied to the actions they perform or observe. By the end of the period, at about eighteen months, children have arrived at a point where they think of themselves as separate objects in a world made up of permanent objects and can perform simple problem-solving tasks. By this age, children begin to view objects as separate from themselves *(14)*.

After the start of the *preoperational period,* which begins at about eighteen months and continues to about age seven, a number of important changes occur in children's cognitive development. The new *cognitive* abilities acquired during this period are determined largely by children's ability to symbolize. Children in the sensori-motor stage learn that objects have permanence; at the beginning of the preoperational stage, they master use of objects to represent other objects and situations in play and thinking. When children pretend that blocks of various sizes "stand" for a family, their symbolic play demonstrates their representation of familiar family groups in another medium. Children at this stage of development also begin to make drawings which help to organize their thinking. Although the drawings may not appear to be realistic to the adult observer, they are intended to be. Drawings help children develop mental images of objects. Finally, during the early part of this stage, children develop the ability to form real mental images of objects not present. Once children have formed mental images and once they have labels for these images, they comment on and describe absent objects and past events *(22)*.

Piaget has been concerned with the role of language in the development of thought for many years. In 1926, he published a book entitled *The Language and Thought of the Child (21)* which examined the function of the speech of children at play with other children. He found a great preponderance of *egocentric speech* among preschool children, with a greater amount of *socialized speech* emerging in children over the age of seven. Egocentric speech is centered essentially on one's own actions; children talk aloud to and about themselves even when in the presence of other children. Socialized speech involves real dialogue; information and questions are provided in an interactive situation. Piaget's later studies *(22)* have shown that the amount of egocentric speech in preschool children diminishes under certain circumstances; for example, when children converse with adults. Generally, though, children appear to talk for and to themselves about their play and activities. It is important to note that, according to Piaget, the egocentric speech of young children does not determine their behavior; it is a *verbal accompaniment to behavior*. Piaget's work suggests that language in its functional use is limited to a level of sophistication which has already been achieved in cognitive development. In his theory, cognitive development determines the course of language growth.

Sinclair-deZwart *(24)* states that human infants acquire language out of the cognitive structures already learned during the sensori-motor stage. Early language is described as one way to represent events and objects in the world. Description of children's early utterances in chapter 2 confirms this view of language. Later growth in language, described by other scholars of child language as phenomenal in extent and rapidity, is interpreted by Sinclair-deZwart as a series of accommodations of experiences to previous structures. Studies conducted by Piagetian scholars on language and its impact on cognitive development de-emphasize the role of language in early learning.

During his forty-five years of study of cognitive growth, Piaget has not drastically changed his position on the role of language in thinking. He continues to believe that language ability is generally determined by the level achieved in cognitive development; however, there are points where language does stimulate cognitive growth to a certain extent. For example, language enables children to detach thought from action at the start of the preoperational stage. Thus, thought becomes symbolic and, because language too is inherently symbolic, it becomes the natural medium for representing absent objects and past events. This ability to represent is a hallmark of the beginning of the preoperational stage, and language is one important source used by children as they move into this stage.

Piaget has found in experiments with older children *(22)* that language does not play an important role in the development of logical behavior. Deaf-mute children do not experience as much delay in their cognitive development in experimental tasks as do blind children the same age. According to Piaget, the absence of vision appears to slow growth more than does the absence of language. He further believes, "Language does not constitute the source of logic but is, on the contrary, structured by it."[1]

However, even if language does not contribute to the development of logical behavior, it is recognized as a tool of instruction in cognitive development for children who are in transition to the *concrete-operational period* of development. In a study conducted by four of Piaget's colleagues in Geneva *(16)*, the effect of language training on success in conservation tasks was examined. Experiments examining the influence of language and other factors on the achievement of conservation of children between ages four and eight showed that:

> First, language training, among other types of training, operates to direct the child's interactions with the environment and thus to "focus" on relevant dimensions of task situations. Second, the observed changes in the justifications given (by the subjects) for answers in the conservation task suggest that language does aid in the storage and retrieval of relevant infor-

---

1. Jean Piaget, *The Language and Thought of the Child* (New York: Meridian Books, 1955), p. 90.

mation. However, our evidence offers little, if any, support for the contention that language training per se contributes to the *integration and coordination* of "informational units" necessary for the achievement of the conservation concepts. Language learning does not provide, in our opinion, a ready-made "lattice" or lens which organizes the child's perceptual world.[2]

The authors of this study agree with an American interpretation of Piaget's work that language does not play a major organizing role in determining intellectual development until children achieve formal, mature thought during adolescence. Furth *(14)* further asserts that because of the rather minor role language plays in cognitive growth during the preschool and primary years, verbal output (oral, read, and written language) should not be emphasized in schools until well after the normal age for initial literacy training.

Piaget's impact has been strongest and most valuable in demonstrating to educators the need to support children's natural reaching out for information to use in structuring knowledge by interacting with objects and people. Kamii and DeVries *(17),* for example, have designed a Piagetian curriculum for preschool education. In practice, they supply children and teachers with various techniques to enhance children's natural induction processes. They include specially designed objects as well as many familiar ones for children to interact with. Teachers are trained to diagnose skillfully the level of cognitive functioning a child has attained and to raise questions suitable for improving development. These teacher-child interactions are viewed as supportive of cognitive, rather than language, development.

Vygotsky

In 1934, a few years after Piaget's *Language and Thought* first appeared, the work of a Russian psychologist named Lev S. Vygotsky was posthumously collected and published as *Thought and Language (27).* Vygotsky's work had little impact on psychology in Western Europe and the United States until 1962 when it was reissued and translated. Since Vygotsky offers an alternative interpretation of the role of adult language in the development of the young child's thinking and his use of language, a summary will provide a good contrast with the work and conclusions of Piaget (see *25*).

In Vygotsky's work, dialogue between adult and child is a critical factor influencing language development and stimulates cognitive

---

2. B. Inhelder, et al., "On Cognitive Development," *American Psychologist* 21 (1966): 160–64.

growth. Children learn names and language structures from this dialogue. Although it takes many years of growth to reach mature conceptual levels, the beginning of language and thought comes from the model provided by adults. The development of concepts is initiated by adult models and structured by the individual with further dialogue as a source. According to Vygotsky, when a mature concept expressed in qualitative language is finally and independently organized by the individual, the final product of cognitive and language development has been achieved.

We will look first at Vygotsky's position on the function of communication in childhood development and then turn to his powerful description of the growth of concepts. In order to summarize Vygotsky's analysis of early communication, we must define his terms *external speech* and *inner speech*. *External speech* is that which can be heard both in dialogue with others and in monologue. Adults provide children who are just beginning to talk with language models in dialogue. As children imitate, begin to respond to the dialogue, and later produce monologues, external speech is evident. Through imitation, response patterns become the habitual patterns that are present in external speech and that are used to structure children's inner speech. Thus, external speech is prerequisite to the inner speech which precedes mature thought. Vygotsky describes *inner speech* as a sort of silent speech that occurs before real thought begins. In fact, inner speech leads to thought.

Thus, for Vygotsky, the model provided by adults is necessary to teach names, to demonstrate language structures to young children, and to provide practice. From the adult model, children acquire form and structure that are the organizing sources for the structuring of thought.

On the other hand, Vygotsky also believed that children develop concepts in inductive processing stages not unlike the stages of development Piaget found. The major difference between the two is that adult naming and talk help in the process of acquiring conceptual sophistication in the Vygotsky model.

Heaps.   During infancy and before language begins, children group objects haphazardly without perceiving stable relationships among objects. Fleeting images characterize their organization of the world.

Complexes.   Complexes are formed early and are observable throughout the preschool period, during which they become increasingly stable. The stage of complexes is comparable to Piaget's preoperational stage. In the beginning, children may perceive shared attributes among objects in a group even though attributes may shift for object groupings. When children achieve what Vygotsky calls the *pseudo-concept,* conceptual thinking begins, as they are able to group objects according to consistently shared attributes. To accomplish this kind of grouping, children must acquire concrete and functional attributes from the adult model. Adults must help children to form this pseudo-concept which is a necessary factor for dialogue and monologue. Dialogue and monologue are, in turn, prerequisites for inner speech.

Concepts.   Finally, during adolescence, individuals develop the ability to abstract attributes of groups independently. As mature thinkers, they are no longer either tied to concrete, functional attributes or dependent on adult naming.

Vygotsky's position is clear. First, language is a major stimulant for conceptual growth; however, conceptual growth is also dependent on interaction with objects in the environment. Second, the strategies used in learning language become a major means for acquiring thought processes. Mature thought is achieved only after acquired language forms have provided children with labels and structures to use as they interact with objects. In contrast to the preschool curriculum designed to realize Piaget's work, a preschool curriculum intended to follow Vygotsky's theory would define carefully the language terms and activities provided for children to maximize their cognitive growth.

Thus, in Vygotsky's model, adults name and help in the development of appropriate concept attributes. To explain, children are apt to use a complex relative term like *more* or *big* with only partial knowledge of the attributes of the relational meaning in these words *(11).* Vygotsky's approach to language growth suggests that the understanding of these terms increases gradually as adults specify in words the relationships between terms. The adult helps the youngster learn the attributes through comments, comparisons, and corrections when relative terms are wrong, in the adult sense of what is correct *(8, 12).* By contrast, in Piaget's view, adult use of these terms and corrections of the child's ''incorrect'' use will not help the child discover the conventional use of the term.

Another major point of contrast between the two theories is the analysis of children's use of speech to communicate. According to Piaget, children's speech with others is partially, though not exclusively, egocentric in orientation until the children have reached the age of seven or eight and attained the concrete operational stage of development. The adult role in providing language models exists, of course, but it does not expand children's thinking beyond the limits they have constructed for themselves. However, in Vygotsky's theory, the role of adult language is clearly critical for all language and thought development. Adult language provides dialogue and monologue forms which help children prepare for inner speech and real thinking.

A preschool curriculum designed to encourage language development and following Vygotsky's model of language would emphasize the adult as language stimulator and resource. It would be designed with lessons on specific language elements with activities to hasten language growth.

Bruner

In his brilliant initial chapters of *Studies in Cognitive Growth (7),* Jerome Bruner discusses his view of the interrelatedness of language and cognitive development. In some respects, Bruner's analysis lies between Piaget's and Vygotsky's, for he believes that language plays a stronger role in stimulating thought than does Piaget but does not give it as preponderant a role as does Vygotsky.

Prior to language development, Bruner *(5)* found that certain mother/child modes of communication precede and may determine types of early child utterances. Mothers encourage joint attention even during the early months; infants as young as four months follow their mother's line of sight to an object. By comments or actions, mothers also encourage attention to specified objects. Further, mothers may help infants learn about the beginnings and ends of actions as they sound or use words to mark the start and finish, for example, of bathing or eating activities. Many of these communications occur just prior to language beginnings toward the end of the first year as mother and child play common games, such as peek-a-boo. In this game, as in adaptations of it, mothers help infants learn about the changing roles of actor, action, and receiver. These roles relate directly to uses for early utterances once language proper has begun. Thus, early adult/infant communication is the precursor of early language; language grows out of the communication experience.

Language becomes a major stimulant to cognition once language acquisition begins, according to Bruner, because the sophisticated strategies used by children as they acquire language (which will be discussed later in this chapter and in greater detail in chapter 2) become available for cognitive learning in general. Children's first language structures are rule-governed. With age and experience, children begin to use sentences based on more specialized rules. These rules are not taught directly from outside sources but are developed gradually through the children's experiences. Bruner suggested that the strategies children acquire as they develop language rules are crucial to cognitive development. Bruner, Oliver, and Greenfield's studies *(7)*, which have shown that the ability to achieve symbolic behavior after school entrance is more apparent in developed, verbal-oriented societies than in primitive ones, suggest that when abstractions described through language are valued—as they are in Western society—language does indeed interact positively with thought.

Language helps in general cognitive development because of its abstract nature. Children begin to perceive object groups during the first years, but this perception is only in terms of superficial appearances. Gradually, children acquire the ability to look beyond the surface and to group objects in terms of inherent characteristics. There is a parallel in language growth: in the beginning of vocabulary learning, the *word* appears to be equivalent to the object. Later, children learn that the word is a *name* for the object. To explain, let us imagine a child who says "ball" for his one red ball. "Ball," to him, means that round thing he can hold. In time, he notices that lots of other round things are called "ball," too. If all those round bouncy things are balls, then "ball" must be a name for round things like that and not just his nice round red thing. This is, of course, a vast simplification of the process, but it is intended to illustrate how *naming,* which is necessary to the establishment of groupings, appears through children's language experiences.

Of course, Bruner recognizes the great impact on language of the development of cognition. During the preschool years, language stimulates thought by providing children with a complex structure which helps in organization of general cognitive structures. However, there is an active relationship between the development of language and thought which continues beyond the preschool period. Later, language helps older children achieve maturity of using language to abstract the features of experience and reorganize them into a rational system.

We believe that a good curriculum combines elements from the views of all of these theorists. A good school program should provide children with independent activity, as would a Piaget-based program, in order to ensure active structuring and involvement in events. In addition, this program should include many opportunities for children to hear and interact with adults and each other in dialogue as Vygotsky recommends. Finally, as Bruner *(6)* suggests, a program of merit encourages children to describe their experiences in their own terms and to build on the language forms used.

The three theorists have been interested in the interplay between cognition and language. The theories are presented here, early in our discussion, to place the development of language in the larger framework of cognitive development. This volume is about language development, and we are concerned with techniques for enhancing children's language proficiency. Other scholars have looked more directly at the beginnings of language and have examined what motivates its growth; we turn now to this discussion.

Motivation for Language Growth

It is helpful to consider the question of motivation in light of the vastness of the learning that takes place. Children begin to combine words at about the age of two, and these first utterances, simple and primitive as they are, are understandable only if the listener is present in the situation in which they occur. By the age of three and a half, many children have acquired enough language to make clear, simple, and complete sentences, some of which are understandable independent of the situation. By five, children are advanced enough to speak with near adult-like sentences, clear sounds, and with fairly complex meaning. These changes, occurring in a short span of time and almost universally among children, are as rapid a growth in ability as humans ever experience. For the most part, this learning occurs without direct instruction. Parents do not herald the growth of language as they later do reading; it appears much as it is expected. However, scholars have begun to pay considerable attention to the motivation for the appearance and characteristics of language growth.

It has long been assumed that language is characteristically human. Study of chimpanzees in the wild *(26)* shows that primates make only a few sounds, each of which is a sign, such as the sound warning others of approaching danger. However, psychologists who view language as an accumulation of knowledge and skill have hypothesized that simple aspects of language can be taught chimpanzees. If such attempts were successful, language might be viewed as a set of skills acquired through the environment rather than a qualitatively different system of communication. Such a view would have radical impact on childhood education; it would raise serious questions about the theories described above.

One chimp trained in the use of language developed enough skill to initiate and to respond to similarly displayed signs *(15)*. Another has learned to combine tokens representing simple concepts and to do so spontaneously (see *1*). Both of these recent training programs by-passed the animals' vocal organ limitations and have shown that primitive language can be acquired by lower animals. Attempts are being made to find if language trained chimps are able to pass on their knowledge to younger chimps. In contrast to human language learnings, however, the rudiments of chimp language have come through direct, intensive training. Brown *(1)* points out that human language is also unique in its power to transmit knowledge and culture, in its astounding variety of structures, and its independence of situation (we can describe a different place and time to another person). In spite of the chimps' impressive learning, the human language learning capacity is significantly different.

To turn now to language-learning children, we first trace the explanation offered for normal language development by behavioral psychologists. This position, like that taken by the chimp trainers, views language as the accumulation of successive skills. Obviously, however, the adult role is not one of direct teaching as with chimps but instead is a modification of children's language from nonlingual sounds to adult forms.

According to this position, youngsters are strongly reinforced for their first words. The reinforcements shape their preferences for making certain sounds over others in the presence of certain objects or persons. As skill in naming grows, children are reinforced for combining words and primitive sentence-making begins. The possibility exists that children simply imitate the sentences adults use and learn language forms through this imitation.

Sometimes children imitate adult sentences, but they reduce the number of words to a few essential ones they can handle. The question is whether, in fact, the apparent imitations children make are just that—imitations—or whether they are based on children's rules for language. Ervin's *(13)* study of the complexities of children's spontaneous imitations revealed that they are never more advanced in syntactic structure than are other nonimitative sentences. Further, she found that there are relatively few direct imitations and therefore concluded that there must be other methods for children to acquire their language. Brown and Hanlon *(3)* found that parents do not even react to the "correctness" of their children's utterances; they are interested in the content, not the form, of the statements. The explanation that the parent is a reinforcer is weakened by this finding and others. An additional reason that scholars generally do not adhere to imitation as a strong explanation for language learning is the extent of children's invented sentences (see chapter 2). Invention would simply not be characteristic of one acquiring language through imitation.

Before we turn to other possibilities, we should recall that language learned by imitation should not be discounted altogether. Certainly, without imitation, there would be no learning at all at the level of vocabulary acquisition. Children must be exposed to adult names for objects, action, etc. in order to acquire a vocabulary. The process may work in this manner: when a toddler is playing with a toy, a pail for instance, an adult or older child will name that object. The child associates the word "pail" with the object. After associating it, he may imitate the spoken word "pail." It is likely that in some way he will be reinforced for saying "pail." Thus, imitation is crucial for word learning; however, it does not appear to be a very productive process in acquiring syntactic rules.

A quite different explanation about language growth comes from linguists and psycholinguists *(10, 19, 20)* who have suggested that children, simply by being human, acquire language inductively from the language in the environment rather than from the particular speech events of individual persons. They explain that this occurs through something similar to the Language Acquisition Device (LAD) which represents language learning children. The reader must bear in mind that this "device" does not exist to any observable degree; it is only a hypothesis. But, as McNeill *(19, 20)* points out, what happens with LAD may well be what happens with children.

In the diagram, LAD receives the input from the language of the environment. LAD analyzes this input and produces a language rule system. (By rules, we mean an implicit sense of how to organize words in sentences. In fact, LAD was proposed as a way of accounting for the developing rule system underlying the language of children.) The rule system then becomes the basis for the form of the speech produced. Only the language LAD "hears" and the speech "produced" are observable. The hypothesis lies within the large closed box (see figure 1).

Children appear to do what LAD does. Children hear the observable language around them. When they are ready, they organize that language input and simplify its complexities so that they unconsciously form a system which is the underlying basis for their language production. As children mature, they are able to receive more complex input. The new input is also organized and the rule system adjusted to new complexities. As a result, the speech produced reflects the new rules and increased understanding of syntactic forms.

Although the concept of LAD is a hypothesis, it demonstrates the relationship between language heard and language produced by children. It stresses the following concepts about language acquisition: language growth results from children's growing ability to hear language forms; children make sense of language input in terms of their level of maturity; they form rules to account for the input; they produce speech based on the rule system.

A similar explanation is that of Lenneberg *(18);* this explanation is often called nativist since it responds to the biological propensities for language found in children. In Lenneberg's view, the motivator for lan-

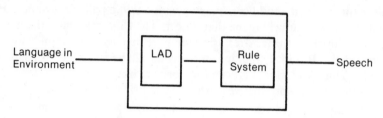

Figure 1.
The Language Acquisition Device

guage acquisition is inside children; it is their natural language learning ability. Lenneberg believes that children are, in a sense, wired for language learning, and draw on a variety of evidence.

For example, if language is specific to the species, then it is not illogical to expect all children to learn to talk. And, indeed, this is usually the case. Most children learn some language without any overt adult training. At this point, the reader probably is thinking of children who cannot talk and is doubting this claim that all children learn language. There are, of course, a very few children who do not learn much language because of severe neglect and some others who do not develop much language because of a physical disorder or a severe nervous disability. However, these children are in a distinct minority when compared with the number of children who learn language normally. Even in the case of disabled children, it is often surprising how much language is acquired; except for severe cases, handicapped and retarded children do learn some language. Studies indicate that comprehension and oral ability do not need to go hand in hand. Lenneberg *(18)* reported a case of a nonverbal boy studied from age four to age nine. At four, he could not babble; he was totally inarticulate. At nine, after intensive training, he could say a word with great difficulty and then only if an adult said it with him. However, tests of language understanding indicated that he had near normal passive comprehension of language and its structure. Apparently, language comprehension develops even under most difficult situations and speech is not necessary for its growth.

Psycholinguists and others who claim that children have an inherent propensity for language have found that language generally begins within a regular range of time regardless of the individual child's environment. Lenneberg *(18)* also reported instances of hearing children born to deaf parents, who cannot reinforce the speech they do not hear, begin to speak at about the same time as children growing up in a normal family. Lenneberg's studies also indicate that position in the family does not appear to affect the time when language begins; the findings show that second and third children begin to speak at the same age as did the first children in spite of the fact that parents of first children often show more interest in their language beginnings. First children may learn more language once they begin, but, according to Lenneberg, all normal children appear to begin to acquire language at approximately the same time.

Lenneberg offers still another piece of evidence for the inductive character of language development in young children by showing that when language changes noticeably, the environment does not appear to change drastically. In other words, it is impossible to find factors in the environment of young children that will account for language change. The home does not provide situations that specifically propel children into new language forms *(18)*. Children's readiness and the provision of language models about them appear to be enough to precipitate language acquisition. In Lenneberg's view, the motivator for language acquisition is inside children; it is their natural language learning ability.

Of the three explanations for language learning, aspects of the last two appear well founded, the one based on linguistic theory (LAD) and the one from a biological background. However, neither of these positions clarifies what adult language supplies for language-learning children to use in inducing appropriate language patterns. Various possibilities for how adults supply children with information to use in producing rule-controlled language have been suggested; unfortunately, there is little empirical support for any *(1)*.

One source for language learning may be by a process of imitation in reverse. Brown and Bellugi *(2)* have suggested that adult *expansion* may provide important data for the language-learning child. An expansion occurs when a child's statement such as "here sock" is repeated by an adult in his form, as "Oh, here is the sock." Thus, the adult displays naturally to the child how his idea is described in mature language. Possibly, the child learns more mature structures by comparing his own sentence with that of the adult. Two empirical studies of the influence of expansion of children's language maturation show opposite effects. Cazden *(8, 9)* reported that deliberate expansion after each comment by the child in short daily sessions is not particularly helpful in advancing syntactic ability when the child is compared with a group of children not treated in this manner. On the other hand, McNeill *(19)* reported a study showing expansion to be very effective for language growth. The main difference in the design of the second study is that *only* the child's comprehensible sentences were expanded. Thus, the authors of the second study avoided probable confusion resulting from misunderstandings of child utterances. We cannot be absolutely sure of the role of expansion since we have contradictory evidence, but because of the more natural situation in the second study, it seems safe to assume that deliberate, meaningful expansion will not harm language growth and may help it. The second study also demonstrates that some training does speed children's syntactic learning.

It is also possible that children learn simply from adult comments on the truth of what they say. This possibility has also been put to test with equivocable results. Cazden's *(8, 9)* study shows strong positive growth from many adult comments, while McNeill's *(19)* shows less. Again, although we cannot be sure about the impact of natural comments on specific aspects of language learning, we do know that such use of language is common in homes where children acquire language facility.

According to Brown, Cazden, and Bellugi *(4),* an additional source for the language-learning child may be adult prompting. For example, if a child says, "I ate (word lost)," the adult might try to increase his understanding by prompting. "What did you eat?" Prompting thus isolates the noun in the child's utterance and also demonstrates the past tense equivalence of "ate" and "did eat" in the statement and question forms. Prompting has not been empirically examined to find out if it offers children language data.

Brown *(1)* concludes that we do not yet know what propels children to produce more and more mature sentences. Children's "incorrect" utterances do not receive disapproval from their parents, nor do such utterances impair communication with them. He suggests, however, that study of children's communications outside the home shows that problems encountered by strangers in understanding children's primitive utterances stimulate use of more advanced language. And, since children at four use less mature language when speaking with two-year-olds than with same-age peers or adults *(23),* there is evidence of preschoolers' sensitivity to communication needs.

It would be easy to design a language curriculum for preschoolers if the research indicated certain kinds of adult language usages to be more helpful than others. Unfortunately this is not the case. There has been little research in the area and existing evidence is equivocal. Interactive dialogue between language-learning children and adults is characteristic in families with children of high verbal skills, however, and fits the theoretical position about motivation for language learning. The program for language development proposed in this volume will stress language interaction between adult and child and among children. Since Bruner found that communication modes initiate language learning, it is supposed that communication on increasingly complex topics and with ever widening circles of people will continue to stimulate language acquisition.

Earlier in this chapter, it was stated that children may acquire a valuable tool for the promotion of their general intellectual development as they acquire the rule system underlying language production. The ultimate goal for education is to promote effective thinking, and by maximizing the language acquisition process through dialogue we may be enhancing children's general intellectual growth.

Selected Activities

At the conclusion of each chapter in this volume is a set of activities designed to extend and apply material presented in the chapter. Since this first chapter is more theoretical than the following discussions, there are fewer activities and more "think" problems than will be found later.

1. If researchers were to discover that chimps can produce longer, more complex "sentences" than has been shown and that they can transmit "chimp" knowledge, which position about language learning is supported, the LAD, the nativist, the behaviorist? Explain your thinking.

2. Why would a Piaget-designed class not have a planned lesson to teach children the concepts of *in* and *out*? Would you find such a lesson in a Bruner-shaped, or a Vygotsky-designed class?

3. Why do researchers in child language propose that the difficulty children have in communicating through language helps them develop more mature language?

4. What are the essential differences between the LAD model and Lenneberg's?

5. Does Lenneberg's finding that nearly all children, regardless of background or place in the family, acquire the beginnings of language at the same time mean that there are no differences in rate of acquisition? When might differences begin? What might affect them?

6. If you were assigned to find out, without using books, what children say as they begin to talk, how would you go about collecting data?

7. Begin to visualize a preschool class with strong adult/child interactions.

References

1. Brown, R. *A First Language: The Early Stages.* Cambridge, Mass.: Harvard University Press, 1973.
2. Brown, R., and Bellugi, U. "The Processes in the Child's Acquisition of Syntax." *Harvard Educational Review* 34 (1964): 133-51.
3. Brown, R., and Hanlon, C. "Derivational Complexity and Order of Acquisition of Child Speech." In *Cognitive and Development of Language,* edited by J. R. Hayes. New York: John Wiley, 1970.
4. Brown, R.; Cazden, C.; and Bellugi, U. "The Child's Grammar from One to Three." In *The 1967 Minnesota Symposium on Child Psychology,* edited by J. P. Hill. Minneapolis: University of Minnesota Press, 1968.
5. Bruner, V. S. "The Ontogenesis of Speech Acts." *Journal of Child Language* 2 (1974): 1-19.
6. Bruner, J. "Poverty and Childhood." In *Preschool in Action: Exploring Early Childhood Programs,* edited by R. K. Parker. Boston: Allyn & Bacon, 1972.
7. Bruner, J.; Oliver, R. R.; and Greenfield, P. M. *Studies in Cognitive Growth.* New York: John Wiley, 1966.
8. Cazden, C. *Child Language and Education.* New York: Holt, Rinehart, & Winston, 1972.
9. _____. "Subcultural Differences in Child Language: An Interdisciplinary Review." *Merrill-Palmer Quarterly* 12 (1966): 185-219.
10. Chomsky, N. *Aspects of a Theory of Syntax.* Cambridge: The M.I.T. Press, 1965.
11. Clark, E. "What's in a Word? On the Child's Acquisition of Semantics in His First Language." In *Cognitive Development and the Acquisition of Language,* edited by T. E. Moore. New York: Academic Press, 1973.
12. Dale, P. S. *Language Development: Structure and Function.* Hinsdale, Ill.: Dryden, 1972.
13. Ervin, S. "Imitation and Structural Change in Children's Language." In *New Directions in the Study of Language,* edited by E. Lennebert. Cambridge: The M.I.T. Press, 1964.
14. Furth, H. *Piaget for Teachers.* Englewood Cliffs, N. J.: Prentice-Hall, 1970.
15. Gardner, R. A., and Gardner, B. T. "Teaching Sign Language to a Chimpanzee." *Science* 165 (1969): 664–72.
16. Inhelder, B.; Bovet, M.; Sinclair, H.; and Smock, C. D. "On Cognitive Development." *American Psychologist* 21 (1966): 160–64.
17. Kamii, C. and DeVries, R. "Piaget for Early Education." In *The Preschool in Action: Exploring Early Childhood Programs,* edited by M. C. Day and R. K. Parker. 2d ed. Boston: Allyn and Bacon, 1977.
18. Lenneberg, E. *Biological Foundations of Language.* New York: John Wiley, 1967.

19. McNeill, D. *The Acquisition of Language : The Study of Development Psycholinguistics.* New York: Harper & Row, 1970.
20. _____. "Development Psycholinguistics." In *The Genesis of Language: A Psycholinguistic Approach,* edited by F. Smith and G. A. Miller. Cambridge: The M.I.T. Press, 1966.
21. Piaget, J. *The Language and Thought of the Child.* New York: Meridian, 1955.
22. Piaget, J., and Inhelder, B. *The Psychology of the Child.* New York: Basic Books, 1969.
23. Shatz, M. and Gelman, R. "The Development of Communication Skills: Modifications in the Speech of Young Children as a Function of Listener." *Monograph of the Society for Research in Child Development* 38 (1973): 1-36.
24. Sinclair-deZwart, H. "Language Acquisition and Cognitive Development." In *Cognitive Development and the Acquisition of Language,* edited by T. E. Moore. New York: Academic Press, 1973.
25. Smith, E. B.; Goodman, K. S.; and Meredith, R. *Language and Thinking in the Elementary School.* New York: Holt, Rinehart, & Winston, 1970.
26. Van Lawick-Goodall, J. *In the Shadow of Man.* Boston: Houghton Mifflin, 1971.
27. Vygotsky, L. S. *Thought and Language,* edited and translated by E. Haufman and G. Vakar. Cambridge: The M.I.T. Press, 1962.

2

How Language Grows

This chapter describes specific aspects of children's language acquisition that demonstrate most clearly strategies and capabilities in language learning. To understand these language-learning milestones in humans is to understand more about how young children seek and find meaning in the events occurring around them. As children grow in their abilities to communicate with others, they gain control and a sense of order of their environment. Teachers who know about language learning can promote growth by providing an appropriately rich atmosphere; they can also determine individual children's levels of functioning; they can apply knowledge of language growth to prepare children for reading and writing.

The first section presents a short introduction to the vocalization appearing during the first year of life. The next section reports major findings of the study of normal language growth through the preschool years followed by a brief review of language development during the school years. The final section is concerned with conceptual learning.

The following questions help to focus on the main ideas of this chapter: What are the general characteristics of the language of the young child? What strategies does the child use to acquire the language spoken by the people around him? From the discussion on these questions will come specific implications for classroom programs to be explored to a greater extent in the material in chapters 4 and 5.

Most of the information reported in this chapter comes from the study of child language that has taken place since the early 1960s. The influence of Chomsky's generative grammar on students of applied language has been enormous; most developmental psycholinguists, researchers of child language, acknowledge the theoretical debt from Chomskian linguistic theory. Beginning in 1970, they began to look at language from an even broader view. Whereas earlier researchers tended to examine the emergence and growth of language from a grammatical, or syntactic, point of view, studying early language to find the rules on which word combinations were based, the later researchers studied syntax in the context of the meaning of the utterances. Thus, instead of a strictly syntactic analysis, developmental psycholinguists now study child language in terms of its syntax and semantics. We begin with the sounds infants make before the occurrence of any discernible structure of words or of meaning.

Birth to 1.0

Prior to the attachment of meaning to vocalizations, language has not really begun. However, in interesting ways, babies represent the language they will later be learning.

During the first year, infants make many different sounds unlike those made after words are acquired. For one thing, we refer to the sounds speakers make to distinguish one word from another as *phonemes*. For example, the initial sounds of "pig" and "big" are phonemes that distinguish the two words and are represented in writing by symbols placed between two slash marks: /p/ and /b/. If the sounds, phonemes, are used only to distinguish words, then babies who have no words have no phonemes. For another thing, we find that the many sounds vocalized during the first year are not used when babies finally do utter words. Thus, while many sounds are produced before referent and utterance coincide, once word acquisition actually begins only a few phonemes are used.

To return to infants who do vocalize, McNeill *(27)* has reported that nearly all human sounds are produced during the first year of life, even though all these sounds will not be used in any one language. During the first three months of life, infants learn to cry in different ways so that parents can often identify one cry as a request for food, another as a complaint about discomfort, and so on. Toward the end of the three months, cooing sounds are used to indicate pleasure.

At about six months or so, infants add to their vocalization repertory. They *babble*. Babbling occurs when the infant combines a consonant-like sound with a vowel-like sound in a syllable which is repeated. Babbling continues after the first words are learned.

An interesting phenomenon about this prelingual stage has been observed. Apparently deaf children go through a similar sequence of crying, cooing, babbling. However, their vocalizations are fewer when others are present *(23)*. The production of these first sounds apparently does not entirely depend on environment or on feedback, but the extent of vocalization is influenced by environment.

Hearing children acquire one important language-like behavior toward the end of the first year—variations in the beginnings of intonation of the language being learned *(15)*. Intonation refers to the stress pattern or emphasis placed on certain words in the rhythm of speech. Thus, a stream of babbling is apt to sound like a statement by a language speaker without words or meaning. After a few isolated words are learned, some babies combine these words into a kind of pseudo-language. They present utterances that sound like speech but with an occasional word. Once the author observed a puzzled three-and-a-half-year-old listening intently to a baby with this pseudo-language. Finally the older child said that the baby was funny because she sounded like she was saying something but it did not come out like talk.

Of the vocalization one hears the infant produce in the first year, only intonations and these few single words mark the beginning of language.

The Acquisition of
Meaningful Talk

The stages of language acquisition in the following pages are designated by age levels in the headings. These ages are approximate. As in other milestones of growth, overlap and individual variation in rate of learning are characteristic.

Single Words: 1.0–1.6[1]

Language really begins with the child's first meaningful words. This fact seems simple enough, but, in reality, it is often difficult to determine exactly when this important event occurs. When, for example, do an infant's babbling syllables take on meaning? When does "pa-pa-pa" begin to mean "Daddy"? In any case, by the end of the first year or the beginning of the second, most children do use a few words meaningfully. Very gifted infants may say words as early as eight months, while handicapped children may not say their first recognizable word until as late as 3.2 *(26)*.

During the six months following initial vocabulary acquisition, there is relatively little change, but after this period, the growth of vocabulary increases dramatically. At age 1.0, the average number of words used meaningfully by a child is three; at 2.0, it is 272 *(24)*. From this point on, vocabulary grows even more quickly. It is difficult to gauge the extent of vocabulary beyond this point, but estimates of the child's understanding at age six of the words others use run as high as 24,000 words *(22)*.

Common first words are "pa-pa," "da-da," "ma-ma," "no-no," "bye-bye," and some infantile word for milk. In most cases, the words are repeated syllables composed of a consonant and a vowel (sometimes called an *open syllable* because of the consonant-vowel combination as in *pa, ma,* and *no*). Infantile single words, like these open syllables, have been called *holophrases,* or single words which express vague, sentence-like meanings. Early in this period, children's words (or holophrases) are usually related to the action the child or someone around him is performing. Children seldom use verbs to express an action; instead, nouns are often the first words learned. A noun-like word also is often used to show emotion; for example, the word for milk may be used to express desire. Sometimes children simply name objects *(28)*. A child may say his word for *dog* when he is loosely naming the dog as well as associating an act he has noted the dog perform. He is unlikely to refer to *dog*

---

1. 1.0 means one year, zero months. 1.6 is one year, six months. This notation is used throughout.

without a picture of the animal, an object associated with it, or the presence of a dog. Because the child can be using a word in any of these ways, in order to paraphrase a holophrase (and understand what the child means), adults need to know the context of its use. At about 1.6 children have acquired fifty words *(31)*.

A curious thing happens in the sounds little ones use when saying their first words. Once words are acquired, the sounds in them become phonemes. In the first words only a few primitive phonemes can be distinguished, but when infants are playing with sounds or *babbling,* they continue to use all kinds of sounds. A number of years ago, Jakobson *(19)* proposed an explanation of this phenomenon. Jakobson showed that many children's first words were similar regardless of the language being learned. According to his theory, since the sounds of language are arranged so that some phonemes are far more distinct from each other than others, the most different sounds are learned first. Later, children learn to differentiate among less distinct phonemes. For example, the two phonemes /p/ and /a/, which Jakobson said would be the first learned, contain a basic distinction which exists in many languages. When producing these phonemes, one uses very different parts of the vocal machinery; /p/ is a consonant made at the front of the mouth with closed lips and with a slight explosive sound when it is the first sound in a word; /a/ is a back vowel made with open lips and open vocal tract. Jakobson stated that, in time, children learn to make more and more differentiation of phonemes which have less and less variation. Thus, the child who has first acquired /pa/ might next acquire a nasal phoneme (/m/, /n/, or /ŋ/), so that /ma/ may be the second word. Next, there would be a division in the vowel system so that /a/ and /i/ (a wide back vowel and a narrow high one) are differentiated and more syllables are possible. With continual splitting of these phonemes, the system gradually is acquired. Ingram *(18)* cites evidence indicating that phoneme contrasts on words are not necessarily stable at first.

While Velten *(35)* has offered some empirical verification for the main points in Jakobson's theory of the beginning of language acquisition, there are less data to support the theory during later development. However, as we see below, there is very rapid acquisition of the phonemes of the language (about 44 in all) so that all are usually acquired by the end of the preschool period.

Beginning Sentences: 1.6–2.6

Between the ages of 1.6 and 2.6, children begin to combine words. According to Lenneberg *(23)* it is consistent among normally developing children, regardless of their language environment, to begin combining words between the ages of 1.6 and 2.6. Table 1 shows representative examples of these "early sentences" taken from one study which examined this particular stage in detail.

Two- and three-word utterances have been described by Brown and Bellugi *(4)* as *telegraphic speech,* and as you read the examples in table 1, you find that the sentences resemble telegrams. There are fewer function words (articles, prepositions, conjunctions, and *auxiliary* verbs, such as *have, be, is,* etc.) than there are nouns and verbs in both the sentences in table 1 and in telegrams. However, as Brown *(6)* has pointed out, there are some function words in these utterances: fall *down* there, boot *off.* To describe these "sentences" as telegraphic is to apply adult thinking about categories of class (nouns, verbs, etc.) to very primitive language. We are mistaken when we view young children's learning from an adult position.

Table 1.
Examples of two- and three-word utterances

all broke	bye bye papa
I see	mail car
no bed	papa away
see train	all gone juice
more hot	fall down there
more walk	airplane all gone
other shoe	outside more
dry pants	there bye bye car
boot off	it doggie

Source: M. S. Braine, "The Ontogeny of English Phrase Structures: The First Phase," *Language* 39 (1963): 1–13. Reprinted by permission of the journal.

The possibility that these two-word utterances may simply be imitations of adult sentences reduced to a few essential words relates to a discussion in chapter 1. However, it is difficult to imagine adult sentences for which the following child utterances are imitations: "outside more," "there bye bye car," and "allgone juice." "Outside more" may be used by the child as he explains that he wants to stay outside longer. An adult would not use the word *more* in expressing the same desire. It could be that just as adults produce an infinite number of new sentences based on a *grammatical rule system,* children's utterances are based on a rule system, too. The novel, nonimitative child sentences listed in table 1 result from children's applications of their system. This interpretation of child language demonstrates that it is quite correct and based on a growing and developing language rule system rather than being incorrect according to adult rules. When a child's rule systems are made explicit, as they are in Bloom's extensive study of the early stages of acquisition *(2)*, the rules appear to vary somewhat from individual to individual; however, there are some common traits found in the sentence structure of various primitive two- and three-word utterances in the many studies of beginning language *(2, 3, 8, 9, 15, 27, 28, 29)*. It is clear from all the studies of language learning that children are learning basic grammatical elements even though their expression is very incomplete from an adult point of view (see more extensive reviews of this point in references *12* and *14*).

Some children show an early use of the subject and object in their sentences. They sometimes produce the subject part of the sentence and the object of the *predicate.* (Predicate refers to the nonsubject part of a sentence.) "It doggie" is an example of a subject plus object sentence. Another early structure includes verb and object ("see train," for example). Sometimes, too, children say the subject and verb part of the sentence (for example, "I see"). In these examples, subject, verb, and object elements are being acquired but are not all combined in one structure. At the same time, children are also apt to be combining words to indicate modification ("more hot"), conjunction, and genitive and locational structures *(2).*

The descriptions of child language (1) as telegraphic and (2) as representative of simple grammatical structures focus on syntax only. As stated in the introduction to this chapter, researchers now examine the meanings of these simple utterances. This is no easy task, however, since the meanings of two- and three-word utterances are strongly tied to the situation in which they are uttered. One-word holophrases can be interpreted only by knowing what was happening when they were uttered; these words are completely context bound. While the longer two-word utterances are more explanatory, they, too, are bound by the context. It is possible to misinterpret a child's "off a this" if one does not know the child is simultaneously removing a toy person from a toy train. Bloom *(2)* was able to interpret the intended meanings of primitive utterances by examining the context, and subsequent researchers have done the same *(3, 4, 6).* Brown *(6),* for example, combined the findings from a number of studies of language acquisition of English-learning children with studies of children learning as diverse languages as Finnish, Mexican Spanish, Samoan, Swedish, and others to find the types of meanings expressed by beginning speakers. Because children appear to use a similar set of meaning expressions in their first utterances, Brown stated that there are certain characteristic meanings expressed across all cultures. The most common are:

1. *Nomination.* Utterances such as "this book," "a truck" which name and include words following "this" or "that" in simple utterances belong in this category and are universal.
2. *Recurrence.* Words which combine with "more" and "'nother" are recurring ones. While this category is not as universal as the first, it is a preferred expressed notion.
3. *Non-existence.* Brown reports that while fragmentary reports do not list statements such as "no more noises," "dog away" in every child, many English-speaking children showed this expression in their language.
4. *Agent and action.* Both Bloom et al. *(3)* and Brown *(6)* found high preference among children for this category ("car go," "me go"). Because such notions are common in different languages, it appears to be part of every language in its incipient form.
5. *Action and object.* There is also a high incidence of expressions such as "close it," "turn it," "make house," "ride Dumbo" in children of many languages. This is a universal category.
6. *Possessor and possession.* As many caretakers of young children know, remarks about ownership are common: "Mommy face," "dolly hat," "dis mine," "girl dress." This is another universal category.

Other categories of language expression have been noted by various researchers, but none have the commonality of those described above. Although scholars do not agree on the exact categories of expression, they do agree that the cognitive level reached during the sensori-motor period influences these universal expressions *(6, 4)*. Sinclair-deZwart *(33)* described the cognitive functioning at 1.6 as showing stable understanding of action on objects and of knowledge of object permanence, including notions of anticipation and of rehearsal. The linguistic expression of these understandings are agent and action, action and object, recurrence and nonexistence. In nomination and possession, children are showing additional awareness of the physical world by labeling common objects and becoming personally attached to objects. Beginning language development appears to be determined by cognitive growth, but Bowerman *(4)* suggests that at later points the learnings acquired through language motivate cognitive growth.

The major points about this first period of word combination are: (1) there are similar expressions made by children learning many languages; (2) these expressions describe universal characteristics of language learning; (3) the primitive utterances also suggest incipient categories of grammatical structures found later in language growth; and (4) the utterances resemble telegraphs. During the following period of language change, children acquire forms of verbs and nouns, prepositions, pronouns, and other functions of the structure of language so that very quickly their language appears like that of adults.

Acquisition During Preschool Period: 2.6–5.0

Because it is difficult to find natural beginnings and endings of language change during the remainer of the preschool period, this rather lengthy section covers the rest of preschool language learning.

During the preschool years, all the sounds of English are acquired by most children. According to Carroll's *(10)* interpretation of a study by Templin *(34),* by the age of six most children have nearly full mastery of the sound system of English. Even at three, most children have acquired many phonemes. Ninety percent of a group of sixty three-year-olds used the following phonemes clearly: /n/, /t/, /g/ (the *g* in *g*oat), /m/, /b/, /d/, /w/, /h/, /p/, /k/. Seventy to 80 percent could also use: /f/, /ŋ/ (ŋ is the sound at the end of ra*ng*), /l/, /s/. Fifty to 60 percent had /v/, /r/, /Š/ (*sh* in *sh*ut), /J̌/ (*j* in *j*udge), /Č/ (*ch* in *ch*urch). Among the sounds causing the most difficulty for children at age three were these: /z/, /Ž/ (*z* in a*z*ure), /θ/ (*th* in *th*ick), ð/ (*th* in *th*en), and /hw/ (*wh* in *wh*ich). These more difficult phonemes are not present in some languages and show less sound distinction from each other than do those learned. For example, the difference between /z/ and /Ž/ is slight; some languages do not have either /θ/ or /ð/. These difficult language specific phonemes are learned late by children, but some adults who are learning English for the first time are never able to learn to use them correctly.

Certain sounds are problems for some elementary grade pupils, such as /r/ and /l/ *(34).* However, as Ingram *(18)* points out, children are able to perceive the acquired sounds as contrasts in the words they hear. Some children can perceive the sounds as contrasts even though they are unable to produce the sounds. Generally, it is important that teachers do not confuse children who are slow in developing the last learned sounds with children who are unable to make the sounds acquired early by most children. Thus, while a teacher does not need to worry about a child substituting /θ/ for /d/ *(this)* in kindergarten, she might become concerned with a child's inability to use/b/.

Even though most phonemes are acquired by age four or five, children still need to learn the pronunciation of longer, multisyllabic words. For example, a substitution one eight-year-old made for *inauguration* was *institution.* Further, some children have difficulty with three-letter consonant clusters as in the beginning of *street.* Finally, children whose dialect is not standard English may have different pronunciation patterns—a topic discussed in chapters 3 and 6.

The set of sounds acquired rapidly during these years is finite. A larger set of finite rules is also relatively quickly acquired during the pre-school period; these rules are the grammatical, or syntactic, rules governing word order, inflections (or endings on words), and combinations of structures. Important grammatical structures appear in children's language just after the early combination of words described in the previous section. Brown *(6)* traced the use of fourteen critical structures in three preschoolers' language. He found that while the *rate* of acquisition of the structures varied among the children, the approximate *order* did not—testimony to the universal quality of language. These structures, in order of acquisition determined by their consistent use in appropriate situations are: (1) the addition of *-ing* on verbs to mark the present progressive as in "Baby sitting in a chair" acquired at ages 1.9, 2.10, and 2.6; (2) and (3) use of "in" and "on" to mark location; (4) plural marking on nouns; (5) past irregular forms of common verbs such as "went," "came," and "did"; (6) possessive markers; (7) the simple unchanged form of the copula—"be"; (8) use of the articles "a" and "the"; (9) regular past tense forms of verbs as in "wanted"; (10) the regular third person singular verb inflection as in "the boy runs"; (11) the third person irregular as in "does"; (12) the uninflected use of auxiliary verbs along with the main verb as in "he do not want"; (13) inflected use of the copula (to be) in "is," "was," etc.; (14) inflected auxiliary verbs with main verbs as in "he does not want." These structures appeared consistently in the "correct" situations in three children by 4.0.

When children use these forms, they are expressing relatively new, complex ideas. For example, the difference between a child who does not yet use the plural inflection on nouns and one who does is the difference between one with no number distinctions and one with beginning notions of number. Again, a child who says "a chair" and "the chairs" can distinguish a particular and a general member of a group. Additionally, the fact that the noun plural inflection is acquired before the third person singular form of the verb, although both the addition of the plural inflection on nouns and the inflection on the singular present verb require the same sounds, demonstrates that the syntax determines order of acquisition, not the ability to make sounds. Thus, in numerous ways the acquisition of these grammatical structures marks the appearance of abstract grammar.

In Brown's list of acquired forms, the *irregular* past tense verb structure *(5)* appears before the *regular* form *(9)*. For irregulars to be acquired before regulars seems counterintuitive. Explanation for this phenomenon comes from Cazden's study *(11)* which found that irregular forms were often used correctly at first but later were used incorrectly. In other words, children at the beginning of this stage might say "he ran," "I did," and "we came" as adults do. A few months later, the same children might say, "he runned," "I doed," and "we comed." This phenomenon occurs because in the beginning, the children are using "ran," "did," and "came" as memorized items and not with understanding of the past tense idea. Later, they learn the past tense concept as shown in the example above, "he feeled it." When they learn the general rule for an inflection (in this case -ed at the end of a verb), they apply it to all verbs, whether or not adults use that general rule or a rule for a variant ending. Thus, children generalize about the formation of inflections and apply the generalization to all members of that class. Later, over time, they learn the rules which apply to smaller and smaller groups of words in that class. Overgeneralized learning also occurs in the acquisition of noun plurals ("wash my feets") and with possessive pronouns ("that's mines").

The learning of inflections is a very efficient process and shows the use of sophisticated strategies. Categorization of items in a class occurs first; in the instance above, for example, a verb class was formed. Then comes the formation of a rule which works in most instances; the addition of -ed to verbs when past tense is intended illustrates this point. The rule is then applied to all members of the relevant category. Only much later and with much experience will children become aware of the idiosyncratic rules of their language. For example, the reader has probably heard youngsters of six and seven saying "brang" for "brought" even though "brought" is the form consistently used by adults around them. A moment's thought will show that such children are sensibly associating "bring" and "ring"; if the past of "ring" is "rang," the past of "bring" ought to be "brang." "Bring" ought to belong to the subgroup of verbs with "ring," "sing," etc. Children are very efficient when learning rules.

More illustration of how children's language matures comes from analysis of their questions and negations. The change from initial two-word questions to almost mature questions is dramatic evidence of the rapidity of language growth.

During the earlier two-word stage, question meaning was realized by rising pitch. A child would say "ball go" with questionlike rising pitch or intonation. This question would mean "has the ball gone?" In the second column of table 2, there are many questions beginning with a wh-word (who, where, why) which clearly ask for a missing object, location, or even a cause. The ability to ask these questions indicates a new awareness of sentence function. With the beginning questions, there are also sentences with -ing. In the last column, however, even more learning has taken place. The most important change is indicated by the word order inversion of newly acquired auxiliary (AUX) verb forms (forms of *have, be, do,* and others used to show verb tense, mood, voice, etc.) and the subject. For example, in the last column, one child asked, "Does lions walk?" In this question, he places the AUX "does" first and the subject "lions" next.The inversion of AUX and subject may be one of the first adultlike word order, or transformational, rules that children learn. Transformations enable children to change words around and put sentence parts together. For example, when children learn to put the auxiliary verb form "can" in front of the subject as in "Can you swim?," they have acquired one of the many transformational rules in our language. Because of the inversion transformation, the first four questions in the last column are remarkably similar to adult questions, and as Klima and Bellugi-Klima *(21)* point out, the child's comprehension of adult questions is increasing. What is still lacking, though, is subject-verb agreement and the elimination of double past tense forms. The wh-word questions in the last column seem immature by comparison with the first four yes/no questions, since inversion of subject and AUX has not yet occured in the wh-word questions. This transformation is acquired in the next few months by most children.

Thus, in eighteen months, children acquire an amazing amount of syntactic knowledge. For example, in asking questions during the two-

Table 2.
Illustrative questions

Pivot Stage	Beginning Questions	More Advanced Questions
Who that?	See my doggie?	Does the kitty stand up?
Ball go?	Dat black too?	Does lions walk?
Fraser water?	Mom pinch finger?	Did I saw that in my book?
Sit chair?	Where my sleep?	Can I have a piece of paper?
I have it?	Where my mitten?	Where small trailer he should pull?
	What my dolly have?	Where the other Joe will drive?
	Why not drink it?	Where my spoon go?
	Why you smiling?	What I did yesterday?
	Why you waking me up?	What you had?
		What you doed?
		Why he don't know how to pretend?
		Can't you work this thing?

Source: E. S. Klima and U. Bellugi-Klima, "Syntactic Regularities in the Speech of Children," in *Modern Studies of English*, ed. D. Reibel and S. Schane (Chicago: Aldine Publishing Co., 1969). Reprinted by permission of the publisher and Edinburgh University Press.

word stage, children can question only generally a thought or an action. Soon after this point, however, they can ask for a specific missing object, person, location, or cause. By the age of about 3.6 years, children are nearly as specific in their questioning as adults. Of course, they still have not learned all the rules the adult knows; for example, they have not mastered the wh-word question inversion and use of the indefinite "any," as in the sentence, "Don't you want any?"

From about 3.5 or 4.0, when basic structures have been acquired to 5.0, child language continues to develop, but in a different way. During this later preschool period, children consolidate previous learnings and combine these basic structures into longer utterances. The rules governing the combinations are called *transformations.* Transformational rules can add elements together as in "you can have it, but remember to give it back to me," where a second clause is added to the first. Transformational rules also govern deletions as in the deletion of "do it" in "I'll show you how to do it, not that way, this way." Transformational rules also govern the reordering of structures as in the passive "she was hit by the boy," but these structures are rare in children's language production.

Menyuk *(29, 30)* has studied the language of nursery school and first-grade children. Although she did not trace a sequence of acquisition of transformational rules, we can get an overview of growth between 3.8 and 6.5 by adapting some other data and comparing the two groups. Table 3 illustrates the number of instances in which certain transformations appeared in the speech of subjects during recorded sessions. Transformations within single sentences are generally more common than are rules which enable simple sentences to be combined into *conjoined* or *complex sentences.* Conjoined sentences are composed of two or more simple sentences joined by "and," "but," "or," etc. Complex sentences have a main clause and one or more subordinate clauses and are also called *embedded sentences.* Embedding takes place when a simple sentence becomes a subordinate clause attached to a main clause; for example, "the dog was barking" is embedded in "The boy ran after the dog that was barking." When two sentences are combined by children of this age group, conjoined sentences occur more often than complex sentences.

In Table 3, relative clauses and "because" clauses are fairly common, but "if" and "so" clauses are not. These last two types of clauses are used more often by the first-grade group than by the nursery-school-aged groups, so they are probably learned sometime during this stage by many children. Although this information does not tell us exactly when and in what order sentence combining transformations are learned, it does show that many common transformations of this sort are learned during this period.

Table 3. Subjects Using Selected Transformations and Sentence Embeddings

Transformations	Nursery School (N=48) (Age Range: 3.1–4.4) (Mean Age: 3.8)	First Grade (N=48) (Age Range: 5.11–7.1) (Mean Age: 6.5)	Examples
Contraction	48	48	didn't
Possessives	48	48	Mary's hat
Pronoun (Transformation)	48	48	. . . and he can . . .
Adjective	48	48	brown hat
Infinitive Complement	48	48	I wanted to do it.
Main Clause Conjunction	41	48	He sang and Mary danced.
Conjunction with Deletion (Sub or VP)	40	47	Mary sang and danced.
Relative Clause	37	46	The man who sang is old.
Because Sentence Embedding	30	46	. . . because he said so.
Particle Separation	41	44	put down the box, put it down
Reflective	29	44	I did it myself.
Imperative*	35	42	Shut the door.
Passive*	23	41	The boy was hit by the girl.
Participal Complement	19	31	I saw her washing . . .
If-Sentence Embedding*	12	30	. . . if you want to.
So-Sentence Embedding*	12	29	. . . so he will be happy
Compound of Nominals*	6	24	baby chair
Iteration	5	13	You have to clean clothes to make them clean.

Source: Adapted from P. Menyuk, "Syntactic Structures in the Language of Children," *Child Development* 34 (1963): 407–22. Copyright © 1963 by The Society for Research in Child Development: Reprinted by permission of the Society for Research in Child Development and the author.
*Numbers are significantly different.

During the later preschool period children also acquire irregular inflections. This later learning occurs after the regular inflectional system is complete and applies to unique subsets of words. In her classic study on inflectional learning in children of nursery school and first-grade ages, Berko *(1)* found, while testing inflections (word endings) on nonsense words, that preschoolers of 4.5 could often correctly use noun plurals and third person singular verb forms, but they did so without the degree of success of children of 6.3. Generally, all children had more difficulty with the plural ending in words such as "glasses" than they did with the endings on "pictures" and "arms." The younger children also had more difficulty than the older ones with the past tense form "rang." The best performance for both groups came when the form was regular. In general, the differences between the younger and the older group were in terms of the number of errors rather than the kind of errors made. Thus, we find the same characteristic as in the previous stage of acquisition; as language is learned, rules are applied to general categories and then are redefined and applied to specific subgroups.

In summary of this rich period of language acquisition, one cannot help but be impressed by the diversity and *extent* of learning that takes place. By the end of the period, most preschool children use all the phonemes of their language. Further, they have acquired all the common grammatical structures and even have figured out how to combine these basic structures so that they can make longer sentences with more than one clause. The process of acquisition is also impressive in that children learn the rules that apply to most members of a class of words before learning rules that apply to a smaller set of that class. For example, it is only during the latter part of the preschool period and into the elementary years that some of the unique inflections are acquired. During the beginning language acquisition, children tend to overextend the general and more productive rules. The process of language learning is an inductive, self-initiating, efficient one. The idea of the innateness of language among humans and the notion of the universality of aspects of language learning are logical given this knowledge of language learning.

Language Development after 5.0

In spite of the extensive language learning before school begins, there are a few unusual and complex structures acquired after school entrance. In addition, language use matures during the early school years. Even though the focus of this book is on the young child, we review briefly here the language maturation characteristics of the early elementary years for those readers interested in older children.

In 1969 C. Chomsky *(12)* published a study of five- to ten-year-old's acquisition of complex structures. Before her study, many believed that language acquisition—the initial learning of structures—was completed before school entrance. After her publication, scholars had to reassess their thinking. In one part of the study, Chomsky asked her subjects to answer the question, "Is the doll easy to see?" when a blindfolded doll was presented. The question applied to the distinction in these two sentences.

John is eager to please.

John is easy to please.

In the first, the person doing the pleasing is John; in the second, someone else is doing the pleasing. To understand the difference is to understand the basic structure of complex sentence relationships. Chomsky's youngest subjects did not understand the second sentence referent and incorrectly answered *no* because they assumed that the doll was doing the seeing. Most of the oldest in the group tested did understand the referent and answered *yes.* There was uneven acquisition between the youngest and oldest subjects; chronological age did not entirely determine acquisition. Kessel *(20)* tested the same structure with a different, and potentially less confusing method and found generally earlier acquisition that was not completely related to chronological age.

Chomsky also found that when the subjects were asked to respond to another set of sentences by activating small dolls, their ability to distinguish between two structures was uneven until the older ages. Sample sentences were:

Bozo promises Donald to do a somersault. Make him do it.

Bozo tells Donald to do a somersault. Make him do it.

Chomsky discerned states of acquisition that were not closely related to chronological age. A different contrast between "ask"/"tell" ("Bozo asked/told Donald to . . .") in the Chomsky study was replicated by Kessel *(20)* whose analysis showed "tell" is acquired first. "Tell" is then overgeneralized to "ask" until "ask" is acquired.

In a later study, Chomsky *(13)* found uniformity across types of structures acquired. That is, children were apt to acquire comprehension of one complex structure at approximately the same time as another complex structure. Furthermore, although the age of acquisition varied among subjects, acquisition related with the exposure to reading the subject had experienced. As in early acquisition, in late language acquisition there is overgeneralizing from the most productive rule to the least. The conclusion drawn from these studies of older subjects is that the processes of language acquisition are similar to that of younger children and relate somehow to reading.

More obvious in school children's language performance than their learning of special esoteric structures is their increased maturing of language use during the elementary years. We combine words in infinite ways based on a set of rules. The capacity for creating new sentences is characteristic of children, too. School children create longer and longer sentences that contain more information. Loban's *(25)* longitudinal study of elementary school children's language showed that there were increasingly longer utterances as children grew older, but that individual variation was extensive. O'Donnell, Griffith, and Norris *(32)* studied the language used by children in oral and, when appropriate, written situations. The subjects (grades K, 1, 2, 3, 5, 7) were asked to tell (and write) about a short film(s) seen without sound. The utterances were marked off by t-units (minimal terminal units which contained at least one main clause and all subordinate clauses attached to it). While there was growth in the length of these t-units throughout the years, the years of greatest gain were between kindergarten and first grade and between fifth and seventh grades. The t-units grew longer as children learned to make more subordinate clauses. That is, subjects became more proficient in embedding clauses into main clauses and in coordinating clauses together. Furthermore, the older children were apt to delete parts of sentences where applicable. In Hunt's *(17)* study, older subjects (high school) were more apt to reduce a simple sentence to less-than-a-predicate than were younger subjects. Thus, as school children become older, they are more apt to combine elements; they can say more in fewer words; and they have more content in longer utterances.

Acquisition of Meaning

In this section we discuss the development of meaning in language—more specifically of vocabulary and concept development. Linguists rightfully stress that full meaning of words comes from the use of words in context of sentences; however, until theory of language provides an agreed upon vehicle for study of semantic development, we must be content to find what we can about how children learn individual word meanings.

Leopold *(24)* has studied in great detail his daughter's language acquisition, and among his chief concerns was her learning of language meaning. He describes the early stages in the following manner:

. . . meanings are necessarily hazy and vague at first; (that) the dearth of vocabulary compels the child to use words for purposes to which they are not adapted from adult point of view; and (that) meanings become progressively sharper and closer to the standard.[2]

The meaning of "hazy and vague" is illustrated in the following example. A small boy of 1.3 who had just learned to say "doggie" for "dog" went with his parents to an art museum. Because he had no name for other animals as yet, every time he saw a four-legged creature in a painting, he shouted "doggie." My daughter visited her grandparents after an eight month absence at the age of 1.6. She could not remember them and, at first, used one word for both of them. In other words, until she learned each of them as an individual, she named them as a set. These two examples with very young children illustrate some of the problems older children have in learning mature meanings of more complex words.

In the long process of acquiring a fixed meaning for a word, one must have a multitude of experiences. For adults, these experiences need not be direct; for young children, they must be direct. In learning "doggie," for example, the young museum visitor had recognized some salient characteristics, or *attributes,* of the concept "dog." He had learned some attributes for dog: dogs have four legs (or at least more than two); they are hairy, etc. However, he had not yet learned which animal attributes do *not* belong to dog but do belong to other animals. Gradually, as he acquired an understanding of the distinguishing attributes and names of other animals, he also learned more about "dog." Every child needs to learn which attributes are attached to a given word as well as which attributes belong not to it but to a similar word. Long after children first use a word, they are still acquiring attributes and experiencing the meaning of the word in various settings, and they continue in this process until a conventional meaning is achieved.

Clark *(14)* devised a theory of concept development she called the Semantic Feature Acquisition Theory (features are equivalent to the attributes described above). According to the theory, in the initial use of concepts children have only some of the attributes adults have. Because there are few attributes, children use a term broadly (they overextend), as the boy described above did. When children use terms inappropriately, as "doggie" was used to name all animals, they exhibit learning processes researchers can study. As learning progresses, more attributes are acquired.

---

2. W. F. Leopold, "Semantic Learning in Infant Language," in *Child Language: A Book of Readings,* ed. A. Bar-Adon and W. F. Leopold (Englewood Cliffs, N. J.: Prentice-Hall, 1971), p. 55.

Diary studies of first word learning show children's overextension of words used. For example, Leopold's child said "tick-tock" originally for "watch," but based on her perception of shape, she soon used the same label for clocks, the gas-meter, buttons on a dress, and a thermometer. Another baby on meeting a young girl, Dina, called all young girls "Dina" (reported in Clark [*14*]). Perceptions of an object's size, shape, feel, sound, and movement direct the overextensions.

When learning relative and relational terms, children often become confused. With terms such as "more" and "less," children first learn that both refer to a quantity. Then they learn that "more" is the positive member of the pair, but are still confused about "less." Finally, the two terms become sorted *(16)*. Similarly, "same" is acquired before "different," although the two are confused for a while *(14)*. "Before" and "after" continue to be difficult relational terms for many preschoolers; in fact, the author observed some middle grade elementary children having difficulty ordering: "before putting the meat in the soup, you have to put in the onions and then the potatoes." Confusions on related terms indicate direction for preschool teachers to take, and these will be specified in chapter 4.

There is still another important distinction to be made in comparing acquisition of semantics with the learnings of the other components of language. We have seen that in acquisition of syntax and phonology, the child appears to use the sophisticated learning strategies of categorization, generalization, and application to new instances efficiently. Our question now is whether the same strategies are used in acquisition of language meaning. Although categorization and application may help in learning vocabulary in some instances (for example, experiences with various household brushes will help a child learn that a painter's tool is also a brush), these strategies will not always work. We can imagine the child's confusion in learning the names for the containers used in the home; some are bottles, some jars, some glasses, some pans, some pots. Some containers are made out of glass but not all glasses are made out of glass. Some pots are large, but there are also small pots such as the mustard pot. And what is the difference between a cooking pot and a pan? Because the strategies for acquisition which work in one semantic cluster may not work with many others, trial, comparison with adult use, correction when mistakes are made, and many direct experiences with objects are necessary before full acquisition of attributes, separation of items, and groupings of words in a cluster reach maturity. Consequently, during the preschool and primary years, there is apt to be some confusion in children's minds concerning the attributes associated with terms and the differentiation of one term in a cluster from others.

Conceptual development is different from that of syntax and phonology both in terms of the sheer amount to be learned and in the continuation of the process beyond early childhood. Although adults help children learn vocabulary items by naming, it is obvious that development of meaning depends upon children's having many experiences. These experiences should ensure that both positive and negative attributes are acquired so that categorization of words occurs. As was stressed by Piaget, Vygotsky, and Bruner, development of language meaning cannot occur in isolation, although much of the motivation for growth of meaning comes from general language development as children use their knowledge of language to order their experiences.

In summary, while we must be impressed with the learning that takes place during the preschool language learning period, we must also remember that young children need help in acquiring important concepts. Before we turn to the instructional implications of this discussion, however, it is important to find out how environmental variation and language difference affect the language-learning process. After discussion of minority children's language learning in chapter 3, we turn in the remaining chapters to diagnostic and instructional application.

Related Activities

1. Some sample beginning sentences are listed below (from Bloom et al., [*3*]). See if you can identify them according to the six categories of expressed meaning: nomination, recurrence, nonexistence, agent and action, action and object, possessor and possession.

Mommy push	see man	this a dump car, too
my blanket	more cookie	can't do dat
sit lap	look at rabbit	sit orange chair
here ball	where's it	dis a my coat
milk all gone	duck water	bit finger
spank me	Gia book	this a bye-bye boy

2. Explain why a child might say, "Mommy came" and later say, "Look, Mommy comed."

3. Before reading chapter 4, speculate about how teachers might help children develop increased understanding of related terms such as "in," "out," "through," "over." Think in terms of Clark's Semantic Feature Acquisition Theory. What feature might all these words share for children learning these concepts? What features not yet acquired would prevent children from differentiating the word meanings?

4. Why is imitation not thought of by many psychologists as a productive explanation for how language is acquired? At what level is imitation necessary?

5. What is the difference between "tell" and "promise" in the sentence on page 38?

6. A preschooler says, "I don't got none." Is he correct?

References

1. Berko, J. "The Child's Learning of English Morphology." *Word* 14 (1958): 150–77.
2. Bloom, L. *Language Development: Form and Function in Emerging Grammars.* Cambridge: The M.I.T. Press, 1970.
3. Bloom, L.; Lightbown, P.; and Hood, L. "Structure and Variation in Child Language." *Monographs of the Society for Research in Child Development* 40 (1975).
4. Bowerman, M. "Semantic Factors in the Acquisition of Rules for Word Use and Sentence Construction." In *Normal and Deficient Child Language,* edited by D. M. Morehead and A. E. Morehead. Baltimore: University Park Press, 1976.
5. Braine, M. S. "The Ontogeny of English Phrase Structures: The First Phase." *Language* 39 (1963): 1–13.
6. Brown, R. *A First Language: The Early Stages.* Cambridge: Harvard University Press, 1973.
7. Brown, R., and Bellugi, U. "Three Processes in the Child's Acquisition of Syntax." *Harvard Educational Review* 34 (1964): 133–51.
8. Brown, R. and Fraser, C. "The Acquisition of Language." In *Monographs of the Society for Research in Child Development,* edited by U. Bellugi and R. Brown 29 (1964): 43–79.
9. Brown, R.; Cazden, C.; and Bellugi-Klima, U. "The Child's Grammar from One to Three." In *Minnesota Symposia on Child Development,* edited by J. P. Hill. Minneapolis: University of Minnesota, 1968.
10. Carroll, J. "Language Development." In *Encyclopedia of Educational Research,* 3d ed., edited by H. Chester, pp. 744–52. New York: Macmillan, 1960.
11. Cazden, C. "The Acquisition of Noun and Verb Inflections." *Child Development* 32 (1968): 433–48.
12. Chomsky, C. *The Acquisition of Syntax in Children from Five to Ten.* Cambridge: The M.I.T. Press, 1969.
13. _____. "Stages in Language Development and Reading Exposure." *Harvard Educational Review* 42 (1972): 1–33.
14. Clark, E. "What's in a Word? On the Child's Acquisition of Semantics in his First Language." In *Cognitive Development and the Acquisition of Language,* edited by J. E. Moore, New York: Academic Press, 1973.
15. Dale, P. S. *Language Development: Structure and Form,* 2d Edition. New York: Holt, Rinehart and Winston, 1976.

16. Donaldson, M. and Balfour, C. "Less is More: A Study of Language Comprehension in Children." *British Journal of Psychology* 59 (1968): 461–72.
17. Hunt, K. W. "Syntactic Maturity in School Children and Adults." *Monographs of the Society for Research in Child Development* 35 (1970): 1–63.
18. Ingram, D. "Current Issues in Child Phonology." In *Normal and Deficient Child Language,* edited by D. M. Morehead and A. E. Morehead. Baltimore: University Park Press, 1976.
19. Jakobson, R. "The Sound Laws of Child Language and Their Place in General Phonology." In *Child Language: A Book of Readings,* edited by A. Bar-Adon and W. F. Leopold. Englewood Cliffs, N. J.: Prentice-Hall, 1971.
20. Kessel, F. S. "The Role of Syntax in Children's Comprehension from Ages Six to Twelve." *Monographs of the Society for Research in Child Development* 35 (1970).
21. Klima, E. S., and Bellugi-Klima, U. "Syntactic Regularities in the Speech of Children." In *Psycholinguistic Papers,* edited by John Lyons and Roger Wales. Edinburgh: Edinburgh University Press, 1966.
22. Larrick, N. "How Many Words Does a Child Know?" *The Reading Teacher* 7 (1953): 100–104.
23. Lenneberg, E. *Biological Foundations of Language.* New York: John Wiley, 1967.
24. Leopold, W. F. "Semantic Learning in Infant Language." In *Child Language: A Book of Readings,* edited by A. Bar-Adon and W. F. Leopold. Englewood Cliffs, N. J.: Prentice-Hall, 1971.
25. Loban, W. D. *The Language of Elementary School Children.* Research Report No. 1. Champaign, Ill.: National Council of Teachers of English, 1963.
26. McCarthy, D. "Language Development." In *Encyclopedia of Educational Research,* edited by W. S. Monroe, pp. 165–72. New York: Macmillan 1950.
27. McNeil, D. *The Acquisition of Language: The Study of Development Psycholinguistics.* New York: Harper & Row, 1970.
28. _____. "Developmental Linguistic." In *The Genesis of Language: A Psycholinguistic Approach,* edited by F. Smith and G. A. Miller. Cambridge: The M.I.T. Press, 1966.
29. Menyuk, P. *Sentences Children Use.* Cambridge: The M.I.T. Press, 1969.
30. _____. "Syntactic Structures in the Language of Children." *Child Development* 34 (1963): 407–22.
31. Nelson, K. "Structure and Strategy in Learning to Talk." *Monographs of the Society for Research in Child Development* 38 (1973).
32. O'Donnell, R. C.; Griffith, W. J.; and Norris, R. C. *Syntax of Kindergarten and Elementary School Children: A Transformational Analysis.* Research Report No. 8. Champaign, Ill.: National Council of Teachers of English, 1969.
33. Sinclair-deZwart, H. "Language Acquisition and Cognitive Development." In *Cognitive Development and the Acquisition of Language,* edited by T. E. Moore. New York: Academic Press, 1973.
34. Templin, Mildred. *Certain Language Skills in Children: Their Development and Interrelationships.* Minneapolis: University of Minnesota Press, 1967.
35. Velten, H. "The Growth of Phonemic and Lexical Patterns in Infant Language." *Language* 19 (1943): 281–92.

3

Language Development Across Social and Cultural Groups

The problems associated with educating children of poverty have been with us since the beginning of our nation's history, but only in recent years have there been widespread attempts to improve and change programs for the education of poor children. Although there have always been individuals who have devoted themselves to the teaching of illiterate adults and poor children, the social unrest and subsequent governmental action during the 1960s resulted in a great number of new educational programs for inner-city schools in the United States. These programs were attempts to counteract the poor performance of inner-city minority children in basic skill acquisition—skills fundamental to the more complex learning required in our technical society. In 1966, Coleman found these programs to be unsuccessful in eliminating the inequality of achievement in basic skills between inner-city pupils and their middle-class peers *(14)*. However, although the reasons are not known, recent reports from the National Assessment of Educational Progress (a nationwide periodic analysis of achievement) indicate that reading comprehension of black nine-year-old children in 1975 was improved over their performance in 1971, reducing the still substantial gap between the reading performance of black and white children *(46)*. Much special program development for minority children has been initiated also for preschool children. Individual preschool programs have shown short-term positive effects, but these effects do not last into the school years *(9)*. Follow-Through projects, meant to continue the special training provided in the preschool programs, have uneven results *(54)*.

During the years of initiation and evaluation of compensatory programs for poor, minority children, many persons have suggested that there has not been enough specific attention paid to their language. But groups of specialists interpret the language needs of minority children differently. Since the topic of this chapter is the language of preschool, minority children, review of these various explanations and research is critical for our understanding. (If the language directly influences the learning to read process is discussed in chapter 6.) The first section of this chapter presents information on language variation: (1) whether the dialect of some minority persons lacks essential characteristics or is simply different from other, prestigious speech and, if so, how it differs; (2) the question of dialect change; and (3) if there are important social and attitudinal factors related to minority language. The second section briefly presents bilingualism and second-language learning in the preschool and early school years; the thrust is toward Spanish/English bilingualism and includes discussion of English language acquisition contrasts between Spanish and English, how literacy training begins, and other instructional implications.

Dialect

Every language spoken in a large country has unique local speech forms. For example, the blending of "you" and "all" into "y'all" is thought of as typical of speakers in the Southeast. Regional variation such as this one are common in the phonological, syntactic, and meaning components of language. These features can also be unique to *socially* identifiable groups. For example, there were social, not regional, dialect features that Professor Higgins changed in Eliza's speech in *My Fair Lady*. He taught her to use the features of the prestigious dialect he used. This dialect, the one spoken by educated persons, is called the standard dialect; the dialect of socially depressed minority persons is called nonstandard. (Of course, what is standard and nonstandard in England is independent of standard and nonstandard in the United States.) The sections below present information about nonstandard dialect and early childhood education. Each section focuses on the approach taken by different specialists.

Study of Verbal Behavior

One major concept included in the discussion of the characteristics and processes of learning language in chapters 1 and 2 was that children have an innate ability for language learning; furthermore, as Lenneberg *(44)* showed, the beginnings of acquisition occur quite regularly regardless of language background. In spite of the fact that the subjects in most of the studies referred to in the previous chapters came from white middle-class homes, we cannot assume that children from diverse backgrounds will learn language by a different process. Nonetheless, while the process of learning will be similar, the result may be quite different. In other words, we can assume that the processes of interaction and natural growth motivate language development for all children regardless of environment. We can also assume that nonstandard dialect characteristics in parent and community speakers will be acquired by language learning children. However, we cannot assume that environmental factors will not adversely affect growth. There are two important questions to explore. Since all children probably acquire language through similar processes, what is the effect of environmental difference on the quality and quantity of the emerging language? Do environmental factors influence children's language development enough to require major modifications in language instruction for minority children? Many, apparently, would answer "yes" to both questions.

A common conception among in-service teachers, as reported in Shuy, Wolfram, and Riley *(52),* is that the language knowledge of poor children, especially black children, lacks some essential characteristics which exist in the language of the middle-class, white children. One text written for preservice teachers even states that overcrowded, noisy homes prevent adequate language learning *(29)*. While more and more educators are accepting a less prescriptive attitude toward the language of various groups, there persists among many the idea that the language of disadvantaged children is deficient. For example, teachers in such diverse locations as Chicago, Memphis, Coney Island, and Michigan hold biased expectations for children's school success because of variations in dialect *(10)*. Before teachers accept the fact that such deficiencies exist, a close examination of the research supporting this view (often called the "deficit theory") is necessary.

A group of studies published during the middle 1960s examined the question of whether or not there is a difference between the amount of language knowledge that middle-class children have and the language knowledge that lower-class, disadvantaged children have at various points during the elementary years. For many educators and psychologists, the conclusion that a language deficit does exist in the language of disadvantaged children indicates a need to intervene in the educational process early in the preschool years to offer the child language experiences he would not receive at home. This conclusion has been reinforced by studies which have suggested there are specific areas of language dysfunction in disadvantaged children.

Deutsch and Brown *(17)* found that when groups were equated by socioeconomic level, the IQs of black children were lower than those of white children in both the first and the fifth grades. The difference between black and white children was greater at the higher socioeconomic levels than at the lower levels. Since IQ is dependent largely on verbal ability, M. Deutsch *(16)* analyzed language data at the first- and fifth-grade levels. He found that being poor and/or a member of a minority group resulted in a tendency to have poorer language functioning than being white and middle class. Although Deutsch found little difference between groups in the ability to label, the differences appeared in the ability to use language for abstract purposes and were greater at the fifth-grade level than at the first. This discrepancy led to the idea that, as these children continued in school, their verbal proficiency fell further behind that of middle-class children. As support, John's study *(34)* comparing first- and fifth-grade black children's performance on various standard measures of verbal fluency showed no difference between lower- and middle-class children at the first-grade level but indicated a significant difference by the fifth grade. Of course, this may be due to inadequate schooling of poor children, as Baratz and Baratz assert *(7)*.

Researchers have also attempted to uncover the *causes* of verbal deficiencies found. John and Goldstein *(35)* analyzed lower-class children's categorization skills and found these children had more difficulty fitting objects into categories than did middle-class children. These authors thought verbal feedback from the home was essential for learning this skill. In a study by Hess and Shipman *(32),* lower-class black mothers tended to provide less verbal explanation to their four-year-old children in problem-solving tasks than black middle-class mothers did.

Another explanation for the supposed language deficiency is impairment of auditory discrimination (perception of phonemic differences). C. Deutsch *(15)* found poor auditory discrimination in lower-class black first-graders who were unsuccessful in beginning reading. She explained that the noise level of slum homes caused difficulties in hearing which produced the perception problem, but this explanation was untested. In fact, Friedlander *(27)* showed that excessive noise is not necessarily uniquely characteristic of poor families. Furthermore, Deutsch used a test for auditory discrimination based on standard dialect.

Conflicting evidence for the language deficit idea comes from study of language structure. Some aspects of nonstandard dialect-speaking preschool children's speech are at least equivalent to standard dialect speakers. For example, Entwhisle's studies *(22, 23)* of word associations showed that poor black and white first graders were superior to white suburban first graders. This superiority of poor children disappeared over the school years. Further, Lacivita, Kean and Yamamoto *(41)* found elementary children equally able to assign meanings to nonsense words that had proper inflections and were embedded in sentences, whatever socioeconomic class they belonged to. Similarly, Shriner and Miner *(50)* showed that white preschool children did not differ by social class in their ability to generalize morphological rules, and Cazden *(10, 11)* reported that very early growth in acquisition of language structures demonstrated that lower-class black children were undergoing the same sequence and kind of acquisition as middle-class whites. Ammon and Ammon *(2)* reported that training young speakers of black English in vocabulary has a more positive effect than training them in sentences. Cazden *(11)* recommends vocabulary training for all children, particularly for poor children.

When we assimilate this information, it appears that a strong case for the existence of a major language deficiency is not possible. Nevertheless, in the language-cognitive tasks of categorization and in parental teaching of problem solving there are social class/racial differences. These differences are not, however, sufficient to substantiate the following claim:

The child of poverty has language problems. These are problems far more crippling than mere dialect problems . . . in brief, the child of poverty has not been taught as much about the meaning of language as a middle-class child of the same age.[1]

In application to preschool education, acceptance of the language deficiency position, as in the Bereiter-Engelmann *(8)* preschool program, would lead to training meant to overcome possibly nonexistent language problems. Children might get the idea that something is wrong with the way they speak, and verbal withdrawal may result. But, as we have seen in chapter 2, verbal activity is necessary for language development.

Study of Dialect Patterns

The view that the nonstandard dialect of minority preschoolers is merely different, not deficient, the view of sociolinguists, leads to different in-structional application. The research into dialect patterns has been done mostly by sociolinguists who have been trained as linguists to find pat-terns and similarities in regional and social dialects. They believe teachers should understand the patterns of language used and historical sources of dialect and adjust to them. Since the nonstandard dialect studied most completely is Black English, the social dialect spoken by many black Americans, the history and feature characteristics of this dialect are available for teachers.

Stewart *(53),* a sociolinguist, has traced the history of the English spoken by slaves during the early history of the country. Stewart finds that many forms of Black English today reflect the early *creolization* of English by slaves. Creole languages are modifications by depressed minority groups of the dominant language. Apparently, slaves in the United States spoke a language similar to that spoken by slaves in Sur-inam and in the Carribean islands which reflected their West African origins. The slaves who worked in the plantation house began to modify their speech toward the British-descended English fairly quickly, while the creolized form of English spoken by field hands changed more slowly. After slavery, continual modification of the language in the direction of the more socially prestigious Standard English continued. Despite the movement toward Standard English, such present-day forms as the Black English use of the verb *to be,* lack of possessives in some in-stances, and uninflected pronouns are, in Stewart's view, all traceable to early creole language spoken by slaves.

However, borrowing has not all been one way. Standard American English shows influences of Black English. For example, the common American use of "uh-huh" to indicate affirmation with rising intonation

---

1. S. Engelmann, "How to Construct Effective Language Programs for the Poverty Child," in *Language and Poverty: Perspectives on a Theme,* ed. F. Williams (Chicago: Markham, 1970), p. 102.

and to indicate negation with falling intonation has been traced by Abrahams *(1)* to language spoken in West Africa. There have been lexical borrowings from Black to Standard English of such terms as *man* in the sense of comrade, *the man* in the sense of white authority, *cool, hot,* etc. Older jazz terms, such as *gig* and *pad,* existed in Black English before they became part of the white person's lexicon. A new expression common to blacks confuses whites; blacks may say "those are *bad* shoes" to mean the shoes are nice.

Despite borrowing back and forth, sociolinguists find many consistent structural characteristics in the speech of some blacks which are caused by dialect. These characteristics are *contrasts* between the Black English dialect and the Standard English one spoken by more teachers.

There are a number of cautions which must be made before we turn to this discussion of Black English forms. First, there are many more points of similarity between the dialects than there are differences, of course; otherwise, we would be discussing different languages rather than dialects. Second, many blacks do not speak or have never spoken Black English. Third, not all characteristics of Black English discussed here are in the speech of all speakers of Black English. Fourth, Black English is much closer to the Standard English spoken in the South than that spoken in the North; therefore, Black English in northern cities is at greater variance from Standard English than it is in the South. Fifth, many blacks speak both Standard and Black English. Sixth, there are many other dialects of English which are at variance with Standard. Finally, many bidialectal persons switch, usually quite unconsciously, from one dialect to the other depending on the context.

There are a number of Black English grammatical factors found in the speech of people in cities such as Detroit by Shuy, Wolfram, and Riley *(52)* and New York by Labov *(38)* which are at variance with the forms of Standard English. Labov *(37)* contends that the major differences between Black and Standard English are phonological. Common phonological patterns in Black English are: reduction of /r/ and /l/ at the ends and in the middle of words, simplification of final consonant clusters so that only the first of the two consonants is sounded, a general weakening of final consonants, combinations of these consonant characteristics, some variation in medial vowel sounds in certain contexts, and, mostly for very young Black English speakers, /f/ instead of /θ/, "roof" for "Ruth." Chart 1 contains phonological differences or contrasts, expressed as word pairs. The two words in each pair are pronounced and perceived as separate in Standard English but as equivalent or as homonyms in Black English. Thus, some Black English speakers will pronounce words such as "guard" and "God" alike because they reduce the /r/ of "guard."

Chart 1.

Characteristics of Black English*

r-lessness

guard = God	court = caught	terrace = tess
nor = gnaw	fort = fought	
sore = saw	Paris = pass	

l-lessness

toll = toe	all = awe
help = hep	Saul = saw
tool = too	fault = fought

Simplification of consonant clusters

rift = riff	box = bock	wind = wine
past = pass	mix = Mick	hold = hole
meant = men	mend = men	

Weakening of final consonants

seat = seed = see	feed = feet
bit = bid = big	road = row

Combination

picked = pick	raised = raise
miss = mist = missed	stream = scream
fine = find = fined	strap = scrap

Vowel sounds

pin = pen	find = fond	sure = shore
since = cents	peel = pail	boil = ball
beer = bear	poor = pour	

Th-sounds

Ruth = roof
death = deaf

---

*Adapted from W. Labov, "Some Sources of Reading Problems for Negro Speakers of Nonstandard English," in *Teaching Black Children to Read,* ed. J. C. Baratz and R. W. Shuy (Washington, D.C.: Center for Applied Linguistics, 1969), pp. 29–67 by permission of the Center for Applied Linguistics.

There are also syntactic contrasts between Black and Standard English, many of which are influenced by the phonological ones. For example, in saying the Black English equivalent for "You'll do it," the characteristic reduction of /l/ and weakening of final consonants would render "You do it." Rather than losing meaning by such reduction, no meaning loss occurs because the statement is embedded in context whether we are talking, listening, reading, or writing. And context explicates meaning. Chart 2 lists major syntactic contrasts.

Chart 2.
Syntactic Differences between Black and Standard English*

Black English	*Standard English*
1. He going.	He is going.
2. He be here.	He is here *all the time.*
3. John cousin.	John's cousin.
4. I got five cent.	I have five cents.
5. John he live in New York.	John lives in New York.
6. I drunk the milk.	I drank the milk.
7. Yesterday he walk home.	Yesterday he walked home.
8. She have a bicycle.	She has a bicycle.
9. You go home.	You'll go home.
10. I ask did he do it.	I asked if he did it.
11. I don't got none.	I don't have any.
12. I want a apple.	I want an apple.
13. He book.	His book.
14. He over to his friend house.	He is over at his friend's house.

---

*Adapted from J. C. Baratz, "Teaching Reading in an Urban Negro School System," in *Teaching Black Children to Read,* ed. J. C. Baratz and R. W. Shuy (Washington, D.C.: Center for Applied Linguistics, 1969), pp. 99–100 by permission of the Center for Applied Linguistics.

The first two contrasts in Chart 2 illustrate a rule which does not exist in Standard English. In the first entry, "He going," the copula is deleted under certain conditions when momentary action is meant. It is present as "be" when habitual action is intended. Note that in Standard English the phrase "all the time" is necessary to translate the full meaning of the second entry. This structure is often used as an example to deny the assertion that Black English is a simplified version of Standard, since, in this case, Standard is simplified to a greater extent than Black English. Further characteristics of Black English are optional deletion of the possessive marker ("John cousin"); deletion of the noun plural in some instances ("I got five cent"); insertion of a pronoun after the proper noun ("John he live in New York"); alternate forms of variant verbs ("I drunk the milk"); different systems of noun-verb agreement ("Yesterday he walk home," "She have a bicycle," and "You go home"); variant structure of embedded questions ("I ask did he do it"); different transformational rules for some negatives ("I don't got none"); indefinite article differences ("I want a apple"); possessive and other pronoun differences ("He book"); and prepositions which vary in some settings ("He over to his friend house").

Teachers unfamiliar with these structural characteristics should listen to Black English-speaking children—good audio tapes are available

(31)—to reduce possible confusions in instruction. As persons unfamiliar with Black English speech listen carefully for the features described above, they discover variations in the number of Black English features children use. Some children use the marked features more often than others.Further, all children are affected by the formality of the situation. School-aged children are apt to use fewer Black English features in oral reading and class talk than when talking with friends or about activities *(33)*. Awareness of pupils' language will increase teachers' sensitivity.

Channon *(12)* illustrated how dialect differences can interfere in communication between pupils and teachers. Her class was asked to suggest examples of words that rhymed with "old." Since in Black English such words often have a reduced final consonant cluster, the assignment was confusing. Channon related how pupils' attempts to offer not only "fold" and "sold" but "bowl" and "soul" appeared to them to be haphazardly rejected. To explain, if pupils rhymed "fold" and "bowl," how could they understand why only one of these was acceptable? From the confusion that resulted the pupils withdrew from participation. Teachers who understand Black English features that might produce confusion in class activities can avoid them.

Although we have not made a strong case for verbal functioning differences due to dialect or for differences in milestones of syntactic development, there are distinct feature contrasts between Black English and Standard English that have given rise to the question of whether schools should teach Black English-speaking children to speak Standard English.

The Question of Dialect Change

Children who speak Black English are rarely taught to substitute Standard English for a number of reasons. For one thing it is impractical. More importantly, such change would distance children from the preferred communication style of family and community. Additionally, sociolinguists have shown that Black English, while different from Standard, is equivalent in its power to communicate (more powerful in many settings). Thus, there is no communication need for dialect change. However, there have been recommendations that Standard features be *added* (not substituted) to the oral repertory of Black English-speaking children.

Shuy *(51)* has reported that employers, even of nonskilled labor, react negatively to a Black English speaker, even though they disclaim any preference for "good" English. Consequently, many educators believe that at some point before the end of the school years, students should have the opportunity to acquire Standard English so that they will not be discriminated against unnecessarily in adult life. Educators ask when such instruction should occur. Athey and Salzberg *(4)* suggest that training in Standard English begin during early preschool, since this is the period of most rapid language growth. But there are more compelling reasons for delaying change. First, research on dialect and beginning reading success shows that general language proficiency rather than dialect preference was related to a successful start in reading *(28)*. Children need ample opportunity to develop language rather than training to change the superficial form of language.

Second, Labov *(40)* showed that not until just before or during adolescence do children become aware of and sensitive to dialect differences. Schools probably should take advantage of this awareness by initiating training later in the school years. However, both Labov *(38)* and Loban *(45)* found a higher incidence of Black English forms just at the onset of adolescence.

A third reason for delaying teaching Standard English is a simple, practical one. It is expecting too much of children preparing to learn to read or just beginning literacy (chapters 7 and 8) to acquire major oral language additions.

Study of Social Aspects of Dialect

The studies of verbal functioning and analysis of dialect patterns offer teachers some understanding of nonstandard dialect; study of the social aspects of language broadens insight into what happens in classrooms. The social aspects of language are of critical importance since the difficulties minority children have in school are influenced by others' perceptions of their language. This discussion examines the effect of immediate environment on nonstandard speakers' language behavior and the attitudes held toward nonstandard dialects.

It appears that the context in which school-aged children talk affects their verbosity. In comfortable street-talk, many Black English-speaking children learn to be competent in culturally preferred styles of oral language. In fact, verbal performance in indirect speech forms determines social status among some adolescent and young adult Black English-speaking groups. Ritual insults, embellished story-telling, nonverbal accompaniments, and the use of nonliteral meaning characterize the verbal games children learn from their older siblings. Expressive language may be highly advanced among these children *(10)*, even though the unfamiliar functions of the content-oriented language required in school tasks may become personally threatening. Many such children respond to school language tasks by withdrawing verbally, even while oral language development in the socially preferred styles continues outside school.

In fact, Houston *(33)* found that rural, Black English-speaking elementary school children produced more mature, complex syntax when talking about family and friends than about school-related subjects. Labov *(37)* described how one pre-adolescent boy's speech production increased when the community-raised interviewer brought in another boy, sat on the floor, and used taboo words. In conditions perceived as favorable, other ghetto youngsters Labov studied were apt to be more logical and analytic than in conditions perceived as unfavorable. Heider *(30)* found direct suggestions to lower-class children that they use explanations were helpful in stimulating more mature language. Ervin-Tripp *(24)* has stated that lower-class children are more sensitive to the language situation than middle-class children; thus, these children are more prone to adverse reaction in situations viewed as threatening.

Context also affects the verbosity of preschoolers in compelling ways. In a study by Schacter et al. *(49)* preschoolers' use of language varied by social and racial groups. When talking to others during spontaneous play at school, advantaged white children directed more mature sounding remarks to adults than did advantaged black children, who, on the other hand, directed more mature sounding remarks to other children than the white children did. Of more importance was the finding that advantaged children of both races used more "modulation" (explanations, justifications, etc.) than did disadvantaged children. The group of disadvantaged black children with lower intelligence made fewer "asserts desire to adults" statements than another group of disadvantaged black children with higher IQs. The researchers suggested the lower IQ children had developed less trust toward adults. The study illustrates that even during the formative years children are diverging by social class in productive use of language.

Applying the findings of this research to classroom practice, encouragement of talk is clearly essential. Because of the evidence that situation affects language production, nonthreatening environments must be established. Preschool disadvantaged children need to learn to ask for things and be praised when they do. In addition, whenever children begin to explain events, praise and reminders to all the children are important. Activities in which children play the roles of adults may develop natural extension of mature language, as Ervin-Tripp *(24)* suggests. Finally, teachers can use extent of language production as a guide to planning. For example, if "Show and Tell" produces tongue-tied children while puppet play does the opposite, "Show and Tell" should be eliminated until children develop more language flexibility. Chapter 4 contains a number of suggestions for specific stimulations of language.

While the research on social use of language is discouraging enough, the study of teacher attitudes toward nonstandard language is even more depressing. Negative attitude toward nonstandard language will surely prevent sensitive provision of a nonthreatening environment. Yet negative attitude appears to be widespread. In one study, teachers held negative judgments toward black children and their Black English dialect *(55)*. In another study by Williams and others *(56)*, younger preservice teachers, who presumably held more liberal attitudes than did older teachers, when viewing video tapes of black, Mexican American and Anglo-white children, made stereotypic responses, showing they perceived ethnic minority children negatively. Additionally, Williams and others *(57)*, in a third study, found that negative stereotypic responses to minority children were associated with low expectation for success in language related learning in school. Low expectation by teachers has been found to result in low achievement (reviewed by Athey [*3*]).

Apparently some teachers are very negative toward minority children and expect little in terms of school achievement. Probably not all teachers are so negative. Indeed, in another study, data showed that if the teacher was of the same race as the children, the bias was reduced, but this was true only if the children were of a higher, not lower, socioeconomic level than the teacher *(26)*. Personal soul-searching examinations of attitudes to minority children help teachers identify their biases. Acknowledgment of bias is productive only when realistic attempts are made to change. Teachers must also realize that when their expectation for children of poor, problem-ridden families is low, the expectation may well contribute to school failure.

In summary of this section on dialect, both substantive and emotive arguments have been presented against the idea that speaking a nonstandard dialect *per se* leads to immature language development. In fact, word association study and study of syntactic acquisition suggests speakers of Black English are at no disadvantage in language development. However, problem-solving modelling from parental behavior is less available to poor than to middle-class children *(32);* this reduction in problem-solving development may lead to depressed ability to categorize *(35)*.

Study of the social aspects of language indicates that the situation in which language functions strongly affects children's production. This is not only true of elementary school-aged children, but preschoolers as well *(49)*. Instruction for poor, black children needs to concentrate on explanation during problem-solving tasks, encouragement of assertive comments to adults, and categorizing activities.

Teachers, too, appear to play a significant role in determining the quality of language production among poor children. Teachers have been reported to be negative in their assessments of minority children, particularly in relation to their assessment of language-related learning

(26). Close examination of attitudes by teachers and during teacher training is needed. It is past time to hear teachers comment, "What can you expect of *these* children; they can't even speak good English?"

Bilingualism

The number of non-English speaking school children in the United States is growing *(36),* and schools need to plan for this growth. In Chicago, for example, large numbers of children speak Spanish, Greek, Oriental languages, or Polish. There are, in all, over forty non-English languages represented in the speech of Chicago school children *(13).* In this section, aspects of instruction for non-English speakers are discussed. Because the largest group of bilingual or potentially bilingual persons in the United States are Spanish speakers, emphasis is placed on Spanish/English bilingual education.

The language situation of our growing Spanish-speaking population is somewhat different from that of Black English speakers. In contrast to dialect difference where the variations are within one language, bilinguals have two language systems. Since the situation for bilingual education differs from the dialect situation, an entirely different analysis is needed. A true bilingual can speak two languages, often equivalently or nearly so. Thus, children being trained to be bilingual must learn to operate with entirely different rule systems. They must learn new sounds and allowable combinations of sounds, new words, and order of words to express sentence relationships *(47).* Hopefully, the children also will acquire literacy in the two languages and will understand cultural behaviors of both groups. Ervin-Tripp *(25)* distinguishes between the *coordinate bilingual* whose two languages are generally used in different settings entirely separately and the *compound bilingual* whose two languages are used interchangeably with some language interference between the two languages.

The problems of developing language facility in English while achieving other goals of bilingualism, literacy in two languages, and biculturalism in a coordinate framework are widespread. Children who grow up in a truly bilingual situation, where both English and Spanish are spoken as native languages, do not have the problems in school of those who grow up in an environment where Spanish only is spoken. Truly bilingual children are relatively rare, however. Most children of Spanish-speaking communities—and there are thousands of Spanish-speaking children in our schools—have only a cursory acquaintance with English. These children will encounter problems in kindergarten and the primary grades unless schools make provisions for their special needs.

This section contains a brief review of second language acquisition, a list of Spanish/English points of conflict for English-learning children, and discussion of two important questions: (1) whether instruction in initial reading should be in the first learned language or in the dominant second language, and (2) the best organizational pattern for developing bilingualism.

Acquisition of Second Language

During the preschool years, children learn a *new language* easily. In fact, preschool children who have equivalent languages have an amazing ability to switch from one language to another to fit the person with whom they are speaking. I knew a two-year-old girl whose father always spoke Italian and whose mother always spoke Spanish. The child consistently spoke Italian to her father and Spanish to her mother. In addition, she knew some English and a little French. Other bilingual families have reported that there is some confusion of vocabulary items at the initial stage of acquisition but that once words are combined, the two languages are not confused. Thus, one way of acquiring a second language is to learn it at home along with the first. In a sense, this is learning two first languages.

Another way of learning a second language is to become completely immersed in it during the school years. Lambert and his associates *(43)* in Montreal placed English monolingual preschool children in a totally French environment for kindergarten and first grade with English taking over some forty percent of the instructional time after grade one. They found at the end of the fourth grade that the children were bilingual and were achieving slightly below equivalent French-speaking children and equally to English-speaking children. A parallel application of this model would be the complete immersion of Spanish-speaking children in English classrooms. Indeed, this was the traditional model for educating non-English children in the United States for many years. However, the model is not now effective in the United States since too many non-English children fail to learn English at acceptable levels, especially children with strong non-English linguistic and cultural ties *(19)*.

For years educators have discussed why the Lambert model has been inoperable in the United States. The explanation is due partly to the social prestige of the home language and the acquired language and partly to the identification with the cultures associated with the two languages. The Lambert children in Montreal already spoke the prestigious language of the country; they came from middle-class families, they had had rich preschool language experiences; they had adult models of bilingualism; and *(21)* their parents were eager for them to learn French. By contrast, the Spanish-speaking children in the United States speak a language of low prestige not essential for business in this country; their Spanish dialect is apt to be nonstandard; the majority of the children are from low socioeconomic homes; they have few close models of true bilingualism.

However, in spite of the inapplicability of the Lambert model for elementary schools, educators recommend something like it during the preschool years, the years of maximum language learning. Guaranteeing the presence of a natural language environment in the preschool classroom seems to be provision enough for preschool children to learn English as a second language if they are required to speak English to communicate. To encourage second language acquisition, Cazden *(10)* recommends that schools create "an educational environment that reactivates the natural language-learning abilities which all children have."[2] Such an environment stresses rich natural dialogue in the new language.

Ervin-Tripp *(25)* has noted a number of characteristic patterns in the language of preschool children acquiring a second language in natural settings such as those described above. For example, she reported about a child acquiring English as a second language who used the negative marker in his primitive English much as a two- or three-year-old who is acquiring English as a first language would (chapter 2). But once he had acquired understanding of the more mature structure of negatives ("I *did* not do it"), he moved more quickly into mature negatives than would a child learning English for the first time. Further, preschoolers learning a second language are apt to stress those second language words that are like first language words (cognates) as they would stress them in the first language. Interdental consonants ($/\theta/$ and $/\delta/$) were acquired more quickly if the sounds were in the first language than if they were not. More importantly, Ervin-Tripp found that second language learners needed to understand semantic relations before they could master the syntactic rules to represent them.

Thus, schools that provide exposure to fairly simplified language spoken by native speakers plus opportunity for children to practice the new language structures are supporting the natural acquisition process observed in bilingual children. On the other hand, drills where the teacher presents a negative sentence for the children to parrot back, do not follow the recommendations for natural environments for language learning. In order for teachers to be prepared to expand and illustrate structures that may cause problems for English second language learners, they must understand what areas cause potential difficulty.

---

2. C. Cazden, *Child Language and Education* (New York: Holt, Rinehart, and Winston, 1972), p. 177.

Spanish/English Points of Conflict

Chart 3 demonstrates areas that may pose difficulty for Spanish-speaking children learning English. Because there are these points of conflict, it does not follow that instruction should be designed to drill on each point. Instead when teachers hear English-learning children making these "errors," they should provide more language data on the English structure so children can induce the form. However, to establish auditory discrimination (ability to hear English distinctions not present in Spanish) and then pronunciation of difficult phonemes of English, preschool and early elementary children should be engaged in many rhyming and sound-emphasized activities. When children achieve the English pronunciation, direct praise and repetition of the sounds give clear feedback that they are developing English correctly. Rarely, when English acquisition is well under way, teachers may contrast the two syntactic systems; that is, they may, on hearing a child say "I have six years," respond first to the content and then compare how the sentence is produced in English. However, much comparative analysis of the two languages is unsuitable for young children because it requires abstraction beyond their cognitive level.

Many of the activities described in chapter 4 on language development are appropriate for second language learners. For productive use of the activities, some issues that concern bilingual educators need attention.

Issues in Bilingual Education

Issues in bilingual education within the scope of this book are (1) the issue of which language should be used for first literacy—the native language or the dominant English language, and (2) the design of bilingual programs.

Under the traditional model of immersion of non-English-speaking children into English-only classes, the language for literacy was, of course, English. As indicated above, this model has not proved effective for school-aged children. Furthermore, many parents want their children to develop literacy skill in the non-English language as well as competence in English. In fact, the Supreme Court ruling in Lau vs. Nichols, 1970, asserts the right of children to enough special language education so they have equivalent skill to native English speakers. The Bilingual Education Act of 1967-68 provided funds for training children in native language until their English is satisfactorily developed; additional moneys were available after 1974. Some states with large non-English populations require bilingual education where there are sufficient numbers of children to warrant it *(36)*. However, there are not enough funds avail-

Chart 3.
Problem Areas in Learning English*

English	Spanish	Problem

Sound System

1. Vowels
   a. Simple

English	Spanish	Problem
/i/ bit	/æ/ *a*lto	Spanish speakers have a
/æ/ bat	/e/ *le*guna	stable set of vowel sounds
/e/ leg	/iy/ aq*ui*	and will have difficulty
/a/ hop	/ow/ herm*o*sa	with the variety of sounds
/u/ full	/uw/ m*u*cho	in English. Some possible
/ð/ duck		homonyms:
/iy/ beet		bit = beet
/ey/ hay		bat = bet
/ay/ spite		hat = hot
/ow/ gloat		fun = fawn
/uw/ fuse		late = let
		fool = full

   b. Diphthongs

/oy/ toy	b*ai*le, c*ua*dro
/aw/ out	d*ia*blo, c*au*sa
/yuw/ few	r*ei*na, c*ue*nto
	b*ie*n, de*u*da
	lab*io*s, ci*u*dad
	c*ui*dado, c*uo*ta

   c. Distinctive features
      voiced/voiceless
      contrast

2. Consonants
   a. Specifics

English	Spanish	Problem
/b/ boy	/v/ between syllables; or /p/ in beginning	boy = poy about = avout
/h/ house	no phoneme	how = ow
/v/ vote	/b/, perhaps	vote = boat
/š/ shoe	/č/ chew	shoe = chew
/j/ jump	either /č/ or /y/	jump = yump = chump
/θ/ thank	either /s/, /t/, or /f/	thank = sank = tank = fank
/ð/ this	/d/	this = dis
/z/ zoo	/s/	soo = sue
/ž/ measure	/č/ or /š/	measure = measher

	English	Spanish	Problem
b. Consonant clusters			
	Many initial ones, many with *s*	few, none with initial s	Apt to add /ðs/ as preliminary syllables to "stop," "station," etc.
	Many final clusters	few	Apt to be reduced to one phoneme
c. Other			
	40 different phonemes at end of words	only 10 phonemes at end	

Syntactic System

	English	Spanish	Problem
1.	Adjective and noun order stable, no agreement	some adjectives follow noun, agreement	Apt to hear structures like "the hat red"
2.	Few inflections on adjectives, pronouns, articles	inflections show gender and number	Expectation that gender associated with nouns: "The table she"
3.	Few verb inflections; auxiliaries show tense, aspects: has, will, had, etc.	tense and aspect shown by inflections	Auxiliaries hard to learn
4.	Always uses subject pronoun	sometimes deletes subject pronoun	Difficult to remember to put "He" in "He is a farmer."
5.	*S* shows noun number and verb person	no such equivalent use of one inflection for two purposes	Difficulty in learning third person singular
6.	Yes/no questions invert subject and verb	not required to invert	May produce questions like "You want my book?" with only intonation to show question
7.	"Do" support for questions and negatives: "Where did you go?" "I didn't do it."	no "do" support	Slow acquisition of negatives and questions

Chart 3 (Continued)

	English	Spanish	Problem
8.	Use of "be" in "I am six" and weather statements	use of "have"	"I have six years."
9.	Cannot delete article	occasionally article deleted	Incorrect omission of article: "He is farmer."

Vocabulary

1. There are many Spanish/English cognates. Difficulty may arise in pronunciation.

2. Many words have different forms.

3. Idioms and alternate connotations can produce difficulty.

---

*Adapted from R. Ruddell, *Reading-Language Instruction: Innovation Practices* (Englewood Cliffs, N. J.: Prentice-Hall, 1974), pp. 273–77 and R. Lado, *Linguistics across Cultures* (Ann Arbor: University of Michigan Press, 1968).

---

able nor enough qualified teachers to realize the law in large urban school systems beset with other problems.

In existing bilingual classes, a pressing question is whether the first language a child learns to read should be the non-English language or English. Much of the research on the question of which language is best for initial literacy has been conducted in other countries with other languages where the social impact of language choice differs considerably from the United States. In addition, the studies have design problems that weaken their generalizability. A thorough review of the research by Engle *(21)* did not produce a clear advantage for learning reading in the first language. On the other hand, it did not reveal any harm resulting from first reading in the first language. Ultimately, starting with the first nondominant language is more likely to result in biliterate bilingualism, an achievement of the educational systems of many other nations. This complex problem is further complicated by the fact that children in the United States come to schools with language skills that may not be fully developed in the first language and that are confused with English structures. Thus, for these children, initial reading in Spanish, for example, will not be the critical instructional question, but language development in both languages.

Thus, the recommendation for young children with no English but sufficiently developed Spanish is to begin reading instruction in Spanish if numbers of children and available teachers and materials allow. At the same time a thorough program to develop oral language skills in English should be initiated prior to reading in that language. On the other hand, for children who have underdeveloped skill in the first and second language, separate oral language development is important; reading could probably begin in either language profitably after the children are deemed ready (see chapter 6 for reading readiness assessment). For older children who have already begun learning to read and write in a non-English language, continuation of that language is called for while initial oral English and reading of simple English begins. These children will be able to transfer their understanding of reading to the new language and will be able to acquire vocabulary through reading as well as through instruction in oral English. Some languages have fewer parallels for productive transfer than others. That is, Spanish literacy skill will transfer to English more easily than will Chinese skill in literacy.

There are innumerable program designs schools use to accommodate to non-English speaking children. Some adjustment to these children occurs with TESL classes (Teaching English as a Second Language) which provide training in English by special teachers who take children out of regular, English-only classes periodically. The TESL plan is often used in schools with multilingual children; it does not develop skill in the non-English language. Another approach in English-only programs immerses children in English for most of each day but trains them in the native language for a small portion of their instruction. Alternatively, those children with little or no English may be placed in full-time bilingual classes. Of course, the children are not initially bilingual, but the goal of the program is to reach bilingual skill. Some of these classes have bilingual teachers who begin training in Spanish (or the language spoken by the children) and gradually develop more and more English language until the two languages are nearly equivalent. When their skills permit, children are often transferred to other English-only classes to make room for new non-English speakers. Sometimes bilingual classes have two teachers, or one aide and a teacher. One adult will teach in one language and the other in the other language. In bilingual classes, the children are expected to move from one language to another and back during the course of a school day.

The most extensive combination of languages in school programming developed some years ago in Miami. The Coral Way School staff recognized that the families of Cuban children were unwilling for their children to be educated only in English and that the English-speaking children were unable to communicate with their new neighbors. The program was designed so that both groups of children studied in English for one-half of the instructional time and in Spanish for the other half. By the end of the sixth grade, both groups became fluent in both languages *(5)*. The design of the Coral Way School has the advantage of clearly demonstrating to children that both languages are respected and worthy of maintenance, an advantage present in none of the other designs. However, Engle *(21)* reports that a change in the school population has reduced the success of the program; children from poorer homes have moved in and do not seem as successful with the two-language maintenance.

Because non-English speaking children have a recurrent problem in continuing to grow in literacy achievement once past the decoding stages of beginning reading, Austin *(5)* made suggestions about methods of teaching and appropriate content. She recommended that children be continually exposed to enriching concept development activities and continual reinforcement of the new language because of the lack of background language support that English-speaking homes provide their children. In addition, while the emphasis on sound/symbol relationships in teaching reading appears successful in teaching Spanish-speaking children initially, teachers are cautioned to pay continual attention to advancing the conceptual level of bilingual children.

To summarize this section, we have seen that bilingual education is an area with many issues, but little research-based direction. While preschoolers seem to profit from early immersion in English, school-aged children do not learn English as easily this way. For these children, some emphasis on the native language in oral language development and in acquisition of literacy skills is desirable. First literacy may be begun in the native language but only when it is clearly the stronger language of the children and when schools can make provision for it. Oral language development is especially needed for children with mixed languages to help them advance in both languages. The kind of program design appropriate for bilingual education is determined by available resources. Generally, given children's rights, social needs, and academic needs, a program which supports both languages is recommended.

Related Activities

1. While observing or teaching in a class with Black English speakers, listen carefully to the speech of one pupil. Make a list of all the Black English structures you hear. Then do the same with the same pupil during play and compare the changes that occur.

2. Ask a number of persons if the way in which people speak indicates their abilities. Include in your sample, if possible, teacher-aides, teachers, business persons, persons in your families, children. What variations are there in people's responses?

3. Examine education materials for descriptions of non-Standard English. How many differ from the position presented here?

4. Visit a bilingual class, if possible, and see if you can relate the organization of activities with the descriptions provided here.

5. Find an adult who entered school with a non-English language. (There are many older persons in the United States who fulfill this description.) Ask this person his or her first reaction to school, how he/she learned English, and what happened to the first language after English became easy to use.

6. When working with Black English-speaking pupils, try to initiate a rhyming activity like that described on page 54 and note responses.

References

1. Abrahams, R. "Welding Communication Breaks." Paper read to Trainers of Teacher Trainers Conference on Language and Cultural Diversity, January 1971, St. Cloud, Minnesota.
2. Ammon, P. R., and Ammon, M. S. "Effects of Training Black Preschool Children in Vocabulary vs. Sentence Construction." *Journal of Educational Psychology* 63 (1972): 421–26.
3. Athey, I. "Reading Research in the Affective Domain." In *Theoretical Models and Processes of Reading,* 2d ed., edited by H. Singer and R. B. Ruddell. Newark, Delaware: International Reading Association, 1976.
4. Athey, J. J., and Salzberg, A. "Language Development." Paper read at American Educational Research Association meeting, April 1972, Chicago.
5. Austin, M. "United States." In *Comparative Reading,* edited by J. Downing. New York: Macmillan, 1974.
6. Baratz, J. C. "Teaching Reading in an Urban Negro School System." In *Teaching Black Children to Read,* edited by J. C. Baratz and R. W. Shuy. Washington, D.C.: Center for Applied Linguistics, 1969.
7. Baratz, S. S., and Baratz, J. C. "Early Childhood Intervention: The Social Science Base of Institutional Racism." *Harvard Educational Review* 40 (1970): 29–50.
8. Bereiter, C., and Engelmann, S. *Teaching Disadvantaged Children in the Preschool.* Englewood Cliffs, N. J.: Prentice-Hall, 1966.
9. Bronfenbrenner, U. "Is Early Intervention Effective?" *A Report on Longitudinal Evaluations of Preschool Programs.* Washington, D.C.: U. S. Dept. of Health, Education, and Welfare, 1974.
10. Cazden, C. *Child Language and Education.* New York: Holt, Rinehart, & Winston, 1972.

11. _____. "The Neglected Situations in Child Language Research and Education." In *Language and Poverty: Perspectives on a Theme,* edited by F. Williams. Chicago: Markham, 1970.

12. Channon, G. "Bulljive-Language Teaching in a Harlem School." *Urban Review* 2 (February 1968): 5–12.

13. Chicago School Board. *Survey of Pupils Whose First Language Is One Other than English.* September 1973.

14. Coleman, J. S., et al. *Equality of Educational Opportunity.* Washington, D.C.: U.S. Government Printing Office, 1966.

15. Deutsch, C. "Auditory Discrimination and Learning: Social Factors." *Merrill-Palmer Quarterly* 10 (1964): 277–96.

16. Deutsch, M. "The Role of Social Class in Language Development and Cognition." *American Journal of Orthopsychiatry* 25 (1965): 75–88.

17. Deutsch, M., and Brown, B. "Social Influences in Negro-White Intelligence Differences." *Journal of Social Issues* 20 (1964): 24–35.

18. deValdes, M. E. "Non-English Speaking Children and Literacy." In *Aspects of Reading Instruction,* edited by S. Pflaum-Connor. National Society for the Study of Education, Contemporary Issues Series. Berkeley, Ca.: McCutchan Press, 1978.

19. Dworkin, A. C. and Dworkin, R. J., eds. *The Minority Report: An Introduction to Racial, Ethic, and Gender Relations.* New York: Praeger. 1976.

20. Engelmann, S. "How to Construct Effective Language Programs for the Poverty Child." In *Language and Poverty: Perspectives on a Theme,* edited by F. Williams. Chicago: Markham, 1970.

21. Engle, P. E. "Language Medium in Early School Years for Minority Language Groups." *Review of Educational Research* 45 (Spring 1975): 238–325.

22. Entwhisle, D. P. "Semantics Systems of Children: Some Assessments of Social Class and Ethnic Differences." In *Language and Poverty: Perspectives on a Theme,* edited by F. Williams. Chicago: Markham, 1970.

23. _____. "Developmental Sociolinguistics: A Comparative Study in Four Subcultural Settings." *Sociometry* 29 (1966): 67–84.

24. Ervin-Tripp, S. "Children's Sociolinguistic Competence and Dialect Diversity." In *Early Childhood Education,* Seventy-first Yearbook of the National Society for the Study of Education. Chicago: University of Chicago Press, 1972.

25. _____. *Language Acquisition and Communicative Choice: Essays by M. Tripp.* Stanford, Ca.: Stanford University Press, 1973.

26. Feijo, T. D. and Jaegar, R. M. "Social Class and Race as Concomitants of Composite Halo in Teachers' Evaluative Rating of Pupils." *American Education Research Journal* 13 (Winter 1976): 1–14.

27. Friedlander, B. Z. "Receptive Language Development in Infancy." *Merrill-Palmer Quarterly* 16 (1970): 7–51.

28. Fryberg, E. "The Relations among English Syntax, Methods of Instruction, and Reading Achievement of First Grade Disadvantaged Black Children." Doctoral Dissertation, New York University, 1972.

29. Greene, H. A., and Petty, W. T. *Developing Language Skills in the Elementary Schools,* 3d ed. Boston: Allyn & Bacon, 1967.

30. Heider, E. R. "Style and Accuracy of Verbal Communications within and between Social Classes." *Journal of Personality and Social Psychology* 18 (1971): 33–47.

31. Hess, K. M.; Maxwell, J. C.; and Long, B. K. *Dialects and Dialect Learning.* Urbana, Ill.: National Council for Teachers of English, 1974. Kit includes tapes, manuals, booklets.

32. Hess, R. D., and Shipman, V. "Early Experience and the Socialization of Cognitive Modes in Children." *Child Development* 36 (1965): 869–86.

33. Houston, S. "A Reexamination of Some Assumptions about the Language of the Disadvantaged Child." *Child Development* 41 (1970): 947–63.

34. John, V. "The Intellectual Development of Slum Children: Some Preliminary Findings." *American Journal of Orthopsychiatry* 33 (1963): 813–22.

35. John, V. and Goldstein, L. "The Social Context of Language Acquisition." *Merrill-Palmer Quarterly* 10 (1964): 265–75.

36. Johnson, L. "Bilingual Bicultural Education: A Two-Way Street." *The Reading Teacher* 29 (December 1975): 231–39.

37. Labov, W. "The Logic of Nonstandard English." In *Language and Poverty: Perspectives on a Theme,* edited by F. Williams. Chicago: Markham, 1970.

38. _____. *The Social Stratification of English in New York City.* Washington, D.C.: Center for Applied Linguistics, 1966.

39. _____. "Some Sources of Reading Problems for Negro Speakers of Nonstandard English." In *Teaching Black Children to Read,* edited by J. C. Baratz and R. W. Shuy. Washington, D.C.: Center for Applied Linguistics, 1969.

40. _____. "Stages in the Acquisition of Standard English." In *Social Dialects and Language Learning,* edited by R. W. Shuy. Champaign, Ill.: National Council of Teachers of English, 1964.

41. Lacivita, A. F.; Kean, J. M.; and Yamamoto, K. "Socioeconomic Status of Children and Acquisition of Grammar." *Journal of Educational Research* 60 (1960): 71–74.

42. Lado, R. *Linguistics across Cultures.* Ann Arbor: University of Michigan Press, 1968.

43. Lambert, Wallace E.; Just, M.; and Segalowitz, N. "Some Cognitive Consequences of Following the Curricula of the Early School Grades in a Foreign Language." In *Twenty-first Annual Roundtable; Bilingualism and Language Contact,* edited by J. E. Alatis. Washington, D.C.: Georgetown University Press, 1970.

44. Lenneberg, E. *Biological Foundations of Language.* New York: John Wiley 1967, chapter 4.

45. Loban, W. *Problems in Oral English: Kindergarten through Grade Nine.* Champaign, Ill.: National Council of Teachers of English, Research Report #5, 1966.

46. *National Assessment of Educational Progress.* "'Johnny,' 'Mary' CAN Read: 9-year-olds Improve Reading Skills." Newsletter 9, October 1976.

47. Pflaum-Conner, S. "Nonstandard Student Language and Reading Achievement." In *Aspects of Reading Education,* edited by S. Pflaum-Connor. National Society for the Study of Education, Contemporary Issues Series. Berkeley, Ca.: McCutchan Press, 1978.

48. Ruddell, R. *Reading-Language Instruction: Innovative Practices.* Englewood Cliffs, N. J.: Prentice-Hall, 1974.

49. Schacter, F. F., et al. "Everyday Preschool Interpersonal Speech Usage: Methodological, Developmental, and Sociolinguistic Studies." *Monographs of the Society for Research in Child Development* 39 (1974).

50. Shriner, T. H., and Miner, L. "Morphological in the Language of Disadvantaged Children." *Journal of Speech and Hearing Research* 11 (1968): 604–10.

51. Shuy, R. W. Untitled paper read at Linguistic Society meeting, February 1971, at University of Minnesota, Minneapolis, Minnesota.

52. Shuy, R. W.; Wolfram, W. A.; and Riley W. K. *Linguistic Correlates of Social Stratification in Detroit Speech.* Final Report, Cooperative Research Project 6-1347. Washington, D.C.: U.S. Office of Education, Part IV, pp. 1–10.

53. Stewart, W. A. "Toward a History of American Negro Dialect." In *Language and Poverty: Perspectives on a Theme,* edited by F. Williams. Chicago: Markham, 1970.

54. Tavris, C. "Compensatory Education: The Glass Is Half Full." *Psychology Today* 10 (September 1976): 63–74.

55. Williams, F. "Psychological Correlates of Speech Characteristics on Sounding 'Disadvantaged'." *Journal of Speech and Hearing Research* 13 (September 1970): 472–88.

56. Williams, F.; Whitehead, J. L.; and Miller, L. M. "Ethnic Stereotyping and Judgments of Children's Speech." *Speech Monographs* 38 (August 1971): 166–70.

57. _____. "Relations between Language Attitudes and Teacher Expectancy." *American Education Research Journal* 9 (Spring 1972): 263–75.

4

Language in the Early Childhood Classroom

There is a curious aspect to early childhood education, at least in my opinion. Although there is a great deal of research and scholarly discussion of language acquisition available, there is relatively little attention to language in the preschool curriculum. For example, even the exemplary programs for young children, described in a volume edited by Day and Parker *(6),* have less emphasis on language development than other areas. The home-based programs described in that volume include principles of interaction and labelling and categorizing activities for families of young children. By contrast, in the school-based programs designed for disadvantaged or non-English-speaking children, language goals are more prominent, and in my experience, tend to be based on assumptions of language deficit. Furthermore, the programs for minority children tend to provide language instruction as repetitive drills without clear documentation that such instruction is successful and in spite of evidence that disadvantaged children acquire language as do middle-class children. In schools for middle-class children, on the other hand, the language goals that exist tend to be much more loosely defined, but teachers are expected to provide considerable interaction with their pupils.

This chapter will do something a little different—provide readers with suggestions for easily combining the language part of a preschool program with other components. Furthermore, this program is suitable for children from different backgrounds; because children learn different dialects is no indication that different approaches to instruction are needed. The content of the chapter, then, concerns the language component of an early childhood curriculum. The material is derived from the discussion of previous chapters modified and enhanced by ideas from some extant language programs. The first section reviews several language programs; the second section presents the assumptions and resultant goals for language development in a preschool curriculum; the third contains assessment and instructional activities for a language program that would follow those goals. For clarity, the last section is divided into subsections on syntax, phonology, and meaning. However, because children do not generally develop skill in one area exclusive of other areas, throughout the discussion there are comments on how an activity designed to support one aspect of language growth will also promote growth in other areas.

Language Programs

The programs described here include those representing different trends in education. A good review of language development growth is found in Cazden *(3);* general references about early childhood programs are in

Day and Parker *(6)*. Articles written in a volume edited by Spodek and Walberg *(18)* raise excellent questions about nonlanguage aspects of early childhood education that are important to consider when designing instruction.

In this section, two highly visible language programs are reviewed. These programs, which are commercially available, are quite different from each other and represent different trends in American education. Both programs have resulted in positive language growth for prekindergarten and kindergarten children. Other programs were initiated for special groups of children, but they have implications for our planning, too. All have resulted in at least short-term benefits for the subjects' language development.

Before the 1960s, most preschool programs were morning nursery schools for the children of the middle classes and emphasized socially oriented goals and some academic study as presented in unit work. The only other common programs were child-care centers which had surrogate mothering as their main goal. During the 1960s, more interest in academic preschool education for all children became evident, and the federal government supported a number of experimental preschool programs designed to serve disadvantaged children.

In 1966, Bereiter and Engelmann *(2)* published a long account of an instructional program they had designed and used successfully with disadvantaged preschool children in Illinois. The Bereiter-Engelmann program received considerable attention from educators and laymen because it represented a radical departure from traditional preschool curricula in terms of both its unique instructional approach and the controversial theory on which this approach was based.

There are two factors in the Bereiter-Engelmann program that demand differential attention. One is the innovative curriculum. Based on the assumption that disadvantaged children lack information and skill, particularly the verbal skill needed for academic work, the curriculum was built to provide compensation for these deficiencies. Thus, rather than measuring general growth in language and cognition by means of the normative tests, as was done in many other research-oriented preschool programs, the authors of this program decided to measure pupil growth by testing acquisition of specified academic skills on criterion-based tests. The curriculum focused on language, arithmetic, and reading of fifteen four-year-old children from "very deprived" families who participated in the project for two years. In the area of language, a major concern was the development of grammatical sentence patterns and use of "precise" pronunciation (Standard English) as a means to that end. The curriculum initially stressed the acquisition of the following minimum language essentials: affirmative and negative statements, ability to use polar sets, correct use of prepositions, ability to classify simple sets, and use of simple *if-then* sentences. As each curricular goal was met, the subjects were trained in successively more complex tasks. Thus, the children were first required to repeat statements as they heard them. They then responded to *yes-no* questions and learned to indicate location. Finally, they mastered the production of sentences and simple deductions.

The other unusual factor in this program was the direct instructional approach. Such direct, systematic instruction created a "highly task-oriented, no-nonsense manner (where) full participation of all children in the learning tasks is treated as a requirement to which children must conform."[1] Attention to the pupils' task, effort, and mastery was considered critical. During the lessons, children were immediately rewarded for making correct responses. If they did not respond correctly, they were told so and, if necessary, even removed from the lesson. Children were rewarded for trying, however. Although this approach is in partial conflict with our discussion, it proved of limited success.

At the end of one year, the children had improved greatly on the subtest of the Illinois Test of Psycholinguistic Ability which examined production of grammatical inflections, an ability stressed in instruction. Although little additional growth occurred in that area during the second year, by the end of the second year, the group was nearly average (in comparison to national norms) in making verbal analogies. Gains were indicated by scores on other tests as well. Furthermore, most of the children achieved the stated objectives.

It should be noted in evaluating these gains that the fifteen children had received two hours of instruction five days a week from four teachers to achieve these gains. In other studies where this curriculum has been used, the results have not been as positive. For example, Day *(5)* found no difference in the gains made by children using this curriculum and those using a traditional unit approach. Where three different prekindergarten programs were compared by DiLorenzo, Salter, and Brady *(7),* both the Bereiter-Engelmann program and a program stressing reading readiness promoted growth for disadvantaged children.

The Distar Language Program *(10)* is the progeny of the Bereiter and Engelmann program. Major aspects of the curriculum and teaching techniques described above also apply to Distar. In Distar language, teachers are advised to use both verbal and physical reinforcement, to move quickly, and to demand attention of all members of the group. Responses are sought both in unison and by the individual.

---

1. C. E. Bereiter, "Academic Instruction and Preschool Children," in *Language Programs for the Disadvantaged,* ed. R. Corbin and M. Crosby (Champaign, Ill.: National Council of Teachers of English, 1965).

In assessing the overall value of the Bereiter-Engelmann approach to language development, we must consider the curricular and instructional characteristics separately. While the curriculum's basic assumption that a language deficit exists is in conflict with the view in this book, the idea of specifying language goals and measuring growth in terms of achievement of objectives is consistent with the diagnostic approach recommended here. Furthermore, aspects of the instructional procedures appear to be alien to the language learning strategies of young children. For example, heavy reliance on repetition of structures that are not part of children's dialects may be questioned. On the other hand, the techniques used in Distar for getting and maintaining attention and the clear verbal feedback system employed may be excellent techniques to draw out nonparticipating children.

Another highly visible language development program is the *Peabody Language Development Kits (9),* developed for children with language handicaps. There are four kits: *P* for prekindergarten level, *K* for kindergarten, *1* for first grade, and *2* for second. As with Distar Language, the teacher using these kits is given explicit directions and structure for teaching groups of children. Pictures of objects and people, plus motivating games, songs, etc., are provided in a program which emphasizes receptive, expressive, and conceptual aspects of language. In sharp contrast with the Distar Program, these kits attempt to train for global language goals; for example, at level *P,* the stress is on developing sentence structures containing major grammatical constructs. Most studies assessing the effect of the kits show that they are effective in stimulating oral language development *(16, 9).* Furthermore, they have been found to produce effective results when used by paraprofessionals.

The major difference between the Peabody Kits and Distar is the encouragement of spontaneous responses. The Peabody program recommends that a gamelike spirit be promoted rather than a work-oriented atmosphere. Furthermore, a wide range of language skills and abilities is involved and organized through twenty-three kinds of activities. Each group lesson involves two or three of the following different activities *(9):*

1. activity time
2. brainstorming time
3. classification time
4. conversation time
5. critical-thinking time
6. describing time
7. dramatizing time
8. following directions time
9. guessing time

10. identification time
11. imagination time
12. listening time
13. looking time
14. memory time
15. pantomine time
16. patterning time
17. relationships time
18. rhyming time
19. speech development time
20. speed-up time
21. story time
22. touching time
23. vocabulary-building time

Many teachers who use the Peabody kits alter the lessons somewhat to reflect the needs of their pupils. For example, one day a teacher might do two of the recommended activities but also substitute another that seems appropriate for the students. Some teachers also specify objectives to be gained from the activities and provide informal assessments of achievement gains with each lesson. In addition, many teachers group children by their language needs and use the kits with smaller groups so that some individual attention is possible. Because the Peabody kits encourage spontaneous language and an open atmosphere for learning, their approach is not unlike the recommendations of this book. Indeed, the teacher who has a kit and wants to use it in conjunction with suggestions made here will find that such adjustments are possible.

In addition to these commercially available programs are interesting instructional approaches used and evaluated in different settings. One *(4)* was designed to improve primary grade children's ability to process and express Standard English but not at the expense of their Black English dialect. The training consisted of language expansion activities in creative drama, puppet use, discussion, and story telling in addition to some structured drills. These activities accompanied a strong emphasis on literature. Control children received the literature component but not the follow-up language activities. All children improved in their ability to repeat Standard English sentences, but the experimental kindergarten children made the greatest gains. Because growth in ability to repeat sentences, as shown in other research *(17)*, indicates growth in language proficiency, application of language activities like those used in the Cullinan et al. study will be included in the recommendations found here. Ervin-Tripp *(11)* also recommends role-playing activities for language expansion, suggesting that children take on more mature language as they play adult roles.

A far different approach to language development training was taken by Lee, Koenigsknecht, and Mulhern *(15)* who developed an effective language interaction program with preschool children whose language was severely delayed. The program consisted of the clinician, working with a disabled child, designing narratives about the client's interest which required that the client respond with appropriate sentences. An example is:

NARRATIVE: This is Karen. Karen is four years old. She is four years old today.
How old is she?
RESPONSE: She is four years old.[2]

In the process of the interactive training, the children's expressive language, that aspect of their functioning most severely disabled, became more mature. Children trained in this program experienced a linguistic growth, as measured on various syntactic tests, greater than that of normal children of the same ages. This study is brought into discussion on language for normally developing children because of the positive effect from interactive dialogue, also stressed in the instructional suggestions found in this chapter.

In these preschool language training programs, one common characteristic is present. Despite differences between the highly structured drill emphasis in Distar and the spontaneous role playing of the Cullinan et al. program, all programs provide for consistent language development activities. Regularity of language instruction is one of the recommendations made here.

Basic Assumptions and Goals of a Language Program

Below are listed the basic assumptions of the recommended program. Beside each assumption is the relevant goal to be set for program design and implementation.

Assumptions	Goals
1. Preschool educators need to provide planned instruction in language on a regular basis.	1. The language program will include a variety of language-enhancing activities which can be expanded to be a part of each day's experience.
2. Adult modelling of language appears to be needed for children to induce linguistic structures.	2. The language program will emphasize the importance of adult interactive modelling.

---

2. L. L. Lee, R. A. Koenigsknecht, and S. Mulhern, *Interactive Language Development Teaching: The Clinical Presentation of Grammatical Structure* (Evanston, Ill.: Northwestern University Press, 1975), p. 75.

Assumptions	Goals
3. Although children acquire language at about the same time and in the same approximate order, the rate of acquisition varies. Rate of acquisition must have something to do with the richness of the language input.	3. The language will insure a rich language input throughout each day and not just during planned language activities.
4. Adults should provide linguistic structures at levels slightly more complex than those produced by the children.	4. The language program will insure that teachers' knowledge of language acquisition is advanced enough to judge the appropriate level of structure for children.
5. Since it is not clear that certain types of adult/child interactions are better at stimulating language growth than others, different modes of interacting are necessary.	5. The language program will include adult expansion of, commenting on, and prompting for child responses.
6. Since there is no evidence that the language of disadvantaged children is acquired differently from language of middle class, the same curriculum is appropriate for different dialect groups.	6. The language program will provide the same approach to instruction whether the student population comes from a poor, minority background or a middle-class background.
7. It appears that many have preconceived notions about the language facility of speakers of nonstandard dialect.	7. The language program will be implemented by persons whose attitudes toward minority speakers are not biased.
8. Non-English-speaking children can learn English well if they are immersed in an English-only program.	8. Non-English-speaking children can acquire English in a regular English program if they are in the minority and if they have a specially designed instructional sequence to enrich their vocabulary.
9. Non-English-speaking children need to have their native language enriched if they are to acquire literacy in it. They can acquire oral English if it is not presented in confusion with the other language.	9. If the non-English-speaking children are in the majority and if their families desire first literacy in the native tongue, the language program will be adapted to that language and presented by adult native speakers. If the program is a bilingual one, the initial teaching of English should be separate in context from the other language.
10. To provide appropriate modelling for the language level of the children, teachers need to know what level of functioning in language children have achieved.	10. The language program will include assessment techniques to uncover children's level of functioning.

11. Phonology and syntax are acquired as a finite set of rules which allow for infinite combinations. The rules are induced by the child from the environment.

11. The modelling aspects of adult/child interaction will be primarily for enhancing acquisition of phonology and syntax.

12. Acquisition of word meaning requires children's active manipulation of objects while using appropriate verbal comments on the differences and similarities of the objects.

12. The language program will include direct teaching activities to help children learn concepts; these activities will focus on concrete experiences as teachers ask questions based on knowledge of children's prior understanding of concepts.

13. The approaches to language training used in other programs include interaction with adults, requests for responses in structured situations from children, drama, role playing, etc.

13. The language program will include many varied activities.

14. Attention to language in the preschool curriculum does not imply that there will be insufficient attention to other goals, including the initiation of reading readiness or actual reading.

14. The language program is one component of preschool education. Often, activities to enhance language will also help in other cognitive and affective learnings.

The Language Program

Of initial importance in program planning is assessment of children's levels of competency. Various standardized and informal assessment measures are available for this evaluation. Some are mentioned and others discussed at length in this section. Also, sample activities used to enhance the developmental process during the years between three and six are included. Each of the activities described ought to serve the teachers as a model for the development of related activities. Thus, while these pages do not include activities for an entire year's program, they do include ideas which are appropriate for expansion to a year's program.

Syntax

Three *assessment procedures* are recommended here as techniques to determine children's level of syntactic functioning. These are tests of language performance, not comprehension, except for part of the second test described below. All require individual observation and/or testing and thus may take considerable care. However, none of the measures takes a great deal of time, and aides can be trained in some testing procedures.

The first test is the Sentence Repetition Test found on pages 81 through 83. It has been used with over one hundred three- to five-year-olds and discriminates especially among the younger children. A number of studies have shown that when repeating sentences so long that they must be processed as language rather than as separate items, children repeat the stimulus sentence in the direction of their syntactic maturity level *(17)*. That is, in repeating a relatively long sentence, a child will interpret it in terms of his grammatical knowledge and use his own structures in encoding.

The sentence repetition test is given individually in a quiet corner of a room by asking the child to repeat a sentence immediately after the teacher's reading of it. The teacher can mark the answers directly on the test, but when she wants to make more careful assessment than is possible with the test, she will want to tape the recorded responses for later scoring. The sentences in the repetition test are in Standard English, and dialect variation should be noted when it occurs. Interpretation should be carefully made so that dialect variation is not interpreted as immaturity. When a child repeats the critical feature in the stimulus sentence, the first blank is checked; if the child changes the critical feature, the second blank is checked; if the child's response has little resemblance to the stimulus, the third blank is checked.

A second measure of syntactic maturity can be made with the *Northwestern Syntax Screening Test* by L. Lee *(14)*. The first section tests receptive understanding of major syntactic structures; in the second part, both understanding and repetition abilities are examined. The test is individually administered and takes up to fifteen minutes. The tasks it presents may be difficult for some children younger than five, and in interpreting the results it is well to remember that the percentiles were established on the basis of scores by upper- and middle-income children.

A third assessment, to be used by teachers with considerable knowledge about children's language acquisition, is the checklist found on pages 84 and 85. With this checklist the teacher tries to establish when she first hears a new structure. Of course, exact dating is nearly impossible, but approximate dating gives teachers ideas about developmental growth. Adjustments for assessing the acquisition of Black English-speaking children are indicated in the checklist by italic type. When an omission or variation noted in syntactic development is traceable to dialect, teachers should not consider this variation an area for instruction. Dialect change is not recommended in this program for young children.

Chart 4.
Sentence repetition test

Name_____ Age_____ Date_____

Sentence	Critical Feature	Repeated*	Partial	Not Repeated**
1. The old man painted a big picture.	man-paint-picture	_____	_____	_____
2. The silly cat runs away very fast.	cat-run(s)	_____	_____	_____
3. The big boy is a very mean boy.	is	_____	_____	_____
4. My mommy told me a funny story.	told (telled)	_____	_____	_____
5. The little girl is brushing her teeth.	(is) brushing	_____	_____	_____
6. We do not want to go home now.	placement of *not*	_____	_____	_____
7. Billy said, "Where is my book?"	where	_____	_____	_____
8. All of the boys and all of the girls are sad.	plural on *boys* and *girls*	_____	_____	_____
9. It's not your book; it's Sally's book.	your–Sally's	_____	_____	_____
10. Susan sings. The girls dance.	sings-dance	_____	_____	_____
11. The man *has been* calling us.	has-been	_____	_____	_____

Chart 4 (Continued)

Sentence	Critical Feature	Repeated*	Partial	Not Repeated**
12. That dirty dog does not want to have a bath.	does-not (doesn't)	_____	_____	_____
13. The lady asked "Do animals talk?"	inversion of *do* and *animals*	_____	_____	_____
14. I can do it. You can do it. He can do it.	I, you, it he	_____	_____	_____
15. The boy shouted at the tired, thin, old man.	tired, thin old	_____	_____	_____
16. The girls said they liked to sing songs and to read books.***	to sing, to read	_____	_____	_____
17. After lunch, we are going to have a nap.	are going to (we'll)	_____	_____	_____
18. The children went to the circus, and they climbed over the seats.***	to, over	_____	_____	_____
19. The children asked, "Where are you going?"	inversion of *are* and *you*	_____	_____	_____

20. The children
     ate all their
     meat and they
     ate their
     apples, but
     they didn't
     drink the
     milk.***   and, and, but   _____   _____   _____

21. The book that
     tells about
     animals in
     the zoo is   the relative
     lost.   clause   _____   _____   _____

---

*If the critical feature is repeated exactly mark the first blank. If it is repeated with a change, write the change in the second blank. If the child shows no sign of repeating the structure, check the third blank.

**The structures in the middle column are the ones being examined. Pay attention only to them.

***The structures being tested in items 16, 18, and 20 are best analyzed in spontaneous speech.

The checklist includes only a summary account of the syntactic forms which children learn between the ages of three and six. However, the syntactic structures included in the checklist are important ones which, if present, probably indicate that other related structures are also present. For example, if relative clauses are apparent in the speech of a five-year-old, it is probably true that he also can use other simple embedded sentences. The content of the instructional program in syntactic development will be similar to the material of the checklist. In other words, the checklist should be used to determine needs, and then to plan instruction based on the outlined structures on the checklist.

Instructional activities to stimulate syntactic growth are included in Chart 6 on pages 86–92. The first activity includes sample expansion, prompts, and comments. Interactive dialogue is the most important activity, but since it occurs throughout the school's day and adults talk spontaneously with individuals and small groups of children, the list of activities can only include these samples. Assessment of children's current level of syntax will indicate which of the other activities are appropriate for different children.

In summary, a program which enhances syntactic growth will emphasize dialogue. Supplementary activities only reinforce structures acquired. These activities and others can be written on cards and filed for easy reference.

Chart 5.
Checklist for assessing syntactic maturity

Name_____	Structure Observed	Date	Age

Ages 3.0–3.6 (Approximate)

Subject-verb-object-sentences	____	____	____
Subject-intransitive verb	____	____	____
Use of copula—*"be" used in habitual action; absent in momentary action**	____	____	____
Past tense when appropriate (overgeneralizations expected)—*absent in many phonological settings*	____	____	____
Appropriate -ing on verbs	____	____	____
Negative word inserted in the middle of sentences	____	____	____
Wh-word in questions	____	____	____

Ages 3.6–4.0 (Approximate)

Plural inflection—*final phoneme missing in some settings*	____	____	____
Possession—*possessive "s" often lost; possessive pronoun not realized*	____	____	____
Subject-verb agreement in present—*"he do," "he have," acceptable; "s" often lost*	____	____	____
Use of AUX forms such as "do," "has," "been"	____	____	____
Negatives attached to "do"	____	____	____
In yes/no questions, subject and AUX inverted	____	____	____

Ages 4.0–6.0 (Approximate)

Pronoun used appropriately with a few exceptions, such as possessive pronouns—*possessive pronoun endings may be lost; subject plus pronoun (John he sang) occasionally inserted*	____	____	____
Adjectives used to qualify nouns	____	____	____
Infinitives used where appropriate	____	____	____
Future tense used—*in contraction future "will" lost*	____	____	____

Prepositional phrases used   ____ ____ ____

Wh-word question subject, AUX inversion used—
*does not occur with many Black English-speaking
children*   ____ ____ ____

Simple sentences conjoined with "and" and "but"   ____ ____ ____

Relative clauses used   ____ ____ ____

---

*Italics indicate some adaptations for Black English-speaking children.

Phonology

On page 93 is a Checklist for Assessing Phonemic Acquisition. This checklist includes only consonant sounds. There are two reasons for the deliberate exclusion of vowels. First, vowel sounds are even more variable than consonants and are very sensitive to the influence of regional and social dialects. Consequently, setting age expectations for acquisition of vowels simply promotes confusion and misinterpretation. Second, little is known about the sequence of acquisition of vowels after the very early stages at the beginning of the second year of life. Nonetheless, we should expect that most children will use the vowel phonemes of their dialect by the time they are six. The *Goldman-Fristoe Test of Articulation (12)* is a good, quick, individualized test of articulation ability.

Another factor about the checklist is that there are alternatives for sounds one might hear from a child speaking Black English dialect. It is especially important that teachers not expect the appearance of phonemes for Black English speakers to be the same as those for Standard English speakers. Specific adaptations are again indicated by italic type in the checklist. In addition, note that Spanish-speaking children will have particular difficulty with the following English phonemes: /ð/, /θ/, /z/, /ž/, /š/, /ǰ/. Again, the checklist provides both the means for assessment of growth and the content material for instruction in this component of the language program.

Finally, continual assessment of slowly developing children is necessary in order to monitor the pattern of growth. Children who continue to be very slow in developing or who have such severe articulation problems that communication is difficult should be referred for special directed training. As will be discussed in chapter 5, the ability to hear phonemic differences is more important in learning to read than is the actual oral use of phonemes; therefore, special strategies for increasing discrimination of phonemes will also be necessary in the prereading program.

Chart 6.
Illustrative instructional activities to enhance syntactic development

I. *Period of Acquisition of Basic Structures (Generally Three- and Four-Year-Olds)*

A. *Topics*

subject-verb sentences
subject-verb-object
-ing on verbs
past tense
use of copula
negative word in middle of sentence
wh-questions
plural inflection
possession
subject-verb agreement
use of AUX
negatives attached with "do"
subject-AUX inversion in yes/no questions

B. *Activities*

The reader may want to refer to the list of topics above when reading the activities since each activity concerns a particular topic. It is easy to identify the topic and to adapt it to another topic when needed in the classroom.

1. *Sample Dialogues*

Interaction at this point will be spontaneous. The following examples are entended to illustrate types of adult responses which are helpful to the child's growing syntactic knowledge.

(a) *Expansion.*   In these responses, adults repeat the child's structure in mature form.

Child: "Look, Teacher. *Smash snake.*" (Another child has just smashed the speaker's plasticene snake.)

Teacher: "Oh, too bad. *Johnny smashed the snake.*" (Teacher emphasizes the exansion of the child's structure.)
"Billy, make a new one, and maybe Johnny will help.

Child: *"Hurt finger."*
Teacher: "Oh, I'm sorry. You hurt your finger. Let's fix it.

(b) *Prompts.*   Adults prompt for words and then repeat the words in mature sentence structure.

Child: "Look, snake." (He points to a plasticene snake before him.)

Teacher:	"Oh, you made a . . . ?"
Child:	"Snake."
Teacher:	"You made a nice snake."
Child:	"Want drink."
Teacher:	(Looking around) "Who wants a drink?"
Child:	"Me."
Teacher:	"Oh, Billy wants a drink."
Child:	"Gimme." (Points to toy.)
Teacher:	"What toy do you want, Billy?"
Child:	"Truck."
Teacher:	"OK, Billy, you want a truck."

(c) *Comments.* With such remarks adults simply engage in dialogue with the child by continuing the child's remark.

Child:	(making a plasticene snake) "Me smash snake."
Teacher:	"What? You are going to smash that snake?"
Child:	"More juice."
Teacher:	"I'm sorry. We don't have any more juice. Do you want some milk?"

2. The teacher shows pictures of people engaged in recognizable actions. He then discusses the pictures with the children.

Teacher:	(showing a picture of a boy crying) "What is the boy doing?"
Child:	"Boy cry."
Teacher:	(showing a new picture) "The lady?"
Child:	"The lady dances."

3. Use of Gotkin's *Language Lotto Set, Actions and More Actions (13).*

4. The children and teacher say favorite nursery rhymes, such as "I Love Little Pussy" and "Simple Simon Met a Pieman," over and over again.

5. A sentence completion game, such as the one which follows, helps to emphasize this sentence structure. First, the teacher says, "I like _____." She then asks for suggestions to fill in the blank. The children all repeat the sentence. Other suggestions: "The dog ate his _____" and "This is a big _____."

6. A rhythm game in dialogue form can provide practice in forming subject-verb-object sentences.

Teacher:	"Who can say, 'You are nice'?"
John:	"I can say, 'You are nice.' "
Teacher:	"John can say, 'You are nice.' Who can say, 'I like you'?"
Amy:	"I can say, 'I like you.'."

7. As a child performs an action in the center of the circle, the others say, "Billy is sweeping"; Donny is crying"; etc.

8. Descriptions of actions or pictured events are used to elicit-*ing* forms.

9. Nursery rhymes, such as "As I Was Going to St. Ives" and "Old Mother Hubbard Went to the Cupboard," are said in unison.

10. A child performs an action before the group and sits down. A dialogue follows:

   Teacher: "Amy ran. What did Amy do?"
   Children: "Amy ran."

   This procedure of action followed by dialogue continues until all the children have had an opportunity to do an action.

11. At the close of the day, the teacher and children should review all their activities in sequence.

12. After a good story book has been read to children, the teacher should encourage the children to use past tense in discussing the events.

13. *Finger play.* For example, "Here *is* the church. Here *is* the steeple. Open it up and see all the people."

14. Not only do children practice placing the negative word in the middle of the sentence, they acquire the beginning development of the concepts *same* and *different* when two identical groupings of objects or pictures are placed on the table and the following dialogue results:

   Teacher: "This pile of blocks is the same as this one."
   Teacher: (adding blocks to one pile) "Are they the same now?"
   Children: "No."
   Teacher: "Right. They are not the same. Say that."
   Children: "They are not the same."

15. In the "foolishness game," the teacher names a well-known object incorrectly. The child responds, "You're silly. That's not a_____. It's a_____." The teacher then encourages the child to be the "silly one."

16. *Songs, nursery rhymes.* In the "question-answer game," each child asks where an object is. The game continues from child to child as children use wh-word questions.

17. During quiet talk times, the teacher asks the children to finish questions beginning with "where," "what," "when," "why." ("Why" is complicated since it represents causality. Teachers are well advised not to expect it to be used with adult understanding.)

18. In a game activity with pictures of various common objects, the teacher says, "Here is a dog." He then shows a picture of one dog. He then says, "Now here is a picture of two of them. There are two of what?"

19. In a game of possession, the following dialogue occurs:

    Teacher: "This is my shoe. It is mine."
    Child: "This is my dress. It is mine."
    Teacher: "This is your dress, It is yours."

20. Any group of pictures of like animals or people involved in action can be used. The following dialogue occurs.

    Teacher: "Look. The ladies dance. What about the clown?"
    Children: "The clown is laughing."
    Teacher: "Right. The clown laughs."

    The conversation continues in this way until the children respond with the present tense. If they do not inflect as adults do, the teacher expands their comments without being negative.

21. Nursery rhymes, such as "Baa, Baa, Black Sheep," "Seesaw, Margery Daw," and "Jack Shall Have a New Master," are helpful instructional aids in teaching the use of AUX forms.

22. Negative games are played in unison by the children. For example, they might say:

    "Look at the horse. He doesn't fly.
    Look at the cow. She doesn't bark.
    Look at the cat. He doesn't_____."

23. In the "I don't" game, the teacher asks the children to answer this question: "I don't want to_____." One child answers, and all the children continue with a statement such as, "Johnny doesn't want to_____."

24. Individual children ask for something to play with. The teacher and the other children repeat the question in unison and the child who asks the question gets a toy. This game continues until all the children have toys.

    Child: "I want the Leggo."
    Teacher: (expanding) "John asks, 'Can I have Leggo?' "
    Children: (in unison) "Can John have Leggo?"
    Teacher: "John can have Leggo."

II. *Final Preschool Period*

A. *Topics*

    pronouns used appropriately
    use of adjectives
    future tense
    prepositional phrases
    wh-word-subject-AUX inversion
    simple sentence conjunctions
    relative clauses

B. *Activities*

As with the previous section, the activities are designed with a special topic in mind but can be modified to develop skill in other topics. Additionally, most of the instruction in this area will be through modelling and interactions as illustrated in Activity 1 under I above.

1. In a rhythm game, the following dialogue might occur.

   Teacher: "Listen . . . I am a teacher. Now you say, 'You are a teacher.' "

   Children: "You are a teacher."

   Teacher: "Now one of you say what you are."

   Child: "I am a boy."

   Children: "He is a boy."

2. To practice using adjectives, the children expand simple sentences by using pictures and objects.

   Teacher: "What do you see here?"

   Child: "A dog."

   Teacher: "Yes. What does he look like?"

   Child: "He's a big dog."

   Teacher: "What else?"

3. On a particularly cold, snowy, rainy, or beautiful day, the teacher asks the children to tell what kind of day it is by using "weather words."

4. The children can be encouraged to use adjectives to describe the characters, settings, and objects from stories read to them.

5. To learn to use adjectives as well as to learn concepts (see Chart 9), unknown objects with distinctive tactile qualities are placed unseen by the children in a cardboard "magic box." Each child in a small group feels one object and says words which tell how the unseen object feels. The teacher reinforces good descriptive terms.

6. To practice use of pronouns and future tense, children can play a game of "wishing" by saying, "When I grow up, I will be a_____" or "On Saturday, I will_____." Another child can continue, "When Johnny grows up, he will be a_____."

7. In projecting from picture stories, the teacher selects pictures which portray events and asks the children to say what will happen. He then expands their comments to include the future tense.

8. To use prepositional phrases as well as to learn their meaning, the teacher or a child places an object *in, on,* or *between* books on a table. Each child identifies an object and describes its location. The teacher expands where necessary and stresses the correct use of prepositions.

9. In playing a rhythm game, the teacher asks, "Where is the_____?" The children reply in unison, "It's on the_____."

10. Gotkin's *Language Lotto* set for prepositions can be used.

11. In playing a "who-what-where" game, the teacher shows the children that they are to ask "who" and "where" questions in the following situations:

    Teacher: "I put the book somewhere."
    Children: "Where did you put the book?"

    Teacher: "I am thinking of a boy."
    Children: "Who is the boy?"

12. In planning a drama following a good story the children like, they should first decide *who* will play *what* roles *where* in the room, and *when*. The teacher might use these wh-words as planning devices with the children.

13. Picture descriptions can help to develop the conjunction *and*. The teacher shows pictures to the children with more than one person or animal. The following dialogue occurs.

    Teacher: "What's happening here?"
    Child: "The boy is sitting down. The other boy is walking."

    The teacher continues the dialogue in this fashion and expands by repeating the single sentences as a conjoined sentence.

14. Picture descriptions also help to develop use of the conjunction *but*. The same system is used here except the teacher starts off by saying, "The little boy is sitting but_____." He then asks who can continue with other pictures using *but*.

    Other, more complex sentence connectives can be gradually introduced after children have skill with *and* and *but* sentences. For example,

    I was hungry, so_____.
    It was raining, so_____.
    I wanted supper because_____.
    It would be nice to go to the zoo if_____.

    After practice the children can try to start sentences for others to finish.

15. To reinforce relative clause embeddings in children's language production, singing the song "This is the House That Jack Built" is a good instructional device.

16. The teacher encourages sentence repetition by showing the children a picture and saying, "Here is a dog who is chasing a cat." The children repeat the sentence in unison.

17. When preparing role-playing situations, as a child takes an adult role, the teacher might encourage the child to "talk like a grown-up." This can be demonstrated to children once one child has used a particularly long, complex sentence, and the teacher says, "Good, Becky said _____ and that sounded like a grown-up."

Some role-playing situations are:

a tired mother trying to find food in the supermarket
three mothers having coffee and talking about their children
the lunchroom lady when the food is late
a mother and father when the laundry is not done
a garage mechanic and a mother when the car breaks down
a doctor and a nurse when a child is sick

In terms of *activities,* since the learning of language phonemes is normally accomplished inductively by the child, adults serve as models so that children can compare their sounds with those of mature speakers. Thus, careful modeling is an important part of the learning environment schools will want to produce. Because children will not acquire sounds they do not perceive, auditory perception will be needed for children who are not acquiring phonemes in the normal sequence and at the expected rate. As in the previous section of this chapter, the techniques suggested here are only the bare beginning of a total program.

The program to promote phonological development will stress clear modeling of important consonant phonemes and phonemic patterns with vowel-plus-consonant combinations. Monitoring of growth continues and supplementary activities which promote active involvement in the sound "games" are introduced when the assessment procedures indicate readiness.

Meaning

We have less documentation of how children acquire knowledge of concepts than we do about their acquisition of syntax. However, as was discussed in chapter 2, we know that children learn the complex attributes of related terms slowly and require considerable experience using terms in many situations. To use one example, although the words "on" and "off" are used early in child language, children need repeated experiences with the words in different contexts before they learn how both words refer to position of one object in relation to another object and before they acquire a sense of how "on" and "off" refer to differences in position of the two objects. In developing a rich store of concepts during the

Chart 7.
Checklist for assessing phonemic acquisition

*Name*_____

	Phoneme Observed	Date	Age

Three- and Four-Year-Olds

	Phoneme Observed	Date	Age
/n/	____	____	____
/t/ — *Often lost in final position**	____	____	____
/g/	____	____	____
/m/	____	____	____
/b/ — *May be lost in final position*	____	____	____
/d/ — *May be lost in final position*	____	____	____
/w/	____	____	____
/h/	____	____	____
/p/ — *May be lost in final position*	____	____	____
/k/ — *In /ks/ for x only /k/ is realized*	____	____	____
/f/ — *May alternate with /v/*	____	____	____
/ŋ/	____	____	____

Five- and Six-Year-Olds

	Phoneme Observed	Date	Age
/v/ — *May alternate with /f/*	____	____	____
/ĭ/			
/θ/ — *Occasionally changed to /f/*	____	____	____
/š/** — *In consonant clusters, next phoneme altered; often lost in final position*	____	____	____
/l/** — *Often lost or reduced in medial or final position*	____	____	____
/r/** — *Often lost in medial or final position*	____	____	____
/s/**	____	____	____
/z/**	____	____	____
/ž/**	____	____	____
/č/**	____	____	____
/ð/** — *Occasionally changed to /d/*	____	____	____
/hw/**	____	____	____

*Italic type indicates adaptations to be made for some Black English-speaking children.
**These phonemes may not develop until after age six.

Chart 8.
Illustrative instructional activities to enhance acquisition of phonemes

I. New Sounds for Three- and Four-Year-Olds: /n/, /t/, /g/, /m/, /b/, /d/, /w/, /h/, /p/, /k/, /f/, /l/

    A. *Expansion*
        1. *Child:*   "Give me my *doy*" (toy).
            Teacher: "Oh, you want your *toy*?" (Stress on initial phoneme)

    B. *Alliteration Fun*
        The teacher uses words that begin with the same initial phoneme in silly sentences just for fun; he does not expect the children to identify or to supply examples at first.

        The nasty neighbor took a nap.
        Find the funny fox, Fred.
        Peggy took a pill for her pain.
        The dizzy dog dragged a door to his den.
        Can the cook cook a cake?
        William wants to wear a winter coat.
        Go away, gorgeous goat.
        Make the mailman mail a message.
        Tilly, the tall tiger, took a test.
        Blow, blow the bubbles out of the box.
        How can the horse be hurt?

    C. *Unison Rhymes and Songs*
        Songs and rhymes that include the phonemes the children need to repeat can be chosen.

    D. *Rhyming Words: From Reading of Books*
        Nursery rhymes should be read to the children regularly before the daily storytime. The children should be allowed to chime in when they are ready. The teacher can encourage this by hesitating just before a rhyming word at the end of a line is reached. Dr. Suess books are especially fun for this exercise as they have a great many rhyming words children love. (As is true with alliteration games, the teacher should not expect the children to supply examples or to identify rhymes unless they have had many prior listening experiences.)

    E. *Rhyming Words: In Oral Language*
        For fun, the teacher can produce rhyming words and ask the children to repeat them again with him. Sometimes, words can be said with particular emotional emphasis. For example, with a frightening face, one can say slowly: "Squishy, squashy, wishy, washy." Or, with a staccato rhythm, one can say: "Stop, mop, flop." Or, with emphatic strength: "Make, cake, bake, stake." After doing this for a time, the teacher should hesitate for a moment at the end to see if the children respond with another example.

II. New Sounds for Five- and Six-Year-Olds: /v/, /r/, /j/, /θ/, /ð/, /s/, /š/, /z/, /ž/, /ð̌/, /c/, /hw/.

    A. (This part of the program begins with the same content as that listed above, but now the children are also expected to supply examples and to identify the repeated sounds.) The teacher demonstrates the exercise in the following way: He has presented four words beginning with /t/, let us say, and then shows a chart with four pictured objects, one of which begins with /t/. He waits expectantly for the children to identify the pictured word that also begins with /t/. If no one does, he prompts. He continues this way until the children respond on their own without prompting.

    B. *Cut-out pictures* can be pasted on large charts which show objects beginning with the same consonant. The consonant grapheme is not identified until the children can supply easily an oral example or can find one in a small group. The children must have plenty of listening experience before they will be ready to identify words which *begin with the same sound.* Furthermore, they will need considerable experience in visual discrimination (discussed in the next section of this book) and ability to name letters before this skill is achieved.

    C. *Rhyming sequences* can be expanded until the children can supply examples.

    D. *Expansion* of sounds, particularly when substitutions are observed, can be continued. *Note should be made of the substitutions the children make* for ongoing assessment of development.

    E. *Alliteration Fun*

The new sounds include some difficult ones which may not be evidenced in speech until later in the children's development. However, they should be presented often in situations where they are clear for discrimination. The following sentences stress alliteration where these sounds are emphasized:

Vera was vexed with her velvet vest.
Ronny, the real robot, ran the race.
Just jingle the gems and the jewel thief will jack them away.
There they go into the thick jungle.
Little Lilly, the lost lamb, limped home at last.
Sam, the silly seal, swam off with the cereal.
The short boy shined shoes in his shack.
Zelda, the zany giraffe, zipped past the zoo.
The churchmouse chewed on the checkered rug.
Where did the whale leave the wheel?

    F. *Auditory Discrimination*

Once the children are familiar enough with the easier consonants and are able to supply words beginning with these more difficult consonants, they can begin preliminary auditory discrimination exercises.

However, it is important that the first groups of words used illustrate only gross differences in the phonemes. A picture can be shown (for example, a picture of a *bee*) and then the teacher can say some other words. When he says the word which shows the named picture, the children raise their hands. An aide can check the children as they respond. The following words might be used on pictures: *bee,* see, bee, fee; *man,* fan, nan, man; *pad,* pad, fad, jad. Gradually, the teacher will want to include phonemic contrasts which are not so diverse. For example: *pail,* sail, whale, pail, bale; *shoe,* Sue, shoe, zoo; *back,* tack, jack, back; *run,* run, won, fun.

G. *Rhyming Fun*

When children have been observed to use many of the phonemes discussed above and have been able to discriminate initial sounds, the teacher can expect them to be able to participate in rhyming exercises. At this point the teacher asks, "Who can hear the word that doesn't belong?" He then says words such as those which follow:

        call, ball, tall, tree
        cat, bat, hat, horse
        boat, coat, goat, bear

When the children become familiar with the game, it can be expanded to include the following:

        hook, come, book, cook
        bear, page, chair, pear
        leg, house, louse, mouse
        luck, duck, now, truck
        pen, cake, rake, make
        clip, clock, lock, block
        train, tape, rain, chain

H. *More Rhyming*

Children ought to enjoy providing examples for nonsense rhymes. To encourage such rhymes, the teacher says: *"Fish, swish, dish.* We all know these words. Say them with me . . . . Now everyone listen to these silly words: *mish, quish, lish.* Who can think of some more? *Mish, quish, lish . . . .* Or *king, swing, ring . . . ding, fing, ting . . . ."*

---

preschool years, adult help is of great importance. This help comes in a number of ways: first, adults provide the words; second, adults provide the materials children need to explore the characteristics of words in relation to concrete experiences; third, adults help when they structure the children's activities with objects so that differences and similarities are noted. The next few pages contain methods for naming and for providing materials and techniques for children to acquire needed concept attributes.

For *assessment* of the extent of vocabulary, teachers can rely on standard measures of vocabulary, such as the *Peabody Picture Vocabulary Test (8),* which measures passive understanding of words and phrases. Norms are set for all ages so that teachers can compare an individual's vocabulary with that of his classmates and of larger groups of children of his age. This test has the great advantage of not requiring oral language.

Informal assessment also could be used in evaluating vocabulary expansion. In talking with children as they play, teachers can ask for names of objects and descriptions of situations in order to assess vocabulary facility. Children can retell a story, thereby demonstrating knowledge of vocabulary items used in the story. Teachers can also set up situations which assess understanding of certain kinds of words which cannot be pictured. For example, if the teacher puts a pencil on a box and asks, "Is the pencil in the box or on the box?" he can discover the child's understanding of the prepositions in the sentence; with similar procedures, he can assess the child's understanding of other prepositions. Sometimes, game situations illustrate vocabulary understanding without the use of oral language. The box and pencil can be used as the teacher directs the child to follow directions stressing prepositions. Games requiring children to find objects or pictures displayed in an array of other objects.or pictures also relate the children's passive understanding. Both oral use and passive understanding should be used in assessment so that noncommunicative children have the opportunity to indicate knowledge. Sensitive teachers use much patience and effort to assure the children's security in the testing situation before they reach conclusions about reticent children's language knowledge. Finally, assessment should be continual to insure a dynamic vocabulary program.

To find if children understand word attributes, teachers should listen carefully to use of words in different settings. Evidence of confusion between like terms, responses to specific questions, and children's comments on the features of words introduced and reviewed become the material for assessment. Because of our knowledge of children's cognitive development, it is important to bear in mind that some kinds of understanding cannot be achieved during the early childhood years. For example, certain relational terms cannot be understood in adult terms. The word "heavy" is not usually understood as a relational term by young children. Such sophisticated terms as "democracy" and "justice" must be used judiciously in determining the limits to expect as children learn the full meaning of words. Cognitive ability provides the boundaries for growth in conceptual attainment.

In terms of *instruction* in vocabulary or conceptual development, consistent, planned lessons for individuals and groups is recommended. These "lessons" can last from five to twenty minutes, depending on the age and attention span of the students and can occur in conjunction with spontaneous play or in a formal lesson; the structure of the lesson should be determined by the age, learning style, and success of previous lessons.

The lessons can involve as few as two words or a review of ten. All these alternatives must be considered by the teacher; her choices of which to use should be based on assessment of needs, understanding of learning styles, and, most importantly, on objective evaluation of previous lessons. For example, shy, reticent children may learn best while engaged in play, while children whose vocabularies are meager and whose attentions wander easily may learn best in an individual directed lesson which lasts for four minutes each day.

There are elements which should be included in every lesson regardless of the instructional situation used. The words to be introduced should have some relevance to the class program. For example, words about farming should precede and follow a class trip to the farm. Furthermore, when the words are presented, children must be provided with concrete experiences that are the media of word learning. The experiences obviously are determined by the kind of word being introduced. If possible, objects should be used in the experience, although clear pictures can be substituted. With words displaying feelings and movement, understanding can be shown by action. The concrete experiences should elicit sense reactions on the part of the students; they should be able to touch, see, hear, and even smell the referent as they learn the word name. After the teacher identifies the word, the children should be encouraged to comment briefly in their own words on the essential features of the word referent. Finally, the new words should be reviewed in a variety of meaningful situations after initial presentation.

Although the words to be taught will be determined on the basis of the assessment of individuals and groups of children and on the basis of the activities in the classroom, research in vocabulary growth and experience with young children indicate that terms from the following word groups provide a good place for the teacher to start:

relational and opposing terms (on-off, small-big, beginning-end, more-less, same-different, affirmation and negation, etc.)
animals
people
family relationships
colors
shapes
prepositions
containers
machinery
clothes
weather
foods
tools

household implements
furniture
body movements
feelings
toys
liquids
plants
temperature

In helping children develop in-depth knowledge of words, their attributes, and the way in which related words cluster, it is *not* recommended that the teacher simply explain the common and distinguishing features. Instead, this kind of help is provided by focusing the children's attention on relevant aspects. Once children have acquired the ability to name a number of terms in a group of words (let us say the words from the group "clothes"), the teacher can place pictures of the known words before a small group and ask questions that will lead them to identify in their own words what is similar about the group and what is singular about each item. Essentially, this procedure is the basic instructional approach to be used with most groups of words.

The specific instructional activities listed in chart 9 include the naming of new words. This is the most obvious role adults play in helping in the acquisition of concepts; and the activities in Chart 1 include words needed in classroom activities, common terms expected of preschoolers, and some less common, but important descriptor words. Thus, field trips, visitors, classroom and home objects will serve as sources for words to extend vocabulary. Throughout this instruction in language, teachers will want to use new words in complete sentences because individual word meaning is strongly influenced by grammatical context.

Other types of instruction in chart 9 include activities involving the classification of important terms and activities to enhance the development of generalizations for clusters of concepts. In these two areas, classification and generalization, interactive involvement with objects and materials of many sorts, with people, with actions, and even with pictures, contributes to cognitive development. The language aspect of this process involves the naming of objects, actions, events, etc., but it also involves the critical elements of description, classification of events, explanation, and communication.

Prompting and probing by the teacher lead children toward desired conceptual understandings. It should be noted that different children will be learning at different levels at one time. Additions to the activities presented is encouraged. Many of the activities are familiar ones in preschool classrooms; the reader should note variations in *instructional method,* since these variations from the common procedures are meant to emphasize meaning.

Chart 9.
Illustrative instructional activities in the semantic sphere

I. Acquisition of New words

A. *Words are introduced as a result of unit study.* For example, as a result of a unit on the circus, the following words might be introduced: clown, all animals, ring, ringmaster, acrobat, parade. A unit on farms might introduce the following: farm animals, farmer, pasture, barn, garden, field, plant, bush, tree, vegetables, hay, grass, dairy, milk, milker, milking machine, bailer, truck, wagon, mowing machine, tractor. A unit on cities might introduce: apartment building, house, apartment, elevator, escalator, skyscraper, warehouse, store, library, school, park, playground, street, sidewalk, highway, superhighway, policeman, cop, fireman, nurse, conductor, bus, car, train, subway, helicopter.

This list obviously could go on forever. Some words can be introduced before a field trip. The teacher might do so in this manner: "I have pictures of some of the animals we will see at the zoo. Do you know the names of any of them?" (Only a few words are introduced at this time.) The teacher names the rest and then continues: "OK. Here is a way to remember. Ronny, pick up the smallest animal. What is it? Dick, pick up the next smallest. What is it?" The teacher continues and then arranges the pictures in a different way, stressing the names of the animals each time. Since it is important for new words to be repeated in meaningful contexts, new and old terms used in a unit or in preparation for a field trip should be used in other activities.

B. *Common clothing, household objects, classroom objects* should be named and practiced until all the children can name these available objects. The teacher will want to vary the practice and the original naming lessons rather than engage in repetitive naming. He can do so in the following manner: "These are old words to us. See how fast you can name these objects. Remember, don't call out the name until I point to you." Or the teacher might say: "Each person in this circle will name an object placed in the middle. The next person cannot name the one the first person named. He has to find another one to name. See, if I point to shoe and say 'shoe,' he must say something else. Carol will name a *different* thing."

C. *Actions are sources for important words.* The teacher pretends to cry and then asks the children what he is doing. Other less actions can be role-played and then named. (Thus, young children learn to abstract their language as they first act and then describe.)

D. *Descriptive terms are important to incorporate into the language program.* The teacher, in talks with individuals and small groups of children, describes the toys and objects they are using. Later, he asks the children, when they review the day (and have further opportunity to abstract), what they played with, what it felt like, how hard it was, its color, its size, etc. In another exercise, the children each touch an unusual object, such as an acorn squash. The teacher then asks:

"Is it soft or hard?"
"Is it smelly or not?"
"Is it smooth or rough?"

Thus, the teacher is providing descriptive terms. Later, he will ask more open questions so that the children can use their own repertoire of descriptive words.

E. *Magic Box, tactile terms.* The teacher places two objects with decisive characteristics in a Magic Box. The children feel one object and then the other and describe the difference. Characteristics, such as hot/cold, smooth/rough, hard/soft, dry/moist, thin/fat, sharp/round, should be controlled so that only one distinctive characteristic is available at first. Some objects that contain only one distinctive feature are a warm moist sponge and a cold moist sponge, a rock and a sponge, a rock and a smooth sponge ball, a dry sponge and a moist sponge, a thin rock and a thick rock (or any other object with this feature distinction), a sharp-edged rock and a round rock. At first, the teacher will ask questions about the distinctive feature: "Is the object *hot* or *cold* (*smooth* or *rough*, etc.)?" Once these terms have been introduced, teacher naming of the descriptive feature should be reduced. When the children have learned to handle these singular distinctions, the teacher can place objects with more than one feature that is different in the Magic Box. For example, the following objects might be used: a warm moist sponge and a dry sponge, a rock and a moist round smooth sponge ball.

F. *Smell Box.* As an alternative to the Magic Box, the Smell Box helps to explore the sense of smell and associative descriptive terms.

G. *Relational terms.* The crucial concepts indicating differences on one dimension, such as on/off, small/big, beginning/end, more/less, same/different, etc., should be used and emphasized in dialogue whenever possible during play. Specific attention to these terms comes at meaning levels beyond the naming level.

II. Classification: In-Depth Understanding of Words

At this level of meaning, expansion, all children are not expected to supply generic terms for the objects they name or even explanations for their groupings, although the teacher will use the category name often as the children develop a sense of the category membership. The major activity at this point is to build categorical *membership*.

A. *Weather chart: classification of clothes.* (Commercially prepared flannel boards.) The teacher explains the problem to the students in the following way: "We're going to talk about what kind of things this boy would wear. We have to plan what's best to wear on different days. We'll put up lots of different things to wear and then decide.'' The teacher then holds up a cut-out jacket.'' Is this something the boy might wear?'' Then he holds up a cut-out kitchen pot. "Is this something the boy might wear?'' He continues until he has a few pieces of clothing. Then, he proceeds to show a picture of a snowy day and the children choose the appropriate clothing for the boy to wear. Thus, the teacher has promoted both the broad classification—clothing—and also the development of the subgroup—warm clothing. Later, lessons will be designed to expand the large set of clothing items and other subsets of clothing for different weather conditions.

B. *Food game.* Toy foods and nonfood objects are placed on a table with a small group of children. The problem is described: "You are planning a tea party for your friends. Let's get all the possible things you might want to have for them to eat or drink and then you can decide exactly which ones you will use.'' The same procedure used in introducing the weather chart will be used with the same objective in mind, the development of the general category as well as subgroups. (Plastic foods are quite inexpensive and can be found in plastic centerpieces in dime stores.)

C. *Clean-up time.* To set up the problem one should note that every classroom has an organization of materials problem; at least this is true in every classroom where there is lots of activity. Over many days, the teacher can collect unused pieces of string, yarn from art projects, small pieces of paper, plastic pieces from games, etc. in a large box. He then asks the children, in small groups, to sort the material so that it can be put away neatly. He places a collection of these materials in front of pairs or groups of children for them to sort. The children can then name each group if they are ready.

D. *Family game.* The problem set-up might be expressed in the following way: "You have all been telling us about your mothers, your sisters and brothers, your cousins. Let's play a game so that we can get all those people straight.'' The teacher has a set of pictures of people of different ages arranged on the edge of the chalkboard. "Now to begin with, this is the family of Ben so we'll put the picture of Ben on the chart (pocket chart).'' He continues with the immediate family, noting that in some families, there is one parent and that not all children have brothers and sisters. Drawing on the children's experiences, the teacher spends one brief discussion on the immediate family, and later proceeds to previous generations. The pictures of the people should be grouped finally on the pocket chart.

E. *Relational terms.* The basic idea that children need in order to deal with these important concepts is that relational terms are used to show *differences* in the same situation. For example, *more* and *fewer* both refer to quantity. "Here are some blocks in this box,'' the teacher says. "Look, I'm putting some blocks in this other box, too. Both have some blocks, but one box has *more* blocks than the other.'' This procedure should be done with questions, of course. Once the children have had experiences with the concept *more*, the idea of *fewer* is begun, first with naming and then with questioning. *Same/different* should be referred to often in discussion. Similar pictures are displayed and the children assert that they are the same. The teacher then marks one and asks if they are still the same using the word *different* at first as an equivalent term for *not the same*.

Beginning/end should be used in reference to stories, time sequence at home (breakfast, lunch, supper) and, later, with the sounds in words. Many other relational words will be introduced as well.

F. *Prepositions*

Naming of prepositions occurs all the time. Explicit instruction is also advised. For example, books, boxes, and small objects can be placed strategically to meet certain prepositional use. Questions and games offer practice with these critical words. Gotkin's *Language Lotto Set, Prepositions (13)* can also be used.

III. *Use of Generic Terms: Generalizations Achieved*

At this level, children are expected to acquire generic terms and to be able to explain their groupings of objects. The main objective is for children to learn the common features that concepts in a category share. For example, children at this level will be able to use *animal* as the term for the members of that set which they can name. In addition, they should be able to explain what all animals have that people, for example, do not have. To be successful in the following activities, children need to have developed in ways other than verbally. These activities require cognitive skill usually found at the end of the preschool period and at the beginning of the primary grades. These activities ought to promote both cognitive and language development.

A. When words are introduced from the unit study, they should be presented so that critical features are emphasized. For example, with the unit circus, the people who work in the circus can be grouped—acrobats, trapeze artists, clowns, animal trainers. Another day, the teacher can remind the children of these words and they might choose pictures of each worker. Then, he might ask them to think up a name for these workers. The name can be discussed until the children use a word which refers to just these people and no others.

B. *Attention to concept attributes. Man* and *woman*—or any similar pair—can serve as the topic for this work. What is different between these two? What is alike? In answering these questions, children identify the critical attributes which separate the two and then identify the shared attributes.

C. *Common object groupings.* The teacher hides a number of pots and pans about the room and puts one pot on a central table. "Who can find another thing which is like this thing on the center table?" he asks. The objects are collected, named, and shared features identified.

D. *Classification by obvious attribute.* Two children are allowed to decide together how to group red and blue blocks. They are asked why they grouped the blocks as they did. They are given some smaller red and blue blocks to be grouped with the others. (They might continue the two color groups or they might form subgroups of large and small red blocks and large and small blue blocks.) Again, the children are questioned simply. If they are skillful, the teacher might ask them if they can think of another way of grouping the objects besides the way they used.

E. *Communication of classification.* Children who can group objects by maintaining a single attribute and who can alter the groupings when another feature is added can try to communicate a similar problem to another child. One child sits on either side of a table which has an opaque mask between them. Each child is told that they both have the same familiar objects—red and blue blocks, for example. One child is designated as the *teller* and the other as the *doer.* The teller is asked to group his objects and then to tell the doer how to do the same. Both children are then allowed to see the results of their work. Once they can communicate a familiar problem, the teacher can try a very simple, but unfamiliar one.

F. *Ten questions (for sophisticated children).* The teacher explains that he is thinking of an object in the room. He gives a couple of broad hints at first and then directs the children to ask him questions. He explains that he will only answer "yes" and "no." (At first, practice is necessary to show the children what the teacher means.) If the children use up their ten questions, they lose the game. The teacher should explain after one trial that some questions are better than others, for if the children begin right by asking about specifics, they will use up their questions too quickly. The children will soon get the idea of questioning for groupings.

G. *Categorizing books.* The teacher explains that a book that the class has just read is a story from the author's imagination; it didn't really happen. Can the children think of other such stories? Are there stories that tell things that really did happen? Are there stories that tell how to do something? Covers of books can be used to help the children recall books read.

In summary, the instructional recommendations made in this chapter must be recognized as only the bare beginnings of a preschool language program. Each teacher will expand these activities far beyond these suggestions if he inaugurates a real language program for his children. Further, it should be noted again that these activities are supportive of other language programs; they do not supplant any program now in use. Where no program in language development is available, the teacher can start from the suggestions given here. Whatever the classroom situation, the teacher will want to make some initial assessment of children's language facility in the areas of syntax, phonology, and meaning. The results of this assessment will indicate, particularly in the areas of syntax and phonology, the direction that instruction should take. Therefore, whether a complete program is available or the recommendations contained in this book will be the basis for instruction, the teacher must make rational decisions based on his children's needs and his understanding of language learning. In the area of language meaning, it is particularly critical that teachers plan for regular instruction for *all* children. Attention to new words, activities to promote groupings of concepts, and activities to help specify concepts and generalizations are critical to all later verbal learning the children encounter. This aspect of the language program should continue through the elementary years and should parallel with instruction in reading. In fact, although the two parts of this book separate language from reading, the two are not distinct in learning strategies, in instructional needs, or in chronological order. We turn now to discussion of reading but with the understanding that reading is a part of children's total language development.

Selected Activities

1. Find a curriculum guide for a local preschool program. Read the section on language development and determine the proportional weight given to language goals.

2. Compare the assumptions made about a local language program for disadvantaged children from one developed for middle-class children.

3. Give the Sentence Repetition Test to a number of different aged preschoolers to see how syntactic processing changes during the years three through five.

4. Imagine a class of five-year-olds who have just listened to a familiar story. The children are preparing to dramatize the story and are doing most of the planning themselves. Finally, they agree on who is to do what, and the drama takes place. Write a list of the language supporting aspects to the planning and implementation.

5. Find a nursery rhyme that stresses a certain sound (e.g., "I Met a Man with Seven Wives . . .") and read it with emphasis on that sound to a three-year-old, hesitate after a few readings before a critical word, and see if he supplies it.

6. Practice expanding, prompting, and commenting on preschoolers' comments.

7. Applying the language assumptions of this chapter to older children, plan an activity to teach a seven-year-old to say *brought* instead of *brang*.

8. Plan a lesson to help four- or five-year-olds to develop a generalization for these terms: rain, snow, sleet, hail, drizzle, fog.

9. Plan a lesson on classification of various simple pieces of hardware (nails, screws, tacks, tools, etc.). Insert in your plan how you will incorporate language learning with the activity.

References

1. Bereiter, C. E. "Academic Instruction and Preschool Children." In *Language Programs for the Disadvantaged,* edited by R. Corbin and M. Crosby. Champaign, Ill.: National Council of Teachers of English, 1965.
2. Bereiter, C. E., and Engelmann, S. *Teaching Disadvantaged Children in the Preschool.* Englewood Cliffs, N. J.: Prentice-Hall, 1966.
3. Cazden, C. B. "Preschool Education: Early Language Development." In *Handbook on Formative and Summative Evaluation of Student Learning,* edited by B. S. Bloom; J. T. Hastings; and G. F. Madaus, New York: McGraw-Hill, 1971.
4. Cullinan, B. E.; Jaggar, A.; and Strickland, D. "Language Expansion for Black Children in the Primary Grades. A Research Report." *Young Children* 29 (1974): 98–112.
5. Day, D. E. "The Effects of Different Language Instruction on the Use of Attributes by Prekindergarten Disadvantaged Children." Paper presented at the meeting of the American Educational Research Association, February 1968, Chicago.
6. Day, M. C. and Parker, R. K., editors. *The Preschool in Action: Exploring Early Childhood Programs,* 2d edition. Boston: Allyn and Bacon, 1977.
7. Dilorenzo, L. T.; Salter, R. T.; and Brady, J. J. "Prekindergarten Programs for the Disadvantaged: A Third Year Report on an Evaluation Study." Albany: University of the State of New York, State Education Department, 1968.
8. Dunn, L. M. *Peabody Picture Vocabulary Test.* Circle Pines, Minn.: American Guidance Service, 1965.
9. Dunn, L. M., and Smith, J. O. *Peabody Language Development Kits.* Circle Pines, Minn.: American Guidance Service, 1965.
10. Engelmann, S.; Osborn, J.; and Engelmann, T. *DISTAR Language, Preschool-Grade 2.* Chicago: Science Research Associates, 1965.
11. Ervin-Tripp, S. "Children's Sociolinguistic Competence and Dialect Diversity. *Early Childhood Education.* 71st Yearbook of the National Society for the Study of Education, Chicago, Ill.: The University of Chicago Press, 1972.

12. Goldman, R., and Fristoe, M. *The Goldman-Fristoe Test of Articulation.* Circle Pines, Minn.: American Guidance Service, 1969.

13. Gotkin, L. G. *Language Lotto.* New York: Appleton-Crofts, 1966.

14. Lee, L. *Northwestern Syntax Screening Test.* Evanston, Ill.: Northwestern University, 1969.

15. Lee, L. L.; Koenigsknecht, R. A.; and Mulhern, Susan. *Interactive Language Development Teaching: The Clinical Presentation of Grammatical Structure.* Evanston, Ill.: Northwestern University Press, 1975.

16. Parker, R. K.; Ambron, S.; Danielson, G. I.; Halbrook, M. C.; and Levine, J. A. *An Overview of Cognitive and Language Programs for Three-, Four-, and Five-Year-Old Children.* Atlanta, Ga.: Southeastern Education Laboratory, 1970.

17. Slobin, D. I. *Psycholinguistics.* Glenview, Ill.: Scott Foresman, 1971.

18. Spodek, B. and Walberg, H. J., editors. *Early Childhood Education: Issues and Insights.* The National Society for the Study of Education. Berkeley, Ca.: McCutchan, 1977.

PART II

Preparation for Reading and Beginning Reading

5

Introduction to Reading: Its Relation to Language

Our main concern in this section is the preparation for and acquisition of reading. In addition, discussion of a number of relevant subtopics is needed to give an overview of beginning reading. One important subtopic is language. The role of language in reading is the major theme of the present chapter. Recent growth of interest in the role of language in reading has provided new theoretical understandings of reading not available a decade ago. This chapter presents a review of the reading process and the influence of language on reading. After this introduction to reading behavior, we turn in chapter 6 to preliterate skill development and related instructional procedures. The question of early readers and approaches to beginning reading is the topic of chapter 7. Specific instructional suggestions for the teachers of beginning readers are presented in chapter 8.

The questions to be answered in this chapter are: What must teachers understand about reading to help maximize children's potentials for reading success? In what ways does language relate to successful acquisition of reading? Does divergent dialect cause reading difficulty?

The Reading Process

The following discussion of the reading process is intended to provide a conceptual framework with which to make judgments regarding the instructional needs and approaches to be used in helping beginners learn to read.

Reading process is a term used often in recent work in the field of reading. It is used to describe what people *do* as they read. To illustrate it, writers have developed reading models of what might be happening from initial perception of written symbols to the point where a meaningful message is understood. Because few of the behaviors involved in reading are observable, it is difficult to uncover what people do as they process written material. We can observe eye movements, of course, but we cannot observe the mental equipment used in translating the written symbols to meaning. There are data, however, which support recent formulations of the reading process, but before we turn to the description of the reading process and these data, we need to understand why it is necessary to discuss theoretical aspects of reading behavior when there is already available a wealth of information about instruction in reading.

Goodman's *(13, 14, 15),* Smith's *(41)* and other educators' thesis is that teachers of reading ought to understand the process of reading so that instruction is not simply a mindless application of instructional programs. The teachers of young children who are getting ready to read must understand what tasks are used in reading if they are to help children acquire reading ability. Knowledge of reading is as important to the teacher as is skill in following a series of outlined skills, since it is the basis on which to make instructional decisions. However, as Jenkinson *(22)* has pointed out, until recently educators have not been as interested in the process of reading as in specific instructional issues.

Reading has been researched more than any other field of education. The bulk of the research has studied topics such as the correct age to begin reading, testing of reading readiness and reading achievement, environmental factors relative to reading, remedial reading, vocabulary counts, phonics instruction, the difficulty of materials. These topics are important but have not evolved from a comprehensive theory. Therefore, reading instruction is often atheoretical. In other words, teachers too often have no explanation for their method or even their choice of content.

Empirical study of the reading process has historical traces. Huey *(19)* published in 1908 a review of work on eye movements which he developed into a theory of the reading act. In the last two decades other major theoretical formulations have been attempted, and models of the reading process have been developed. These models are diagrams of known and hypothesized activities that occur from the eyes' first encounter with graphic information to comprehension. Research is conducted on aspects of hypothesized behaviors described in the models. Reformulations of theory are caused by mismatch of theory and study results. Most models describe the reading activity of skilled readers (see *38*), not beginners; however, this trend is changing.

In this section we contrast skilled and beginning reading behavior. The discussion is meant to increase understanding of the task learning facing preliterate and beginning reading children.

Skilled Readers

The analysis of skilled reading provides us with insights into what reading is and suggests to us direction for instruction. In reading, skilled readers perceive as meaningful communication the little black marks on paper that are combined into clusters to represent words that are in turn combined into word groups to represent events and ideas. Reading is gathering meaningful messages from the graphic presentation.

Recall your reaction to a novel you recently read and enjoyed. Were you lost in the material once you "got into it"? Do you remember being annoyed when practical matters called you away from your book? Were you reading so fast that you finished in very little time? Most of you probably will respond "yes" to these questions; and if you answered yes, you were engaged in skilled reading of easy material. On the other hand, you probably experience a different manner of reading preparing for an examination or when reading unfamiliar content. Slower, careful reading can be skilled too; for skilled readers the speed of reading varies according to the purposes. Unfortunately many adults never read in a swift, skilled manner, nor do they adjust speed for purpose. On the other hand, a few children as young as seven or eight read easy (for them) material as skilled adults read.

Skilled readers who are reading easy material clearly do not read every word. These readers bring a great deal of information to their reading. Some of the information comes from within themselves and some from their experiences with the world; much information comes from building up knowledge from the material being read—the plot movement, the characters, the setting, the mood, and style. As a result of outside knowledge, language ability, and familiarity with the material, readers build up expectations for the material which reduces the need to read every word. These expectations are treated as predictions to be tested. Readers swiftly sample the written material and use as little data as possible to verify predictions. Skilled reading behavior has been called a *psycholinguistic guessing game* by Goodman *(14).* It involves a steady reduction of uncertainty *(41)* as the reader actively communicates with the author. In communicating through reading, according to Hochberg and Brooks *(18),* the reader is not just *absorbing* the information present; he is also *supplying* information from a variety of sources.

Carroll *(4)* has described two levels of activity in skilled reading. The first level is perception of written symbols. For skilled readers, perception is immediate; most of us do not use spelling and phonic generalizations or analyze closely any of the words except unfamiliar or proper nouns. Smith *(40)* has distinguished between immediate and mediated word recognition. Skilled readers perceive and name (or know) most words immediately. Unskilled readers have to mediate (puzzle out) many new words.

Carroll's second level of reading is immediate grasp of the meaningful message contained in the material. Skilled readers use expectation and prediction, understanding of grammatical structure, semantic familiarity with language knowledge of the world, and personal reaction to grasp the author's meaning. Goodman *(13)* uses the diagram to illustrate the behavior of the skilled reader.

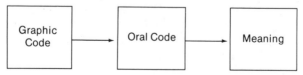

It is important that skilled readers communicate actively with the writer by matching their predictions with enough features to verify them in terms of their knowledge *(18, 5)*. As Ruddell *(34)* has pointed out, a high interest level is essential to achieve this behavior.

Figure 1 shows how skilled reading occurs. The first section, "Before Reading," indicates what the writer and the reader share. First and foremost, they share a language system and thus whole sets of shared rules—syntactic, semantic, word/sound relationships, vocabulary. They must also share at least some information; if one imagines reading an advanced treatise on biochemistry, for example, one can see that for comprehension to occur, some shared information is required. In addition, the reader must have the intent to read and learn or interest in the content as well as ability to attend to the task of reading.

"During Reading" the reader focuses on the print, and a trace of the letters or letter combinations of a word or word unit remain in brief storage. The reader, while holding the trace in storage, searches for the possible word(s) that will fit both the trace and the predictions made from meaning and grammatical structure in prior reading. The predictions are then matched with known word(s). The information is grouped into larger and larger language units. Interpretation of these units occurs in the "Feedback System." When the language structures, grouped according to syntactic constituents, are found to be meaningful, the process continues and the new material is used for further prediction. If the material is meaningless to the reader, he regresses (goes back) to a point where rereading might clarify and repeats the process.

A digression here might help clarify the prominent role language has in reading. Smith, Goodman, and Meredith *(39)* described readers' use of a series of cues. Readers use punctuation to find sentence units; they use spaces to know word boundaries; they use inflections on the ends of words to find plurality of nouns, tense and aspect of verbs, and comparison of modifiers; they use knowledge of acceptable English word order to cue expected words to follow, such as where subject and predicate are likely to appear, and how articles and prepositions indicate following nouns. Thus, every piece of graphic material does not need to be analyzed for meaningful interpretation; readers supply their language expectation and find the information necessary to confirm.

As a "Result of Reading," a number of events may occur. As mentioned above, meaningfully processed material is used for further predictions. Large groups of material may be stored in memory and readers may experience a change in knowledge. They might also use the reading to direct future reading. There are additional results of reading, but they are beyond the scope of this book.

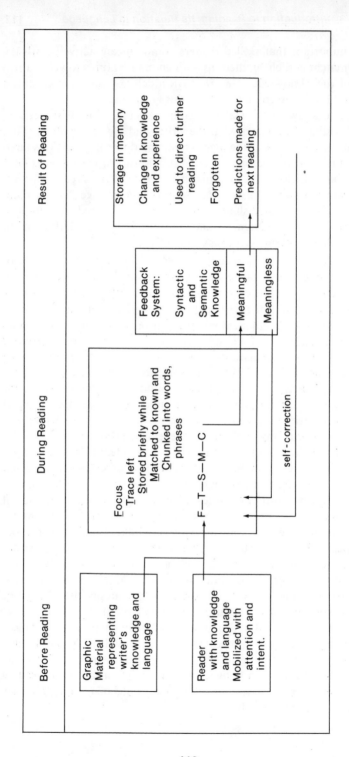

Before Reading

Graphic Material representing writer's knowledge and language

Reader with knowledge and language Mobilized with attention and intent.

During Reading

Focus
  Trace left
  Stored briefly while
  Matched to known and
  Chunked into words, phrases

F — T — S — M — C

self - correction

Feedback System:
Syntactic and Semantic Knowledge

Meaningful

Meaningless

Result of Reading

Storage in memory

Change in knowledge and experience

Used to direct further reading

Forgotten

Predictions made for next reading

Figure 1.
Skilled readers

In sum, this sketchy hypothetical description of how skilled readers read emphasizes (1) that a shared language system between writer and reader is required; (2) that graphic information is immediately processed; (3) that the feedback system depends on language structures and on the reader's continual predictions; and (4) that there are a variety of results of reading. This description was influenced in its language base from the word of Goodman *(15)* and of Ruddell *(35)*. The description of processing of the graphic information was influenced by models of information processing from Mackworth *(26)* and Gough *(16)* and others. As is true of all models, the description seems more complete than is perhaps justi-fied. For example, scholars disagree whether during the brief store, readers must rely on some auditory input or whether the material is processed strictly visually. Thus, the description is a hypothesis.

One way to test the hypothesis is to find if known information of eye movement validates aspects of the description. And there is some sup-port for it. The visual aspects of reading actually complement skilled reading behavior. The eyes stop or fixate, and during fixation written symbols are perceived. Skilled readers reading easy material fixate three or four times a line. Only part of the total information (the letters of a word or words) is necessary for the brain to translate the symbols into meaning. The eyes somehow select just enough material in these few in-stantaneous fixations to provide the information needed. Hochberg *(17)* suggested that peripheral vision supplies the brain with information about where the eyes should fixate next, and McConkie and Raynor *(25)* report that peripheral vision may influence fixation position and duration. These writers state that "the amount of visual information required de-pends on the amount of redundancy in the language."[1] Language redun-dancy exists when there is more than one cue to syntactic/semantic meaning; for example, tense and noun markers in "they are" are redun-dant cues to plurality.

Between fixations, the eyes move jerkily or with *saccadic* rhythm. Although most reading is in a left-to-right direction, regressions also oc-cur. Sometimes, regressions are caused by lack of comprehension. Smith *(26)* suggested that skilled readers also regress to pick up needed infor-mation. So what seem, on introspection, to be regular, smooth eye movements are actually jerky movements to the right with occasional movement to the left and few fixations. The brain does a great deal more work than the eyes, Smith stated, because the brain stores grammatical knowledge, semantic experience, and broad reading experience.

---

1. G. W. McConkie and K. Raynor, "Identifying the Span of the Effective Stimulus in Reading: Literature Review and Theories of Reading," in *Theoretical Models and Proces-ses of Reading,* 2d ed., ed. H. Singer and R. B. Ruddell (Newark, Del: IRA, 1976), p. 159.

Beginning Readers

These abilities—grammatical knowledge, semantic experience, and broad reading experience—enable skilled readers to read printed discourse with immediate understanding. Normal children who approach the task of learning reading have two of these abilities—grammatical knowledge and semantic experience. Given simple materials with simple syntax, vocabulary, and ideas, then, the beginning reader only lacks ability to identify the printed words as words he knows to be able to read. This comparison suggests that beginners need to be taught to recognize words or to *decode*. Decoding by using phonics is a major part of beginning reading, and as Samuels and Schachter *(35)* pointed out, can be taught effectively when organized as a hierarchy of subskills. Additionally, the syntactic and semantic knowledge young children have can help them read words. Because of this, reading instruction should encourage use of context from the start as well as decoding skills.

As we describe the reading behavior of the beginner and contrast it with the skilled reader, we are impressed by the vastness of the task of reading acquisition. Remember, however, that, just as *all* normal children learn to talk and to understand language, *nearly all* normal children learn some reading despite a variety of approaches to teaching (see chapter 7), and despite variance in pupil ability and in teacher skill. We should not, on the other hand, feel satisfied with accomplishments in teaching reading since there are wide inequities in reading achievement. Nor should we assume that reading is acquired naturally like language because it is not. However, reading should be viewed as one aspect of verbal communication which builds upon already acquired speech and listening abilities. As a first step in understanding instruction in reading, we will present major areas of concern in beginning reading instruction.

First, there is one potential stumbling block to reading acquisition that teachers can clarify easily for their pupils. Educators are becoming more knowledgeable about children's inability to understand the task of reading and the language adults use when teaching reading. For too long teachers have mistakenly assumed that adult concepts of reading were shared by children. We neglected to look at the problems of instruction in reading from the child's point of view. And, apparently, the view is often confused. Studies indicate that when we speak of "words," "sounds," "phrases," "sentences," etc., preliterate children do not know what we are talking about. Downing and Oliver *(11)* found that in oral tasks children between five-and-a-half and six-and-a-half have difficulty distinguishing short words, much difficulty with long words, with phrases, with sentences, sounds and syllables. When one thinks about it, why should we expect an illiterate youngster to know that "going to" is made up of two words when he usually hears them combined into "gonna" as in "I'm gonna go to the store." (If you do not think you say it this way, turn to a member of your family and announce this intention as you normally would and listen to yourself.)

When presented with similar tasks in written form, first graders who were slow in developing reading skill equated *words* and *letters* and did not know that spaces mark off word boundaries. Even advanced first graders had difficulty identifying long words with tall letters in the middle *(28)*. For teachers to give directions about circling words, finding words with similar sounds, etc., to youngsters who may not know what is being talked about unnecessarily compounds the difficulty of the first months of reading instruction. Downing *(10)* wisely counseled teachers to teach children *directly* the terminology (or school register) of reading instruction.

Second, preliterate children need to know what reading is—a meaningful communication between writer and reader. Children should understand that the markings on paper can be transformed into sensible oral language. Thus, teachers must help children understand that reading is meaningful. Otherwise, the task of becoming literate produces confusion that may prevent adequate learning *(10)*.

In addition to instruction about terminology and the purpose of reading, there are many other aspects of reading required prior to and during beginning reading. Such instruction includes experiences with units smaller than words as pupils learn to relate to the two-dimensional world of print. Smith *(40)* pointed out that before children can read, they must be able to discriminate the essential features of written symbols. In the beginning, discrimination of features is necessary for differentiation of letters. Also, since prereading children do not easily segment oral words into parts—syllables, beginnings, and endings—analysis of word parts and association of analyzed parts with sounds to be blended together into words is helpful to reading acquisition *(12)*.

The findings of a series of studies examining the errors first graders make while reading orally reveals what children do when they meet unknown words. These studies indicate children need skill in subword analysis as well as context.

Weber's study *(44)* demonstrates that grammatical context is a major cue used by first-grade readers. Of all oral errors made by first graders during many months of study, 91 percent were grammatical according to the preceding context. In fact, the children studied either used context or responded to the graphic code of the word, and they used context far more often. Weber analyzed the spontaneous corrections and found that the better readers corrected only 27 percent of their errors that did not affect the grammaticality of the sentence but corrected 85 percent of the errors that adversely affected the grammaticality of the sentence. By contrast, poorer readers corrected only 58 percent of the errors that changed the sense of the sentence. This was the only discovered difference in the use of context between successful and unsuccessful first-grade readers.

Clearly, the successful readers use language knowledge productively. The difference between Weber's children's use of context suggests teachers ought to help the less able children distinguish sentences that make sense from sentences that do not and to distinguish words that are sensible in a given context from those that are not.

More study of beginners' oral reading showed stages of use of cues in beginning reading *(3)*. Biemiller found beginners would first use context to figure out unknown words and next would either skip the word because they knew they were supposed to figure it out and could not, or would use some letters to pronounce a word. Finally, by the end of the first year of reading instruction, many children were able to relate the letters of the unknown word to the oral word. Cohen *(9)* found it takes many months for successful readers to integrate what they are being taught about letters and sounds (phonics) for pronouncing words with use of context. It is interesting to note the combination of phonics and context use by beginners. Even if children are trained in a program emphasizing phonics over context and meaning, the good readers still use context *(9)*, testimony to children's natural application of language to reading.

To turn now to a general description of beginning reading behavior, we begin with Smith, Goodman, and Meredith's *(39)* approximation of the major components of beginners' reading behavior:

The beginning reader must enter the words into his oral code to receive the meaning. For example, imagine a youngster haltingly reading word-by-word the sentence, "A . . . long . . . came . . . a great . . . big . . . f . . . fish." After hesitating in this manner, the child repeats, "Oh, along came a great big fish!" The first time through, he is busy using all his memory and word attack skills to figure out the words. When the words are put together, either aloud or subvocally, their combination incites understanding of the meaning as children "hear" the language being used.

We know from the oral reading studies that children make a number of different errors, thereby illustrating different strategies. Children might quickly name words they have memorized; they might try to figure an unknown word from its letters and produce a nonsense word; they might put in another word they have been taught in place of the unknown word; they might guess the word from the context for one that would make sense; they might make a wild guess that does not make sense; they might skip the word; they might make any one of a variety of errors, realize their mistake, come back and correct, or try to correct, the word.

Obviously, there are a number of additions which need to be made to the diagram so that it reflects major strategies possible for children to use in perceiving graphic symbols as words. Figure 2 represents a hypothetical view of the beginning reader. As is clear, the beginner's activities "During Reading" contrast the most with the skilled reader. In fact, the only difference between the skilled and beginning reader "Before Reading" is the emphasis with the beginner on whether he has *sufficient* language, knowledge, ability to attend, and the intent to read successfully.

Within the "Graphic Code" are a number of components that look complex, but are not difficult to understand. First, beginners focus on the graphic material. In order to make sense of the print, they must be able to perceive the features of letters and letter combinations that distinguish them from other letters and other combinations of letters. Also, beginners often focus on familiar ending patterns ("at" in "fat") or on word shape, although shape is not a very productive feature.

Under "Analysis" is the description of what the beginner does with the perceived features. If, after going through the process of focus, trace, store, the reader can match with a known, memorized, sight word, the process of analysis and word naming is similar to that of the skilled reader, except that the beginner has to do this for each word rather than only for essential words as the skilled reader. When the word perceived cannot be matched with a known word further analysis is required. Such words can be anlayzed in a variety of ways (reading under "Unknown" on the figure). First, the beginner can use the phonics method of blending each letter/sound together, or he can substitute a sound element from a known word into this unknown word. For example, he comes to the unknown word "mast," relates the "ast" to the known word "fast," and then substitutes /m/ + ast for "mast." The third method of analysis is the use of a rule that operates when the reader meets the unknown word "Cindy," remembers "C" with "i" after it is pronounced /s/, and fits the parts together. Another analysis technique breaks the word into morphic units ("outside" into "out" and "side") or smaller pronouncable parts. Another technique uses grammatical context. Finally, beginners make wild guesses—a questionable technique. Some of the appropriate techniques should be combined as, for example, when use of letter and sound combines with use of context by successful readers.

The analyzed words are named, either correctly or incorrectly. The incorrectly named words might be nonsense words, sensible word substi-

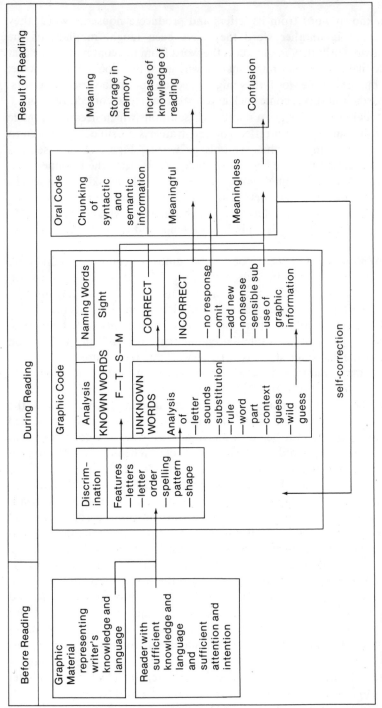

Figure 2.
Beginning readers

tutions with no relation graphically with the text word, or word substitutions with some graphic relation with text word. Other errors include words that are skipped or added words the text does not have.

Once named, the words are coded. Beginners hear the words to determine the meaningfulness of the material and while doing that beginners are applying prediction and confirmation strategies used so productively by skilled readers. If the material is meaningful, it becomes part of the child's knowledge about reading and is stored. If the material is not meaningful, a beginner may regress and self-correct. If meaningless material is not corrected, confusion results.

A note about sense and self-correction: sight words and correctly named analyzed words obviously produce meaningful material. But sensible contextual substitutions do, too. For example, when a reader substitutes "small" for "little" in "The little girl went to the store," there is no meaning change. Omission of "and" in "The hen ran down the road and the man ran, too" results in no change of meaning. Conversely, correct naming may result in meaninglessness. Thus, a word reader (the term implies that the reader is not good at successful coding of pronounced words into language) may correctly pronounce all words in "An unusual happening forced a change in plans" but he may understand little because in the grouping, the oral code is not mature enough to process the following complexities: word order, the relationships of complex structures, the implied but unstated information, and the sophistication of the words. Directional arrows on the figure indicate that both incorrect and correct naming result in meaningful or meaningless coding.

Finally, as a "Result of Reading" the beginner who has read successfully learns more about how to read. He has experienced more word order arrangements, and more description of events and characters each time a new piece of discourse is read.

When we compare the visual behavior of skilled with beginning readers, we find expected differences. Beginning readers fixate many more times in a line, sometimes many times on a single word as it is analyzed. Brown *(5)* has pointed out that the fixations do not last longer for young children, but the amount of information perceived is much less. Because beginning readers need to recode material through the oral code, regressions necessary to attain comprehension are plentiful. Since habitual eye movements of left to right and the return sweep from the end of one line to the beginning of the next have not been established, children often lose their places in the material. Thus, the visual requirements for beginning readers are generally greater than for skilled readers, since it is necessary to obtain more information to achieve comprehension.

The description of the beginning reader presented in figure 2 demonstrates how the oral code is used to interpret the words named. There are a variety of techniques for naming words. Not every beginning reader can make use of every technique. It is the goal of instruction to develop in beginners flexible use of profitable techniques.

Beginning reading, when viewed in light of skilled reading behavior, appears to be more than a series of discrete skills. Children need to be helped in their development of behaviors that will be of lasting importance, and natural language ability is a force to be generated to this end. Youngsters who are ready to read have a store of sophisticated syntactic knowledge which Weber has shown they use to uncover unknown words; we must improve this use through instructional techniques. Once children understand that reading is a form of communication just as talking is, and once they know that oral and written language is made up of *words* that convey meanings, they develop consistent expectations for meaningfulness in reading. Aided by instruction that probes into their knowledge of syntax, children ought to search for a match between their language knowledge and the written language. In this way, context becomes an important and acceptable technique for uncovering unknown words. Since context is one source for the searching behavior of skilled readers, beginning reading instruction should emphasize the syntactic cues adults use. Decoding skills stressing sound/symbol correspondences should be combined with contextual analysis to increase the accuracy of children's testing procedures. With experience, children will begin to realize the specific roles that word order, function words, and inflections play as cues to structure and meaning. Strategies to promote syntactic prediction and verification through meaning should be promoted, practiced, and reinforced. Chapter 8 combines specific suggestions for instruction in use of context with awareness of sound/symbol correspondence.

Language Variation and Reading Achievement

Thus far, the discussion of reading and language has made claims about the *beginning reader* as though all children could be categorized together. But there are widespread differences in children's reading ability even at the beginning. Further, there are group differences in reading achievement, for such achievement is very closely related to socioeconomic status. A pertinent question is: How much does language ability relate with beginning reading achievement?

Loban's *(24)* longitudinal study of children's language from kindergarten through the sixth grade examined the relationship between reading achievement and language. The measures of language included vocabulary and syntactic measures. In this study, highest and lowest scoring subjects were placed in high and low groups for analysis on the basis of language. From the end of the third grade through the sixth grade, those subjects who scored high in language also scored high in reading achievement. As additional evidence for the relationship of language and reading, Strickland's *(43)* study showed that there was a positive relationship between sixth graders' oral language complexity (syntactic measure) and their reading achievement. Evidence of the relationship between early reading and language is provided by Brittain's *(4)* study which shows strong positive correlations between second graders' ability to use inflection and their scores on general reading achievement tests. In Chomsky's *(7)* study of five- to ten-year-old children's comprehension of certain specific syntactic structures, individual variation was found. Further analysis by Chomsky *(8)* indicated that those subjects who were advanced in syntactic knowledge also had had more reading exposure than those whose syntactic comprehension was slower.

Research indicates what one would suspect—that ability in language tends to relate with reading achievement; however, much more work in the area is needed to discover the specifics of the language/reading relationship. We need to know what kinds of differences exist in children's syntactic comprehension at the start of reading. Further, study of the effect of literacy on language development is necessary.

A critical issue in reading has been the question of whether the presence of nonstandard dialect adversely affects reading achievement. Some writers assumed that the identifiable English dialect spoken by many black American children with features different from the written language of books would cause difficulty for Black English-speaking children learning to read *(1)*. Alternatives were suggested to counteract the supposed difficulty. For example, Wolfram *(45)* suggested these alternatives: (1) that teachers teach standard dialect features to Black English-speaking children; (2) that Black English speakers should be allowed to pronounce words in oral reading as they would in speech; (3) that texts be written to avoid the points where the dialects differ; or (4) that texts be written with Black English features especially for Black English-speaking children. A number of sociolinguists favored the last alternative *(1, 41)*.

However, consistency in the studies examining the possible difficulty because of dialect raises questions about the necessity of the four alternatives. First, research in the listening abilities of Black English speakers indicates they understand oral Standard English as well as Black English *(30, 32, 44)*. Second, study of reading demonstrates that dialect does not interfere with beginning reading. Although children in primary grades tend to pronounce material when reading orally similarly to the way they do when they speak *(20, 33)*, there is no evidence that comprehension is improved if the material is written with Black English features *(37)*. Silent reading comprehension is also not improved for primary grade Black English-speaking children when they read material written to represent their dialect *(29, 21)*.

An excellent study by Melmud *(27)* investigated specific sources of dialect interference in auditory discrimination when hearing words in oral context, when reading word lists, and when reading in context. When lower-class white and black third-grade children were tested, it was found that Black English did not interfere with reading comprehension; however, there was interference caused by dialect at the level of auditory discrimination and oral production. Confusion at the phonological level due to words that are homonyms in Black English but are distinguishable in Standard English (see chapter 3) disappeared when contextual cues were available. This study demonstrates that while dialect does not cause comprehension problems, it does account for auditory discrimination confusion. To explain, some Black English-speaking children will not necessarily encounter difficulty distinguishing "cents" and "since" when these words are in oral or written context, but they may not *hear* the difference when the words are presented to them orally in isolation. Further, when they read the words, a standard speaker (the teacher) may not be able to distinguish them. Thus, if teachers are not able to either adapt instruction or avoid tasks with dialect confusing words, there may be an indirect source of interference produced in instruction *(31)*. Suggestions about how to avoid this confusion are included in the following chapters in reference to auditory discrimination and phonics.

The idea that dialect readers are needed for Black English-speaking children still persists in spite of research evidence that no direct interference exists and practical and social imperatives against their use. Since there are wide variations in Black English, it would be difficult to make a match between every individual's dialect and materials. In addition, the problems of developing reading materials for all the people who speak certain dialects make such a project an insurmountable chore: southern mountain, Spanish-American, American Indian, Hawaiian pidgin, and southern rural (black and white speakers). Further, the social implications of dialect-based readers in integrated schools are particularly unhealthy ones. Teachers should not divide children according to their dialect for reading instruction. Finally, attempts to test the use of dialect readers have not been fruitful *(2, 23)*.

In sum, the relationship between language proficiency and reading is strong. To use that relationship to explain completely the low reading achievement of poor, inner-city children is, however, unwarranted. Poor, inner-city children need good instruction to build language and reading skill, not special materials.

Summary

This chapter has presented concepts about reading as a background for the chapters that follow and as a framework for analysis of methodology in reading instruction. Since the skilled reader effectively uses language knowledge to predict and to confirm predictions, it is reasonable that such strategies should be taught beginners. Beginners apparently use grammatical knowledge when figuring out words; successful beginners use this knowledge to self-correct. In addition, instruction in beginning reading provides beginners with techniques for relating symbols with sounds that children use more and more effectively in identifying words as they gain reading experience. Teachers need to help children combine these important techniques for early success.

In order to prepare children to combine productive techniques, a number of preliminary skills should be developed. One area involves understanding of tasks and terminology used in reading instruction. There are other, subword units that should be understood before reading instruction begins. These skill areas—feature differentiation, segmentation of words, sound associations of letters and letter combinations—are discussed more completely in the chapters that follow as we attempt to relate the theoretical presentation of beginning reading capsulized in figure 2 with practical application in teaching.

We also considered language development and its relationship with reading achievement. Language skill and reading development may be reciprocal skills—development in one skill may precipitate growth in the other. This idea will also be developed in later chapters.

Although language development and reading are related, research does not demonstrate a direct interference in reading learning because of dialect. However, since Black English speakers may not auditorially discriminate sounds Standard speakers do, teachers will need to pay particular attention to the auditory discrimination of certain contrasting sounds. This and other prereading skills are described in the next chapter.

Selected Activities

1. Compare your reading time (words per minute) when reading a difficult textbook with the reading time for recreational material.

2. Examine the purposes you have for reading these kinds of materials: instructions to follow (a recipe, dress-making instructions, how to clean a machine, etc.), reading for an examination, reading a front-page newspaper article, reading aloud to a child, or a relaxing novel. Ask another adult to do the same and compare the results.

3. In the sentences below, try to figure out what kinds of words can fit in the blanks:

   __(a)__ very old __(b)__ __(c)__ home in the __(d)__ . Where __(e)__ you __(f)__ when __(g)__ met you? __(h)__ put the dish in the __(i)__ cupboard.

Could (a) be a noun? A verb? An adjective? (b) could only be a noun. Why? If (b) is a noun, then (c) must be what? What is the clue that (d) is a noun ("in")? You might have difficulty with (e) except that it cannot be a noun, an article, an adjective, a conjunction, a preposition, etc. It must be a verb. Once you put a verb in (e), you find that (f) relates strongly with (e). The clause needs a subject, so (g) is obvious. (h) is a typical structural pattern of English. The only possible word type that can go in (i) is what?

4. Or in this example, determine how punctuation and spacing help you read.

iwishthepainterswouldfinishsoicangetallmythingsbackinorderimtiredof movingfromplacetoplace.

5. Follow each word that the child reads through figure 2. The text says, "Terry and Daddy looked at the camera. They smiled." A beginning reader reads, "Ter . . . Terry and Dad looking . . . looked at the ca . . . crama they smiled." Where might the material be processed as meaningful and what as meaningless?

6. If a Black English-speaking beginning reader read the sentence "Freddy stopped when he saw Mr. Mays" as "Freddy stop when he see Mr. Mays," what interference is there to disturb comprehension?

References

1. Baratz, J. C. "Teaching Reading in an Urban Negro School System." In *Teaching Black Children to Read,* edited by J. C. Baratz and R. Shuy. Washington, D.C.: Center for Applied Linguistics, 1969.

2. _____. "The Relationship of Black English to Reading: A Review of Research." In *Language Differences: Do They Interfere?* edited by J. L. Laffey and R. Shuy. Newark, Del.: International Reading Association, 1973.

3. Biemiller, A. "The Development of the Use of Graphic and Contextual Information as Children Learn to Read." *Reading Research Quarterly* 6 (Fall 1970): 75–96.

4. Brittain, M. "Inflectional Performance and Early Reading Achievement." *Reading Research Quarterly* 6 (1970): 34–48.

5. Brown, R. "Psychology and Reading." In *Basic Studies on Reading,* edited by H. Levin and J. P. Williams. New York: Basic Books, 1970.

6. Carroll, J. P. "The Nature of the Reading Process." In *Individualizing Reading Instruction: A Reader,* edited by L. A. Harris and C. B. Smith. New York: Holt, Rinehart, & Winston, 1972.

7. Chomsky, C. *The Acquisition of Syntax in Children from Five to Ten.* Cambridge: The M.I.T. Press, 1970.

8. _____. "Stages in Language Development and Reading Exposure." *Harvard Educational Review* 42 (1972): 1–33.

9. Cohen, A. S. "Oral Reading Errors of First Grade Children Taught by a Code Emphasis Approach." *Reading Research Quarterly* 10 (1974-5): 616–50.

10. Downing, J. "How Children Think About Reading." Paper presented at International Reading Conference, New York, 1975.

11. Downing, J. and Oliver, P. "The Child's Conception of a Word." *Reading Research Quarterly* 9 (1973-4): 568–82.
12. Gibson, E. and Levin, H. *The Psychology of Reading.* Cambridge, Mass.: The M.I.T. Press, 1975.
13. Goodman, K. S. "A Communicative Theory of the Reading Curriculum." *Elementary English* 40 (1963): 290–98.
14. _____. "Reading: A Psycholinguistic Guessing Game." *Journal of the Reading Specialist* 7 (1967): 126–35.
15. _____. "Behind the Eye: What Happens in Reading." In *Theoretical Models and Processes of Reading,* 2d ed., edited by H. Singer and R. B. Ruddell. Newark, Del.: International Reading Association, 1976.
16. Gough, P. B. "One Second of Reading." In *Theoretical Models and Processes of Reading,* 2d ed., edited by H. Singer and R. B. Ruddell. Newark, Del.: International Reading Association, 1976.
17. Hochberg, J. "Components of Literacy: Speculations and Exploratory Research." In *Basic Studies on Reading,* edited by H. Levin and J. P. Williams. New York: Basic Books, 1970.
18. Hochberg, J., and Brooks, V. "Reading as an Intentional Behavior." In *Individualizing Reading Instruction: A Reader,* edited by L. A. Harris and C. B. Smith. New York: Holt, Rinehart, & Winston, 1972.
19. Huey, E. B. *The Psychology and Pedagogy of Reading (1908).* Cambridge: The M.I.T. Press, 1968.
20. Hunt, B. C. "Black Dialect and Third and Fourth Graders: Performance on the Gray Oral Reading Test." *Reading Research Quarterly* 10 (1974-5): 103–23.
21. Jaggar, A. M. "The Effect of Native Dialect and Written Language Structure on Reading Comprehension in Negro and White Elementary School Children." Unpublished doctoral dissertation, New York University, 1973.
22. Jenkinson, M. D. "Sources of Knowledge for Theories of Reading." *Journal of Reading Behavior* 1 (1969): 11–29.
23. Leaverton, L. "Dialect Readers: Rationale, Use, and Value." In *Language Differences: Do They Interfere,* edited by J. L. Laffey and R. Shuy. Newark, Del.: International Reading Association, 1973.
24. Loban, W. D. *The Language of Elementary School Children.* Champaign, Ill.: National Council of Teachers of English, Research Report No. 1, 1963.
25. McConkie, G. W. and Raynor, K. "Identifying the Span of the Effective Stimulus in Reading: Literature Review and Theories of Reading." In *Theoretical Models and Processes of Reading,* 2d ed., edited by H. Singer and R. B. Ruddell. Newark, Del.: International Reading Association, 1976.
26. Mackworth, J. F. "Some Models of the Reading Process: Learners and Skilled Readers." In *The Literature of Research in Reading with Emphasis on Models,* edited by F. B. Davis. New Brunswick, N. J.: Graduate School of Education, Rutgers University, 1971.
27. Melmud, P. J. "Black English Phonology: The Question of Reading Interference." *Monographs of the Language-Behavior Research Laboratory.* Berkeley: University of California, 1971.
28. Meltzer, N. S. and Herse, R. "The Boundaries of Written Words as Seen by First Graders." *Journal of Reading Behavior* 1 (1969): 3–14.

29. Nolen, P. S. "Reading Nonstandard Dialect Materials: A Study at Grades 2 and 4." *Child Development* 43 (September 1972): 1092-97.
30. Peisach, E. C. "Children's Comprehension of Teacher and Peer Speech." *Child Development* 36 (June 1965): 146-80.
31. Pflaum-Connor, S. W. "Minority Student Language and Reading Acquisition." In *Aspects of Reading Education,* edited by S. W. Pflaum-Connor. Berkeley: McCutchan, 1978.
32. Ramsey, J. "A Comparison of First Grade Negro Dialect and Standard English." *Elementary English* 49 (May 1972): 688-96.
33. Rosen, C. L. and Ames, W. S. "Influence of Nonstandard Dialect on Oral Reading Behavior of Fourth Grade Black Children under Two Stimuli Conditions." In *Better Reading in Urban Schools,* edited by J. A. Figurel. Newark, Del.: International Reading Association, 1972.
34. Ruddell, R. B. "Psycholinguistic Implications for a System of Communication Models." In *Theoretical Models and Processes of Reading,* 2d ed., edited by J. Singer and R. B. Ruddell. Newark, Del.: International Reading Association, 1976.
35. Samuels, S. J. and Schachter, S. W. "Controversial Issues in Beginning Reading Instruction: Meaning Versus Subskill Emphasis." In *Aspects of Reading Education,* edited by S. W. Pflaum-Connor. Berkeley: McCutchan, 1978.
36. Shuy, R. W. "Some Conditions for Developing Beginning Reading Materials for Ghetto Children." *Journal of Reading Behavior* 1 (1969): 33-43.
37. Simons, H. D. and Johnson, K. R. "Black English Syntax and Reading Interference," *Research in the Teaching of English* 8 (Winter 1974): 339-58.
38. Singer, H. and Ruddell, R. B., editors. *Theoretical Models and Processes of Reading,* 2d ed. Newark, Del.: International Reading Association, 1976.
39. Smith, E. B.; Goodman, K. S.; and Meredith, R. *Language and Thinking in the Elementary School.* New York: Holt, Rinehart, & Winston, 1970.
40. Smith, F. *Understanding Reading: A Psycholinguistic Analysis of Reading and Learning to Read.* New York: Holt, Rinehart, & Winston, 1971.
41. Stewart, W. "On the Use of Negro Dialect in the Teaching of Reading." In *Teaching Black Children to Read,* edited by J. C. Baratz and R. Shuy. Washington, D.C.: Center for Applied Linguistics, 1969.
42. Strickland, R. G. "The Language of Elementary School Children: Its Relationship to the Language of Reading Textbooks and the Quality of Reading of Selected Children." *Bulletin of the School of Education, Indiana University* (1962): 1-131.
43. Weber, R. M. "First Graders' Use of Grammatical Context in Reading." In *Basic Studies in Reading,* edited by H. Levin and J. P. Williams. New York: Basic Books, 1970.
44. Weener, P. D. "Social Dialect Differences and the Recall of Verbal Messages." *Journal of Educational Psychology* 60 (1969): 194-99.
45. Wolfram, W. "Dialect Training and Reading: A Further Look." *Reading Research Quarterly* 5 (1970): 581-89.

6

Before Reading

All the language and cognitive abilities acquired during the first years of life help prepare children for reading. The previous chapters have analyzed language growth and its relationship with reading. We turn now to instructional procedures that promote learning certain skills that have been found to be helpful in the beginning of reading.

Instruction in specific prereading skills traditionally took place at the end of the kindergarten year and/or at the beginning of first grade in a period of instruction called reading readiness. The first section of this chapter reviews background material concerning the tradition of reading readiness. The second section presents the skills, assessment techniques, and methods of instruction for different prereading areas.

Reading Readiness

The term *reading readiness* was first used in the 1920s to describe the instructional period which prepared children for reading. From this period until the end of the 1950s, research studies were undertaken to find answers to the questions: When is the best time to begin reading instruction? How can an individual's readiness be determined? Although it may appear that the following discussion applies only to instruction which occurs *before formal reading instruction,* many of the readiness skills described here continue to be useful to children *after they have begun to read.* In fact, it is often difficult to know whether training in the association of sounds and symbols, for example, is a readiness or a beginning reading activity. Thus, readiness instruction begins well before reading and continues afterwards.

Reading readiness instruction traditionally includes story-telling and listening activities as well as auditory training in sounds of letters, visual training, and the naming of letters. It sometimes includes eye movement training and practice in writing letters. While *testing* to determine if children are ready to learn to read has consistently been a part of the application of the readiness concept to classrooms, *training* to prepare children for reading has varied greatly. To illustrate, two different trends in early childhood education have led to very different concepts about readiness.

One important trend in early childhood education dates back to work begun in the 1930s. During this period, Gesell *(22)* examined in detail the motor, cognitive, and social development of children from birth through adolescence. From the observational records of children seen at various chronologically determined intervals, the researchers searched for common growth patterns which they then combined into descriptions of typical behavior of children at each interval. As a result of this study, childhood was described as a period of natural movement from one discernible stage to another. Children would be "ready" to learn new skills when genetically determined growth developments allowed new learning to take place. Gesell's work influenced educators for many years and is still considered important; however, researchers and educators alike accepted this approach, particulary in reference to reading readiness, more than empirical study and classroom experience justified.

During the 1950s—especially at the end of the decade when the launch of Sputnik redirected their attention—educators began to look more closely at environmental influences on learning. As a result, educators and psychologists outlined alternate approaches to curricula matters during the late 1950s and 1960s. For example, Bruner *(6)* stated that by closely analyzing the conceptual framework of a field, it was possible to find hierarchically arranged material which could be adapted appropriately to the learning level of all students. In other words, the new thinking required analysis to find, first, the components of prereading; these components were ordered as a series of steps. Second, the topics were specified, or operationalized, in hierarchical fashion so that each step was presumably dependent on mastery of the previous one. Theoretically, any preliterate child could then be tested and assigned lessons on the skills he needed. A major implication of this approach was that schools began to prepare young children for reading and to teach reading when children appeared to be ready.

A schism developed between the earlier "developmental" advocates who preferred stimulation of natural growth processes and were therefore reluctant to hurry children into early reading and the other school of early training advocates. This latter group recommended earlier, structured sequential preparation for reading and early reading instruction. In recent years, the developmental point of view has received support from educators influenced by Piaget. These scholars note that the time common for preparation and beginning reading typically occurs just before acquisition of the concrete operational stage (chapter 1). They doubt if children should be expected to read when their cognitive level of functioning is still immature. Elkind *(15)*, for example, pointed out that beginning reading instruction requires a level of abstraction beyond the ability of the preoperational child. As a result of similar thinking, Furth *(18)* recommended that reading instruction be postponed for a year or two. However, research does not consistently support the idea of reading delay.

Bradley *(5)* delayed instruction up to a half year for some children and studied the effects in comparison to a control group. Her conclusions, based on tests made at the start of third grade, were that the children whose instruction had been delayed were better readers. Spache et al. *(40),* using a far better research design, found that at the end of first grade the children in the experimental groups where reading instruction had been delayed if warranted were not significantly superior to the children of the control groups who were all taught reading at the beginning of first grade. The experimental children with low readiness in this study, though, showed gains over the controls as a result of delayed reading and extended readiness. It would be difficult to measure the effect of a more extended delay in reading given societal expectations. Few parents and children would be willing to agree to planned delay of a year or more, and quite understandably in light of research discussed in chapter 7 in reference to early reading.

Disagreements among scholars about the role of early education is reflected in disparate curriculum designs found in kindergartens. For example, the author has observed in three schools located within a ten block urban area three drastically different approaches to kindergarten instruction. In the first school, the children all begin to read in a highly structured phonics-oriented program after a minimal preparatory period during which they learn letter sounds and names. These children are expected to read grade one and grade two level materials at the end of the kindergarten year. In the second school, much of the children's time is spent in a different commercial program, highly directive or structured, but focusing on the development of prereading skills rather than on actual reading. In the third school, children do building, categorizing, and problem solving activities. Teachers provide good materials to work with and ask questions appropriate to the activities. These children are not expected to read during kindergarten, although by the end of the year some readiness begins. With teachers in many schools there seems to be a growing tendency to design programs like those in the first and second schools, the Piagetian influence notwithstanding.

The kind of prereading instruction described in this chapter applies more to kindergartens designed like the second and third schools than to kindergartens designed for early reading acquisition. However, the suggested assessments and teaching ideas presented here are also suitable for kindergarten programs that emphasize early reading and for beginning first grades in that the assessments can point out important information about strengths and weaknesses in pupils' preparedness, and the teaching ideas are helpful in supplementary activities.

Determining Children's Readiness for Reading

Educators in the 1920s, 1930s, and later used standard methods to determine achievement levels of groups of children. During the twenties, large-scale testing of school achievement and of intelligence uncovered reading problems among American children Since the thesis that stressed ripening within the child influenced how these test findings were interpreted, it was thought that failure to read well in first grade must be due to the imposition of reading instruction before children were ready *(27)*.

In order to prevent further reading problems, researchers believed that they should find a Mental Age (MA) at which reading would be most effectively taught. Morphett and Washburne's *(32)* 1931 study supplied an answer, but not conclusive evidence, to this question. Based on the first-grade reading achievement in one school system taught with one approach, this study found that those children who had achieved a mental age of 6.6 were more successful than those whose MA was below this point. Morphett and Washburne stated that teachers should wait until children had a mental age of 6.6 before beginning reading instruction. This one study influenced reading instruction more than was warranted, particularly since Gates *(19)* reported that postponing reading for all children who did not have a mental age of 6.6 was not necessary. In a later study, the effectiveness of the teacher and the method he used was found to be far more crucial to reading success than was a 6.6 MA *(20)*. The Gates and Bond studies were virtually ignored, though, while textbooks *(22, 25)* continued to inform readers that reading instruction should be delayed until children achieved a mental age of 6.6. Fortunately, educators today are quite willing to accept the idea that teacher skill does matter in developing successful beginning readers. In fact Bond and Dykstra *(3)* found that instruction is a major factor determining first-grade reading success.

Reading Readiness Tests

An important development begun in the 1930s and continued later was the production of standardized tests used to gauge reading readiness. The *Lee-Clark Reading Readiness Test* (California Test Bureau), the *Monroe Reading Aptitude Tests* (Houghton Mifflin), and the *Gates Reading Readiness Tests* (Teachers' College) all originally date from the thirties era but have been revised in recent years. The popular *Metropolitan Readiness Test* (Harcourt, Brace, Jovanovich) was developed in 1950. These tests are given at the end of kindergarten or the beginning of first grade. Usually they are group paper-and-pencil tests, although the Gates and Monroe Tests have individually administered subtests of visual discrimination ability (the ability to differentiate among pictures, shapes, letters, and words), and oral comprehension as well as a subtest on auditory discrimination ability (ability to hear differences in the sounds of words). The Monroe Test also includes subtests of auditory blending, motor coordination, visual memory, and maze tracing.

Since readiness tests require paper-and-pencil responses, they pose problems for young children who have not had practice in following complex directions on paper. As discussed in chapter 5, children are confused about the technical words used. As a result, poor performance on tests may indicate lack of ability to *understand the language of the test directions* rather than lack of ability to *understand the task being tested.* For example, a bright child with little prereading experience asked to circle words, underline, match, etc., may score low because he does not know how to follow the directions. Because of problems such as this, psychologists and educators have tried to avoid confusions in new tests. For example, the Goldman, Fristoe, Woodcock *Test of Auditory Discrimination (24)* begins by training children to point to the picture which represents a spoken word before the actual testing is begun.

Research studies on the effectiveness of readiness to predict reading success have not been very encouraging. Gates, Bond, and Russell *(21)* pointed out that only if the tests represent the method of instruction to be used in teaching reading are they useful diagnostic instruments. Comparisons of readiness tests with teachers' judgments indicate that teachers are at least as good as readiness tests in predicting which children will have success in beginning reading. Kottmeyer *(29)* compared teachers' ability to predict with that of intelligence tests and readiness tests and found that teachers' judgments were not significantly improved when the scores from intelligence and readiness tests were added. Teachers who had been teaching for ten years or more were better predictors of reading success than were less experienced teachers. Annesley, et al. *(1)* and Koppman and Lapray *(28)* also reported that teacher assessment of children's probable success in reading is as good a predictor as a readiness test. Spache and Spache *(39)* stated that helping teachers judge children's competency in language and readiness through the use of informal techniques of assessment will increase determination of readiness.

On the other hand, in a recent study by Fishbach, Adelman, and Fuller *(17)*, teacher observations, while better than standard measures as predictors, were by no means flawless. Teachers used a carefully designed instrument to rate kindergarten children's probable success in reading. Overall, the teacher predictions related significantly with reading achievement; however, teachers only identified half of the children who later experienced failure in second and third grades. Thus, careful observations make sense for group prediction but are questionable when used to make exact identification of children who may develop difficulties.

Despite the fact that we do not have exact measures for prediction, we do know some are better predictors than others. Many studies show the ability to name letters predicts reading success *(13)*. Boney and Lynch *(4)* and Durrell *(13)* concluded that ability to retain words after initial presentation shows readiness for reading. Farr *(16)* suggested that examination of ability to retell stories and to describe events would help in identifying ready-to-read children. In a study by Richek *(36)*, preliterate children were taught six words by two methods, and the skills that predicted successful learning were analyzed. Like others, she found that ability to name letters predicted successful learning whatever the method of teaching words. If the words were taught as whole units to be memorized—sight words—visual discrimination and recall of digits also predicted success, but to a smaller degree. If the words taught belonged to a rhyming group and were therefore related in terms of sound and symbol, in addition to letter naming, ability to name sounds and to blend sounds related to successful learning. This study suggests that the ability to predict reading success is partly determined by the approach to be used in teaching reading.

There are a number of prereading assessment procedures included in the second section of this chapter. Some of the assessments predict well; others are included for their value in planning instruction before reading rather than as predictors.

Effect of Training on Readiness

There are two critical questions of current interest to teachers. One is whether participation in a readiness training program before reading helps children acquire reading skill. The other issue is whether readiness training is preferable to early reading without prior readiness training. Only the first question has been studied empirically.

The question of whether readiness training in kindergarten or first grade really helps children learn to read can be answered affirmatively based on the available data. In fact, Teegarden *(42)* and Pratt *(35)* show that attendance at kindergarten alone is helpful for first-grade reading, whether a planned readiness program has been included or not. However, Morrison and Harris *(33)* show that by third grade inner-city children who did not attend kindergarten are equal to their classmates who attended kindergarten in reading. However, if the language experience method was used, a residual gain for the kindergarten children remained in third grade. Blakely and Shadle *(2)* and Ploghoft *(34)* have also shown the beneficial effects of planned readiness programs.

In spite of its advantages, there were relatively few classes with readiness training in kindergarten a few years ago. LaConte *(30)* found that 57.3 percent of the kindergarten teachers who responded to his survey disagreed with the statement that reading had no place in kindergarten classrooms. Nonetheless, planned instruction was found to be minimal. Teachers provided instruction in naming letters, writing words, word discrimination, and reading words, but only occasionally.

LaConte also found that teachers depended on popular reading readiness workbooks accompanying basal reader sets far more than they did a decade earlier. Allen [reported by Spache and Spache *(39)*] found that the workbooks are similar; they include "reading" of pictures, some visual discrimination exercises, and some auditory discrimination exercises. Although Ploghoft *(34)* found no difference in the preparation of children taught with and without workbooks, Blakeley and Shadle's *(2)* study indicates that teacher-planned activities and language experience both are superior to workbooks in helping children prepare to read. Hillerich *(26)* also found language experience better as readiness training. Although a workbook program was better than none, it appears that use of workbooks should be supplemented with other teacher-planned activities.

Governmental agencies have become interested in early childhood education and have funded many programs. The first such program was Head Start. Head Start was not designed specifically for readiness training, but the findings of the Westinghouse-Ohio study of 1970 indicated that full-year Head Start children approached the national norms on the Metropolitan Readiness Test *(38)*.

Perhaps in response to parental sensitivity to national media and to local changes *(12)*, many families now emphasize early academics. Of course, the availability of television's *Sesame Street* and *Electric Company* and supermarket workbooks remind parents of fairly typical prereading instructional areas. Another indication of increased focus on early reading preparation comes from published readiness materials. Basal reading texts published since 1968 include more extensive workbook and kit prereading materials than in the past.

To summarize the prereading period, the original concept of readiness, fostered by the testing movement of the 1920s and 1930s, was defined as the period of natural development in cognitive, language, auditory, visual, and motor capabilities. Piaget's theory and supporting data encourage some educators to adhere to this developmental model today. On the other hand, both the curricular changes of the 1960s and public interest in comparative achievement of individuals and groups have increased the emphasis on academic preparation for reading. These influences have also changed the focus of testing. Instead of using tests simply to determine a child's readiness, we now use them to determine instructional needs as well. Overall research on the effectiveness of prereading training demonstrates it has a positive influence on achievement. We now turn to the specifics of prereading testing and teaching.

Prereading, Skills, Assessments, and Instruction

For many years, educators debated the value of various kinds of reading readiness skills. The most important factors that appear to be related to reading success are those in the auditory sphere, in the visual sphere, and in language and listening. *Auditory discrimination* is the ability of young children to hear significant phonemes in words. For example, if children can tell that "bat" in the sequence "bet, bat, bet, bet" is different when the words in the sequence are spoken, they can discriminate auditorily the vowel phonemes. Other auditory skills support the development of auditory discrimination. *Visual discrimination* is the ability to distinguish one visual form from another. When children can tell which letter is different from "b" in the sequence, "d, b, b," they can visually discriminate "b" and "d." In addition to the four main skill areas, there is brief reference to a related area.

The Prereading checklist, chart 10, is included as an outline of the skill areas discussed below, and this section is organized into the five areas listed in the checklist. The discussion of each area includes a general introduction, assessment recommendations, and teaching suggestions. In practice, the checklist is an efficient summary of assessed reading behaviors. It has been used with over three hundred four- and five-year-olds and has been found to differentiate training needs effectively. Some of the assessment instruments can be used with groups (and are marked "group" in the relevant parts of the discussion) and some are individual. On the checklist the columns "Above Average," "Average," and "Below Average" present approximate criteria to use in judging children's performance. The numbers next to each "4" row are allowable *errors* in each category for four-year-olds. The numbers next to the "5" rows are criteria for fives. In some cases the criteria for rating are included in later discussion.

Chart 10.
Prereading checklist

Skill Area		Above Average	Average	Below Average
I. Language Production				
A. Syntax	4	2,3	4,5	6 or more
	5	none	1–3	4 or more
B. Vocabulary	4	1,2	3,4	5 or more
	5	none	1,2	3 or more
C. Storytelling, language experience		Described in text		
SUMMARY				
II. Listening				
A. Recall of story detail		Described in text		
B. Recall of sequence		Described in text		
C. Following directions	4	1	2	3 or 4
	5	none	1	2 or more
D. Understanding vocabulary of reading	4	5,6	7,8	9 or more
	5	1–4	5,6	7 or more
SUMMARY				
III. Auditory Skills*				
A. Discrimination of sounds		Described in text		
B. Initial sound analysis	4	1–3	4,5	6 or more
	5	none	1,2	3 or more
C. Rhyme	4	1,2	3	4
	5	none	1	2 or more
D. Association of sounds and letters	4	1–5	6–10	
	5	0,1	2,3	4 or more
SUMMARY				
IV. Visual Skills*				
A. Discrimination of letters	4	1–6	7–9	10 or more
	5	1–3	5–8	9 or more
B. Discrimination of words	4	1–6	7–9	10 or more
	5	1–3	5–8	9 or more

C.	Names/Sounds of letters	4	half (18)	few (5)	
		5	few (5)	half (18)	most (20)
D.	Identification of	4	16	all	
	common words	5	16	18	
	SUMMARY				

V. *Related Skills*	
Small motor coordination	Described in text

*The skills under "Auditory" and "Visual" are arranged from simplest to most complex In actual testing, it is best to test the most complex first. If a child achieves highly in the complex area, the teacher can assume mastery of the subordinate skills and not test them.

I. *Language Production*

In part I of this book, the language development of young children was discussed, and chapter 5 stated that general language ability appears to relate to reading success. Consequently, teachers must be conscious of the great importance of the language aspect of their readiness programs. Indeed, language should be included not only during prereading stages but also at the start of reading acquisition and throughout developmental reading.

A. Syntax

—One method of assessment uses the Sentence Repetition Test in chapter 4. Chapter 4 also presents other methods for assessment.

— Instructional activities are described in chapter 5.

B. Vocabulary

— A simple assessment procedure is included in Test 1.

Test 1

Materials: 2 cigar boxes, small ball, different colored blocks.
Preparation: First, play with objects and make sure child understands their names. Then set up each situation and ask the questions as indicated.

SITUATION	QUESTION
1. Slowly place a block on top of the box.	"Where is the block now? Is it under the box? Where is it? (*on*)"

SITUATION	QUESTION
2. Place block inside the box.	"Now where is the block? (*in*)"
3. Place block under box.	"Where is the block now? (*under*)"
4. Slowly put the ball in the box. Say, "Watch me now," as you slowly take it out and ask . . .	"Now I'm taking the ball _____(*out*)."
5. Toss the ball over the box.	"Look, I'm throwing the ball where? Is it going in the box? No, it's going _____ (*over*)."
6. Slowly fill one box with blocks and explain what you are doing. Place an empty box next to the full one, but do not use these words.	"Now one of these has blocks in it and the other doesn't, right?" Point to one and say, "This box is what _____ (*full*)? So this one must be what _____ (*empty*)?"
7. Put one block before (in front of) one box and one block behind the other box.	Point to one box and ask, "This box has a block where _____ (*in front of it*)?" Point to the other and ask, "This box has a block where _____ (*in back of it*)?"
8. Push a block with one of the boxes. Ask the child to do the same.	"What are you doing to the box? (*pushing it* or *using it to push*)"
9. Fill one box with many blocks and the other with few to elicit more and fewer or less.	"See how many blocks are in this box. This box has _____ (*more*) than this. So this other box has _____ (*fewer* or *less*)."
10. Arrange three differently colored blocks in front of child.	Point to first (on child's left) and ask, "This is what, the *first, second,* or *third?* Which one is last? Which one is in the middle?"

— Activities to expand vocabulary should be an important part of every classroom's activities. As described in chapter 4, there are two types of instruction needed. One introduces new words in the context of related words from the same semantic cluster. For example, if children do not know "moist" but do know "wet" and "damp," the lesson would begin with the known words and their common shared meaning and then move to the unknown. After stating in their own words that "wet" and "damp" mean there is liquid on objects, children can be introduced to the word "moist."

— New words are best learned when children have direct experiences with them. When it is not possible to have direct experience (e.g., with "crocodile"), teachers should develop vicarious experience by using pictures and other simulations. With the example above, the teacher asks the children to feel three sponges and tells the children that one is a "wet" sponge, one a "damp" sponge, and one a "moist" sponge. The children learn that a "moist" and a "damp" sponge are alike and both different from "wet."

— A second type of word learning clarifies partially known words. These already known but incompletely understood words can also be introduced within a semantic cluster. Attributes of each word are clarified as concepts are compared. Children at five or six have incomplete understanding of the concepts of familial relationship, for example, although they use "father," "sister," "aunt," etc. appropriately in their families. Young children are apt to understand the idea of "brother" and "sister" as they relate to themselves, but they are unable sometimes to understand the adult-sibling relationship and are often confused about the reciprocity of the relationship *(9)*. Teachers can begin with the known attributes as children explain about their siblings, then show adult-sibling relationships, and discuss carefully the reciprocal attribute.

C. Story Telling and Beginning Language Experience

— First attempt stories should not be rated since some children may have had no such experience at home. The stories used for rating can come from dictated and recorded language experience stories. An above average five-year-old storyteller has a recognizable sequence of events and consistent characters with clearly expressed development. An average storyteller demonstrates some sequence understanding but perhaps an unclear plot. A below average story may include change in theme, unnamed characters, and/or illogical sequence of events. A four-year-old's above average story is like that of an average five-year-old. An average story is apt to have little logical plot sequence, but clear characters. A below average story has two or more of the weak story characteristics.

— In this area teachers may want on-going records of growth. For example, teachers can keep a copy of the dictated stories so that sentence structure and vocabulary development is monitored. A carbon copy provides the child with the original and the teacher with a copy for the file. Once real reading occurs, this filing system becomes extremely important since it contains the reading vocabulary of each child. But even at the prereading level, teachers can look for evidence of conjoined and embedded sentences, use of inflections, and appropriate use of new vocabulary words. Important to the implementation of these language experiences is stimulation of output.

— Work with children after writing down dictations helps them develop increased understanding of what reading is. In helping children to perceive that their oral words can be represented by printed symbols, the teacher should immediately reread their stories to them asking if he has written the story as it was said. The words are read as the teacher slowly moves his hand in a *left-to-right direction* across the page. He can ask, "Is this what you said? See this word. It is *umbrella*. Look at how long it is on the paper." The sentences should each begin a new line and the teacher can point this out by saying, "You started a new idea here."

— Another important understanding is that stories can be shared. The teacher can encourage this idea by asking a child with whom he wants to share his story. Then both children listen to the story and, perhaps, even illustrate it together. Or two or three children who have "written" (dictated) a story about the same event can listen to all the stories and talk about how they are different and alike.

II. *Listening*

Ability to comprehend what one hears is similar to comprehending what one reads; both require analysis in terms of one's own language knowledge. Various listening experiences will help children develop ability in skills which will be stressed later during reading instruction.

A. Recall of Story Detail

— Assessment of this ability can be accomplished with the whole group. The teacher can prepare a ditto to be used after reading a story. For example, if Ezra Keats' *The Snowy Day* is used as the story, the format shown below will indicate how well children recall details.

Ditto

Questions

(Identify all pictures first.) Look at the pictures next to the ball. Draw a line around the one picture that shows what Peter used to mark the snow.

Look at all the pictures next to the box. Draw a line around the picture that shows where Peter put his big snowball.

Look at the pictures next to the tree. Draw a line around the picture that shows what Peter did the next morning.

In a simple assessment such as this, one error indicates below average performance for four- and five-year-olds.

— Instructional activities for recalling details include discussion after reading the story, discussion of details from a story the children dictated the previous day, and discussion of past events. Occasional assessment may help determine how much attention is warranted in this area of listening comprehension.

B.   Recall of Sequence

In order to understand sequence, children must be able to decide which events in a story are important. Then they have to remember the order of the events.

— Again, assessment of this ability can be made with *The Snowy Day,* as children are presented with a dittoed copy of the material shown below. Of course, the teacher will want more than one example to assess ability in this area.

Ditto

Questions

Put a circle in the picture that shows what the story of Peter is mostly about.

— Assessment of order (*group*) can be accomplished in a large group by using a ditto which requires that children put the numbers 1, 2, and 3 next to the pictures in the order they occur in the story. This task may require practice by teacher and child together before assessment becomes reliable. After practice, most average and above average five-year-olds can put two or three events in order.

— Instruction occurs in discussion of material read and in telling the order of events in, for example, the child's household in the morning before he comes to school.

— Instructional activities designed to improve identification of a main idea will come largely through discussion of poems, other stories, and dictated stories ("What's the most important idea in your story?") the teacher has read to the children. Since young children often do not want to continue to sit still after hearing a story, the teacher can form little groups of children to discuss a story later in the day. This practice has the advantage of promoting memory and of encouraging more opportunities for each child to talk.

C. Following Directions

— Test 2 (*group*) can be used to assess children's abilities to follow one-, two-, and three-step directions.

Test 2

Directions: Hand out a drawing paper to each child that has already been folded and each fourth numbered as shown.

Ask children to listen to all your directions before they start to follow them. Say the directions only once. Practice one on another sheet first.

1. In square 1, draw a ball and put a dot in the middle of the ball.
2. In square 2, draw a line. Then draw a ball on the line.
3. In square 3, draw a big ball. Now draw a box in the middle of the ball. Now put a tiny ball in the middle of the ball.
4. In square 4, draw a line. Put a box on top of the line. Put a ball next to the box.

— It is important that the activities with young children to promote following directions be mostly in the realm of physical activity even though the assessment is a paper-and-pencil affair. (Use of paper and pencil enables many children to be assessed at one time.) Practice in both following and giving directions is important. Play with objects on a table, marching around the room according to simple directions, organizational procedures, cleaning up—all these provide opportunity for following and giving directions. The teacher can also have a child give directions for others to follow.

D. Understanding Vocabulary of Reading

Discussion in chapter 5 described difficulties young children have in understanding the terms used in teaching prereading and reading. One set of words is included in Test 3. Other words are found in the materials children use.

— Test 3 demonstrates if children understand the terms "word," "word part," "sound," "sentence" in oral and/or written form.

Test 3

Directions: Say the following items.

ORAL

1. *Words:* Count the words I say.

   Let me help you.   _____
   What is your name?   _____

2. *Word Parts:* Count the words I say.

   grandfather   _____
   outside   _____

3. *Sounds:* Say the first sound of these words.

   boy   _____
   Mom   _____

WRITTEN (Put this part of test on plasticized cards)

1. *Words:* Draw a line between the words on this card.

The boys saw the
elephant.   _____   _____   _____   _____   _____

2. *Sentences:* Put a big X at the end of each sentence.

The girls went home.
They ate some cookies. Then   _____
they went out
to play.   _____

— Instruction should be direct and simple. For example, to teach "word," the teacher explains that we use "words" when we talk and that usually there is a pause after each word. He then pronounces distinctly "I like you" and asks the children to count on repetition, "I (1) like (2) you (3)." After much practice, the children can give sentences for classmates to count words.

— When children dictate stories, the copy of the story is good for teaching words written down as the dictated sentences are read back and words are counted and marked in some way. The teacher makes sure children learn that spaces mark off words on paper as pauses do when talking. The teacher can also show that each of the children's names is a word. Finally, children can cut words from a sentence strip to show mastery of concept.

— Many other common terms to be used in teaching are: "underline," "match," "find words that—," "draw lines to—," "circle," "list," "around," "on top of," "under," "over," etc.

III. *Auditory Skills*

It is important for teachers to discover if auditory impairment will hinder reading. Acuity, the ability to hear varying pitch (high and low), and loudness may affect children's ability to discriminate, although this is not always true. Spache and Spache *(39)* recommend that teachers test children's *discrimination* of sounds and use the results of the test as determinants of possible reading difficulty. Some children learn to read easily in spite of acuity problems; others have slight acuity difficulties which cause considerable confusion. Unusual difficulty in auditory discrimination may indicate need for referral for more testing for possible auditory impairment.

There are different methods for testing auditory discrimination. The *Wepman Auditory Discrimination Test (44)* presents pairs of words; some have different phonemes, while others are identical. The child responds "same" or "different" after presentation of each pair. Another test is the Goldman, Fristoe, Woodcock *Test of Auditory Discrimination (24)* which requires that the child associate a spoken word with the correct picture from a group of four pictures "with names differing by only one phoneme."[1]

Auditory discrimination subtests in reading readiness tests have been analyzed by Dykstra *(14)*. He found that in seven tests, there were six ways of testing discrimination and that most of the subtests were very poor predictors of reading success. However, if the test measured the ability to hear the beginning sound, then the test could predict reading achievement to some extent. IQ tests were better predictors than all the auditory discrimination tests. Dykstra's study may indicate that auditory discrimination ability is not a very important predictive factor even though other studies have shown a strong positive relationship between high auditory discrimination and reading success. For example, the Spache, et al. *(40)* study shows auditory discrimination to be a very good predictor of reading success.

Although children may be able auditorily to discriminate "bag" and "back," they may *not* have the analysis skills that Gibson and Levin *(23)* point out are required in learning to relate sounds of spoken words to reading. "The child must develop the ability to hear *segmentation* in what is spoken to him before we can reasonably expect him to learn to map the written code to speech or vice versa. . . . But . . . young children do not automatically analyze the phonemic information in speech."[2] In other words, children must understand that oral words consist of ordered sounds which can be removed from word context. Especially important, Gibson and Levin found, is the ability to remove the sound at the end of a word and say a new word with that sound or to rhyme.

However, the importance of auditory skill to reading ultimately depends on the amount of dependence on sound/symbol correspondences that is present as an aid to word recognition in the beginning reading program. Duggins *(10)* has shown that auditory dis-

---

1. R. Goldman; R. Fristoe; and R. W. Woodcock, *Test of Auditory Discrimination* (Circle Pines, Minn.: American Guidance Service, 1970), p. 6.

2. E. Gibson and H. Levin, *The Psychology of Reading* (Cambridge, Mass.: The M.I.T. Press, 1975), p. 228.

crimination training at the start of first grade resulted in superior reading achievement. If a school stresses phonics or a linguistic approach during the first and second grades, strong auditory discrimination is probably important. On the other hand, if visual techniques are stressed in the beginning reading program, auditory discrimination will be of lesser importance. Chall's *(8)* analysis of studies that examined the effect of various kinds of phonics programs has shown that a heavy phonics program has a salutory effect on reading achievement. Editions of basal reader sets published since 1968 reflect a greater amount of sound/symbol correspondence instruction than did earlier basals. Partly because of these developments toward increased use of sound/symbol correspondences in beginning reading, it is important to include a strong auditory component in the readiness program.

In all auditory training, teachers should remember the analytic skills required. For example, imagine a teacher working with the initial consonant sound /b/. He may ask children to listen to a group of words which begin with /b/—"big," "bat," and "boy"—and then ask them for other words that begin the same way. In order to respond, they need to be able to *isolate the beginning sound of a word* and then find another /b/ beginning word in their own vocabularies.

Other lessons will concentrate on rhyming words or the end sounds of words. For example, the teacher may ask children to tell what is similar about these words: "fat," "pat," "mat." They must then be able to *hear the end component of words* to be able to provide such other rhyming words as "sat," "Nat." Again, children may be asked to tell which of the following words rhyme with the presented words: "bat," "song," "flat." Accomplishing this task requires that the end components be *compared and likenesses and differences identified.*

Later, these exercises are combined with the visual presentation of the letters and words so that sound and sight correspondences are built up. Depending upon the method used, additional auditory perception may be needed. For example, many phonics programs require *blending of separate sounds,* while other programs require *substitution of one sound for another* in a known word to make a new word. Basic concepts and skills needed for auditory training are listed below with a few suggested teaching activities.

A.   Discrimination of sounds
   — This skill underlies all other prereading auditory skills. In the actual assessment (Test 4), teachers would test this skill only after they have found children to lack the superordi-

nate skills (B, C, and D) on the Checklist. In testing, the teacher says the pairs of words in Test 4 while the child is turned away so he cannot see the teacher; this arrangement assures that mouth movements do not provide information. The child being tested decides if the two words spoken are two different words or if they are one word repeated. Prior practice with these words helps: mother/table, man/said, dog/dog.

Test 4

man/nan	sip/ship	lamb/lamb	pan/pan	fat/vat
top/dop	ran/rin	dig/dig	pin/pen	shin/chin
bad/pad	sat/zat	gap/cap	scheme/cream	
tag/tag				

If any five-year-old makes more than two mistakes, further testing with standardized measures is called for. Four-year-olds with more than five errors also need further testing.

— This skill is difficult to teach. Basically, children in need of instruction in discrimination need to repeat words with very distinct sound contrasts (dog/fog) and begin to identify where their tongues are when saying each word. Gradually extension into closer and closer phonemic contrasts (gap/cap) should help develop discrimination.

— As stated in chapter 3 and referred to in chapter 5, Black English-speaking children may not distinguish phonemes that are distinguishable to Standard English speakers. This is especially true of medial vowels, final consonant clusters and specific phonemes (/r/, /θ/, and (/ð/) in some settings. Teachers may decide to develop auditory discrimination of these sounds later when reading has begun or to ignore phonic instruction requiring these sounds. Since the first alternative is preferable, teachers should plan for much practice prior to expectation of mastery of difficult sounds.

B. Initial sound analysis

— Test 5 demonstrates a simple individual assessment of this skill.

Test 5

Directions: Ask children to say the sound that comes first in each word: man, lamb, picture, house, goat, fat, oatmeal, door, nut, sink.

— At this level, it is important that children understand that the same sounds are used over and over again. Although later experiences will present phonemes systematically for discrimination, brief informal attention to this concept is very appropriate at this point. The teacher can slowly pronounce B . . . o . . . b . . . b . . . y with an emphasis on initial /b/ and ask, "Does anyone else's name begin like this? Listen, B . . . obby . . . Bill."

— At this point, children should supply similar examples in a systematic way. Children's names are an appropriate place to begin. The teacher can hold up a ball, ask for it to be named, and then ask everyone whose name begins in the same way "ball" does to stand up. He can refer later to the "ball" boys and girls (Bobby, Bill, and Betty) and the "sock" boys and girls (Sammy, Sally, and Sue).

— Classification and initial phoneme production is appropriate for this activity. The teacher can say at lunch, "Look, we have cookies for lunch. What other foods begin like cookie?" (The children might answer with "cake," "candy," etc.)

— Some good commercial materials for these children are: *Building Pre-Reading Skills* (Waltham, Mass.: Ginn and Co.), *Sounds for Young Readers Series* (Baldwin, N. Y.: Educational Activities, Inc.), *Auditory and Visual Discrimination* (Plainwell, Mich.: Richards Research Associates, Inc.), and *Elementary Phonics Program* (Chicago: Bell & Howell Co.).

— Learning activities designed for very young children are best done with objects. The teacher places a set of objects before a small group of children (a dollhouse *bed,* a *cup,* a *sock,* a toy *goat,* a *rock,* a *mitten,* etc.) and asks the children to find something that begins like "boy," for example. After each choice, the teacher and children say the stimulus word and name of the object together slowly to check the correct choice.

C. Rhyme

— In assessment of rhyming, teachers should not use the word "rhyme" since most four- and five-year-olds do not know it. The teacher asks children, when preparing for Test 6, to listen to the similar endings of "cat," "fat," "bat." Then the teacher asks the child to add another word. The teacher then repeats the stimulus words and hesitates for the child's addition. If there is none, the teacher supplies it. Then he should move to the test.

Test 6

Directions: Ask the child to say another word that ends like each of these: "dish," "man," "bell," "ring." Accept nonsense words.

— For teaching, before children can supply rhyming examples, they need to understand order of sounds in words and they need to have heard many rhymes in listening experiences. Thus, one instructional technique is to read rhyming poems, nursery rhymes, etc. to children.

— Instructional activities to develop perception of rhyme can include participation in and sharing of poems, riddles, and jingles. The teacher reads each poem or jingle with stress on the rhyming word. When the children develop favorites among the poems, the teacher hesitates at the ends of lines for children to say the rhyming word.

— At this point, *all* the children should learn to use the word "rhyme." The teacher can hand each small group an object (such as "sock") and ask them to think of a word that rhymes with their object. After the children are familiar with this process, the teacher can ask each child to supply a rhyming word for a pictured or real object. When each child presents his pair (the teacher should make sure the child will be successful before he participates in such a group presentation), the rest of the class tries to think of other words that rhyme.

Object	New Word	Other Word
fish	wish	dish
pot	not	got
hand	band	sand

D. Association of Sounds and Letters
    This skill should be attempted only after children have developed visual skills described in the next section.

    — Test 7 (*group*) is a common procedure used to assess this skill. When administering the test, each of the pictured objects should be named to avoid undue identification confusion.

Test 7

Directions: Ask children to circle the letter that stands for the sound in the beginning of the word. Include a practice example.

m s b	h t f
f l r	c n m
o k h	e u i
z s a	j v l
a o g	d p b

— Once children have mastered skills A through C and have learned letter names or sounds, they can begin learning to associate the two. This skill area takes them into beginning phonics instruction. A child who can supply words "boy" and "bat" as beginning like "ball" and who can say /b/ for *b,* merely needs to practice putting the two together. Children need to move ahead slowly, concentrating on one sound/symbol relationship at a lesson with reviews at regular intervals.

— A sample practice with /b/*b* (sound/symbol) follows. First, the teacher is assured there is mastery of prerequisite skills. Second, the teacher asks children to find a card with *b* on it. He tells the children that *b* stands for the sound at the beginning of "boy," for example. Next, the teacher asks children to hold up the *b* card every time they hear a word beginning like "boy": "box," "bottle," "paper," "book," etc. Next, the teacher provides individual practice with worksheets such as those in Test 7.

IV. *Visual Skills*

Many teachers and most beginning reading programs teach children to name letters. In order to have learned each letter, children must have required enough perceptual knowledge to distinguish the differences among letters which have fairly similar construction. For example, the lower case *i* and *l* are similar, as are *b, d, p,* and others. Further, children are expected to respond to a letter in all its forms, so that, for example, *a* is recognized in its printed form, its manuscript form *a,* and upper case form *A.* In order to do this, children need to be able to perceive both the total form and the critical features within the whole. In other words, children need to know that the *stick* and *circle* placement of *b* helps them distinguish it from *p* or *d.* The placement is the feature which differentiates these letters; it is therefore critical.

Many children appear to develop the ability to discriminate single letters naturally. Gibson and Levin *(23)* reviewed studies of visual discrimination and found preliterate children had difficulty with few letters except for the mirror reversed letters (*b* and *d*) and, to a lesser extent, rotated letters (*n* and *u, p* and *d*). As Gibson and Levin explain, when children learn to discriminate objects in the real world, it does not matter if an object is reversed or rotated. A key turned around is still a key. Only in the two-dimensional world of print do reversal and rotation discriminate.

On the other hand, preliterate children have considerable difficulty in matching a string of letter combinations to a stimulus: CQ–OQ OC QC CQ CO *(7).* The difficulty lies in perception of letter order, not the letters themselves. Similarly, when the sequence of assessment instruments described below has been used with prereading children, many children who cannot discriminate real words can discriminate single letters easily.

Nevertheless, some children have problems discriminating single letters and need to learn this skill. Most of the children tested in the published studies of discrimination were from middle-class homes where familial prereading experiences may have prepared them more than is true in lower class homes. According to Gibson and Levin's *(23)* suggestion, children learn to discriminate as they practice writing letters; perhaps some children are encouraged more than others to learn to write letters. Research indicates successful discrimination training includes learning the distinguishing features of letters *(37).* Stallard's *(41)* first-grade children benefitted from experiences discriminating single and combined letter-like forms. Thus, discrimination training suggestions are included below.

A perennial issue in prereading development is whether learning letter names helps in reading acquisition. There is far more convention on this question than research supports. For centuries the first step in learning reading was to learn letter names *(31)*. Parents today consistently teach letter names if they teach prereading skills at all. However, although studies *(8)* show a strong relationship between knowledge of letter names before reading and early success in reading, this relationship does not mean learning letter names causes children to read well. Since the abilities to recall an associated name with a letter is similar to remembering words, the strong relationship may result from similar underlying abilities, or parental interest exhibited in teaching children letter names may encourage interest in reading.

On the other hand, children do profit from learning letter *sounds* *(43)*. Many commercial programs include both letter sound and name activities. In an effort to help teachers prepare for teaching both sounds (because it helps in reading) and names (because school programs may require it), both types of learning are included below. Further, because knowledge of letter names is the best single predictor of reading success, it is an important assessment technique but not necessarily an important instructional area.

A. Discrimination of Letters
   — The first items of Test 8 (*group*) are easier than the last ones. The test should be duplicated on two papers with clear letters and clear demarkation between items.

Test 8

Directions: Ask children to circle the letter that does not belong. (Be sure they know *letter.*) Practice with *m m m a* together.

1.	L	O	L	L	10.	E	E	E	F
2.	b	b	b	n	11.	i	j	j	j
3.	s	t	t	t	12.	p	p	d	p
4.	f	p	f	f	13.	u	n	u	u
5.	c	o	o	o	14.	h	h	n	h
6.	A	H	A	A	15.	B	B	R	B
7.	k	k	k	h	16.	z	s	s	s
8.	M	M	N	M	17.	b	d	b	b
9.	g	a	g	g	18.	q	q	g	q

   — For children needing instruction, matching activities are best, preferably with wooden or cardboard forms raised from a base so letters cannot be reversed. Beginning with easy contrasts like *c* and *o,* the teacher asks children to point out what *o* has that *c* does not. In order for children to develop strategies for comparison of letters, simple feature contrasts (*i* and *l, m* and *n*) along with verbalization of the differences should precede study of more difficult contrasts. Children do not need to discriminate the very difficult letter contrasts in order to read.

B. Discrimination of Words
— Test 9 (*group*) uses similar procedures as in Test 8.

Test 9

Directions: Ask children to circle the one word that doesn't belong. Show them how "on" doesn't belong in the sequence "supper" "supper" "on" "supper."

1. tree tree apple tree
2. man man man seed
3. lady friend lady lady
4. can baby baby baby

5. cute cute fly cute
6. box box box fox
7. blow blue blue blue
8. girl gift girl girl

9. moon money moon moon
10. whale whale while whale
11. float flat flat flat
12. snowman snowman snowman snowball
13. feet feet feet foot
14. big dig big big
15. much chum much much
16. saw was was was

— Instruction for children who have difficulty with this skill will begin with discrimination of individual letters and then continue with activities that concentrate on the specific distinctive letters which differentiate words.

It may help for children to do tactile activities with words that are formed with cardboard letters and placed in this way.

cat

cap

The teacher shows the two words and names them. The children trace each letter of the word "cat," then each letter of the word "cap." The letters *c* and *a* are then placed over each other to show that they are the same. Finally, *p* and *t* are identified as different.

— Further practice occurs when children write over (directly superimpose) with a pen the printed words and then write under the words:

cat   cap

cat   cap

C.   Names/Sounds of Letters

This section is presented so teachers who want to teach letter names or letter sounds can adjust assessment and instruction either way.

— In order to assess knowledge of names/sounds, teachers should arrange upper and lower case letters in random order on plasticized cards.

— Table 7 presents a recommended order for teaching names/sounds.

— Durkin *(11)* suggested that learning letter names in conjunction with learning to write letters is beneficial. Teachers should focus children's attention on the critical features of letters as they write them. Developing the concept that the upper case, lower case, and printed forms of the letters have the same name demands additional practice. Children enjoy learning how to make letters in the context of words so teachers might teach the letters in words of objects and people in a room.

boy   table

— Various senses should be involved in practicing letters and numbers. Three-dimensional letters are helpful if children match the three-dimensional and the two-dimensional. In this way, the transition to the two-dimensional world of literacy is eased as letter naming or sounding is practiced.

— Letter lotto games can be devised or bought. Matching cardboard letters with their printed forms facilitates the transition to a two-dimensional sphere.

— When further practice with letters and numbers is needed, Bingo is a common activity.

— Another practice game involves placing letters and numbers on paper fish to which a paper clip is attached. The "fish" are put in a "pond," and a magnet is used as the "fish hook." Children then name the letters of the fish they catch. It is important to indicate the mouth and eye of the fish for direction. (These games and others, such as Climbing a Ladder, can be used for practice with sight words, too.)

Table 7.

h	H	i	L	o	O
a	A	c	C	x	X
l	L				

Note that in this first group are some like letters (*o* and *c*, *A* and *H*). The distinctive feature, whether the line is closed or not, is not difficult for four-year-olds. Review these letters before moving to next group.

s	S	t	T	y	Y
b	B	e	E	g	G
k	K				

Review all letters.

j	J	r	R	m	M
f	F	d	D	z	Z
q	Q				

Review all letters.

n	N	u	U	v	V
w	W				

Note the confusion inherent in these final letters. Review all letters.

— Durkin *(11)* suggested that learning letter names in conjunction with learning to write letters is beneficial. Teachers should focus children's attention on the critical features of letters as they write them. Developing the concept that the upper case, lower case, and printed forms of the letters have the same name demands additional practice. Children enjoy learning how to make letters in the context of words so teachers might teach the letters in words of objects and people in a room.

boy   table

— Various senses should be involved in practicing letters and numbers. Three-dimensional letters are helpful if children match the three-dimensional and the two-dimensional. In this way, the transition to the two-dimensional world of literacy is eased as letter naming or sounding is practiced.

— Letter lotto games can be devised or bought. Matching cardboard letters with their printed forms facilitates the transition to a two-dimensional sphere.

— When further practice with letters and numbers is needed, Bingo is a common activity.

— Another practice game involves placing letters and numbers on paper fish to which a paper clip is attached. The "fish" are put in a "pond," and a magnet is used as the "fish hook." Children then name the letters of the fish they catch. It is important to indicate the mouth and eye of the fish for direction. (These games and others, such as Climbing a Ladder, can be used for practice with sight words, too.)

— Motivational devices may help the learning process. For example, every child can be given a card on which the letters named are attached to a piece of yarn tied to his chair or coat hook; or once a letter is named and is maintained, the child may keep it in a Letter Bank. Each named letter can be pinned to his jacket for him to wear home.

— When teaching letter sounds, teachers should take care that the sounds of consonants do not include a vowel sound. In other words, the sound of *d* should be a brief /d/, not /da/. Most programs using a blending of sounds/symbols approach include practice in individual letter sounds.

D.   Identification of Common Words

— Test 10 lists simple words, some of which preliterate children may recognize. The teacher should carefully print or type the words with large type on a plasticized card and circle unknown words on prepared worksheets while testing.

Test 10

Directions: Ask the child to pronounce words. Assure the child that he should not worry if he doesn't know the words.

in	a	it	me
to	the	mother	I
at	not	big	look
do	good	red	walk
go	is	stop	see

— When children can identify a few words they have experienced previously, they are ready to begin reading instruction. Some readiness activities should be continued, especially those that encourage the development of sound/symbol understanding and of other visual/perceptual activities.

— Children should learn to recognize their own names in print for practical as well as educational purposes. Preschool teachers use name labels for many purposes: jobs, coathooks, supply drawers, etc. Small photographs of each child can be attached to their names at first and then removed when each child is able to find his name among the others.

— To teach the words "stop" and "go," which have practical importance, a Musical Chairs game is fun. When the "go" sign is up, the children march about the room; when the "stop" sign appears, the children must find a chair.

— Teachers often label room furniture and learning centers. After these labels have been displayed, they can be removed, placed in a pile, and identified by the children.

— The dictated stories described in the section of this chapter on storytelling include many words that are used frequently in the language. As the teacher rereads a dictated story, he can ask children to "read with him." This practice may be sufficient to allow some children to find words they can recognize alone. (The use of these stories as reading material is described in detail in the next chapters.)

E.   Memory of Words Learned

— This last component of visual skill development is simply an assessment technique. (Instruction in words is reading and is discussed in later chapters.) To accomplish this assessment, teachers teach three words at one sitting by showing the word on a card, pronouncing it, matching it with a picture if possible, saying it in a sentence, matching it in a list of other words, and practicing it with the other two learned words. If a five-year-old recalls all three the next day, he is above average. The recall of two is average. Memory of one or none is below average. Four-year-olds who remember one or two are above average.

V.   *Related Skills*

Motor coordination does not necessarily relate with later reading achievement *(17),* but small motor coordination does relate to school readiness *(27).* Thus, assessment of this ability is included below.

Before turning to that assessment, some nonassessed areas of prereading development deserve attention. There are other areas of visual development which should be of concern during the reading

Test 11

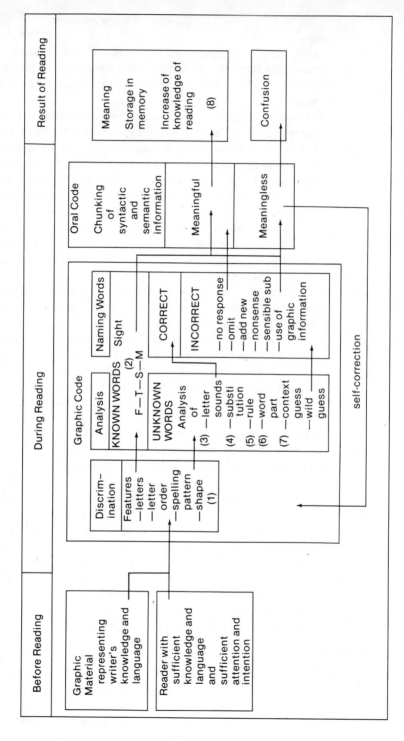

preparation period. We have discussed form perception, but according to Spache and Spache *(39)*, directionality and eye coordination are also important visual factors in reading. In chapter 5, we discussed the habitual left-to-right eye movement of reading. Nonreading children have the muscular ability to move their eyes in left-to-right direction, but they are not practiced in it. In fact, many children are not even aware of consistency in the direction of print. For example, a five-year-old told me that he could write the word "eel." I encouraged him to show me, but before he began, he asked, "Do I start with the *e* or with the *l?*" A very few words of explanation about how placement is coordinated with the sounds one hears in words were sufficient for him to proudly write "eel" for me.

Teachers can help detect eye problems that need correction. Unfortunately, not all schools provide adequate testing for visual defects and not all parents are able to make provisions for such testing themselves. In addition, since visual screening tests used in school vary in effectiveness *(39)*, children need the attention and diagnosis of specialists whenever possible. Knox (as reported by Spache and Spache) found that besides screening with visual tests, teachers through their observation provide additional information helpful in finding children with visual problems. Symptoms that may indicate difficulty include facial contortions, tilting of the head, indication of tension during close work, consistently holding close material near the eyes, and rubbing the eyes. Kindergarten teachers must attend to the matter of visual difficulty before reading instruction begins so that, if possible, all children can be free of visual distortions.

— Test 11 (*group*) is used to assess children's small motor coordination. The teacher should ask the children to draw a line *inside* the path from the mouse to the clock in the first two items and *on* the dotted lines in the next. Above average and average five-year-olds are able to do this unhesitatingly with no movement off the track. Below average five-year-olds have great difficulty staying on a clear path. Four-year-olds are not expected to do this task easily.

— Ability to copy simple geometric shapes and large letters is also used to assess eye/hand coordination.

Summary

The discussion of prereading preparation has reviewed some traditional issues and raised new ones of concern for teachers. Underlying the presentation of assessment and teaching activities was the assumption that determination of needs and appropriate instruction before reading is important and can be accomplished through planned activities. It is not recommended that the instruction be in long lessons unsuitable for young children or that formal teaching methods be used; rather, appropriate teaching is planned for short periods in game-like formats. Successful teachers integrate activities among the different areas listed here. There should be a good mix of language, listening, auditory, visual, and other activities. Teachers will want to remember that early prediction is not always accurate when applied to individuals and, therefore, will refrain from final judgments about children's development and avoid making critical comments on youngsters' productive work.

Children who have mastered most of the skills described in this chapter are ready to begin to learn to read. In fact, some skills described here (association of sounds and letters, identification of words) are beginning reading skills. In a program responsive to children's growing abilities, the line between prereading and real reading is difficult to determine.

Selected Activities

1. How can the concept of reading readiness be applied to more advanced levels of reading?

2. Imagine having to learn the following printed message.

$$\triangle \perp \;\; \mathsf{T} \mathsf{U} \;\; \square \triangleright \;\; \triangleright \square \sqcap$$

Prepare a list of the information and skills you need in order to read it. At what point does this information in your list of skills help?

$\triangle$ /ð/　T /b/　$\square$ /i/

$\sqcap$ /k/　U /oy/　$\triangleright$ /z/

3. Plan a prereading activity that combines learning concepts about words and storytelling.

4. Plan a lesson of association of /p/*p* like that of /b/*b* found on page 154.

References

1. Annesley, F.; Odhner, F.; Madoff, E.; and Chomsky, N. "Identifying the First Grade Underachiever." *Journal of Eudcational Research* 63 (1970): 459–62.

2. Blakely, W. P., and Shadle, E. M. "A Study of Two Readiness-for-Reading Programs in Kindergarten." *Elementary English* 38 (1961): 502–5.

3. Bond, G. L., and Dykstra, R. "The Cooperative Research Program in First-Grade Reading Instruction." *Reading Research Quarterly* 3 (1967): 5–142.
4. Boney, D., and Lynch, J. E. "A Study of Reading Growth in the Primary Grades." *Elementary English Review* 19 (1948): 370–75.
5. Bradley, B. E. "An Experimental Study of the Readiness Approach to Reading." *Elementary School Journal* 56 (1956): 262–67.
6. Bruner, J. *The Process of Education.* Cambridge: Harvard University Press, 1960.
7. Calfee, R. C.; Chapman, R. S.; and Venezky, R. L. "How a Child Needs to Think to Learn to Read." In *Cognition in Learning and Memory,* edited by L. W. Gregg. New York: John Wiley, 1972.
8. Chall, J. *Learning to Read: The Great Debate.* New York: McGraw-Hill, 1967.
9. Clark, E. "What's in a Word? On the Child's Acquisition of Semantics in His First Language." In *Cognitive Development,* edited by T. Moore. New York: Academic Press, 1973.
10. Duggins, L. A. "Auditory Perception in the Beginning Reading Program." *College Bulletin Southeastern Louisiana College* 113 (1956): 1–45.
11. Durkin, D. *Teaching Young Children to Read.* Boston: Allyn & Bacon, 1972.
12. _____. "A Six Year Study of Children Who Learned to Read in School at the Age of Four." *Reading Research Quarterly* 10 (1974–5): 9–61.
13. Durrell, D. D. "Success in First-Grade Reading." *Journal of Education* 140 (1958): 1–48.
14. Dykstra, R. "Auditory Discrimination Abilities and Beginning Reading Achievement." *Reading Research Quarterly* 2 (1966): 5–34.
15. Elkind, D. "Cognitive Development and Reading." In *Theoretical Models and Processes of Reading,* 2d ed., edited by H. Singer and R. B. Ruddell. Newark, Del.: International Reading Association, 1976.
16. Farr, R. Untitled speech read at Chicago Area Reading Association meeting. May, 1972.
17. Feshbach, S.; Adelman, H.; and Fuller, W. "Early Identification of Children with High Risk of Reading Failure." *Journal of Learning Disabilities* 7 (1974): 639–44.
18. Furth, H. *Piaget for Teachers.* Englewood Cliffs, New Jersey: Prentice-Hall, 1970.
19. Gates, A. I. "The Necessary Mental Age for Beginning Reading." *Elementary School Journal* 37 (1937): 497–508.
20. Gates, A. I., and Bond, G. L. "Reading Readiness: A Study of Factors Determining Success and Failure in Beginning Reading." *Teachers' College Record* 37 (1935–36): 679–85.
21. Gates, A. I.; Bond, G. L.; and Russell, D. H. *Methods of Determining Reading Readiness.* New York: Bureau of Publications, Teachers College, Columbia University, 1939.
22. Gesell, A. L. *The First Five Years of Life.* New York: Harper, 1940.
23. Gibson, E. and Levin, H. *The Psychology of Reading.* Cambridge, Mass.: The M.I.T. Press, 1975.

24. Goldman, R.; Fristoe, M.; and Woodcock, R. W. *Test of Auditory Discrimination.* Circle Pines, Minn.: American Guidance Service, Inc., 1970.
25. Harrison, M. L. *Reading Readiness.* Boston: Houghton Mifflin, 1936.
26. Hillerich, R. L. "An Interpretation of Research in Reading Readiness." *Elementary English* 45 (1968): 359-64; 372.
27. Ilg, F. L.; and Ames, L. B. *School Readiness.* New York: Harper and Row, 1965.
28. Koppman, P. S., and LaPray, M. H. "Teacher Ratings and Pupil Reading Readiness Scores." *Reading Teacher* 22 (1969): 603-8.
29. Kottmeyer, W. "Readiness for Reading, Part I and Part II," *Elementary English* 24 (1947): 355-66; 528-33.
30. LaConte, C. "Reading in Kindergarten." *The Reading Teacher* 22 (1969): 116-20.
31. Mathews, M. M. *Teaching to Read: Historically Considered.* Chicago: University of Chicago Press, 1966.
32. Morphett, M. V., and Washburne, C. "When Should Children Begin to Read?" *Elementary School Journal* 21 (1931): 496-503.
33. Morrison, C., and Harris, A. J. "The Craft Project: A Final Report." *The Reading Teacher* 22 (1969): 335-40.
34. Ploghoft, M. H. "Do Reading Readiness Workbooks Promote Readiness?" *Elementary English* 36 (1959): 424-26.
35. Pratt, W. E. "A Study of the Differences in the Prediction of Reading Success of Kindergarten and Nonkindergarten Children." *Journal of Educational Research* 42 (1949): 525-33.
36. Richek, M. "Readiness Skills That Predict Initial Word Learning by Two Different Methods of Instruction." *Reading Research Quarterly,* in press.
37. Samuels, S. J. "Success and Failure in Learning to Read: A Critique of the Research." In *The Literature of Reseach in Reading with Emphasis on Models,* edited by F. B. Davis. New Brunswick, N. J.: Graduate School of Education, Rutgers, 1971.
38. Smith, M. S., and Bissell, J. S. "Report Analysis: The Impact of Headstart." *Harvard Educational Review* 40 (1970): 51-104.
39. Spache, G. D., and Spache, E. B. *Reading in the Elementary School,* 2d ed. Boston: Allyn & Bacon, 1969.
40. Spache, G. D., et al. "A Longitudinal First-Grade Reading Readiness Program." *The Reading Teacher* 19 (1966): 580-84.
41. Stallard, C. "Effect of Selected Prereading Skills and Subsequent First Grade Achievement." Paper at Illinois Reading Council, March 1977.
42. Teegarden, L. "Clinical Identification of the Prospective Nonreader." *Child Development* 3 (1932): 346-58.
43. Venezky, R. S.; Calfee, R. C.: and Chapman, R. S. "Skills Required for Learning to Read." In *Individualizing Reading Instruction: A Reader,* edited by L. A. Harris and C. B. Smith. New York: Holt, Rinehart, & Winston, 1972.
44. Wepman, J. M. "Auditory Discrimination Speech and Reading." *Elementary School Journal* 60 (1960): 325-33.

7

Beginning Readers and Beginning Reading

At some point during the years between ages three and seven, most children become ready and show interest in learning to read. After they begin reading instruction, children ought to continue with oral language development so that vocabulary continually expands and so that growth toward increased language complexity is assured. If teachers neglect these language activities, long-term growth in reading may suffer, since reading achievement ultimately depends on vocabulary and general language facility. Thus, the total program should include reading instruction as well as on-going instruction in language. Reading instruction is presented here with the realization that although many children do begin to read at the first-grade level, some are ready earlier, while a few will profit from delayed reading.

No area is as replete with advice to teachers, research data, commercial interests, and varying instructional systems as is beginning reading. Since analysis of various approaches to beginning reading is needed in order to make critical judgments, this chapter reviews various reading systems, and provides a framework for analyzing beginning reading approaches.

The first section of the chapter attends to the question of early preschool reading. For many years, teachers were either strongly in favor of early reading instruction or, more commonly, strongly opposed to reading before first grade. However, in recent years educators in general have altered their thinking and their classroom instructions to include earlier reading. This section will attempt to answer the questions: Does early reading instruction have any place in the program for four- and five-year-olds? Will early reading affect children adversely or will it, in the long run, help them?

The second section of the chapter describes beginning reading programs organized into separate categories; thus, the programs in one category share critical design features. Variations in extent of vocabulary control, choice of vocabulary in stories, extent and time of beginning phonics instruction are some of the critical factors on which beginning reading programs differ. Such differences are described here so that readers can understand the instructional intent of programs in order to use them to fullest advantage by becoming more aware of the design characteristics of the reading materials they use in class than they appear to be *(53)*. The emphasis in this discussion is on categorical variations rather than on individual program characteristics since there are too many commercially available beginning reading programs to review here. The third summary section relates the beginning reading programs with the theoretical description of the beginning reader of chapter 5. It is a preparation for the presentation of specific teaching activities that follows in chapter 8.

Early Reading and Early Readers

Educators, parents, and press have argued for a number of years for an early beginning to reading instruction. On the other hand, others have stated strong reasons against early reading. Because practices in other countries differ as to the age at which children enter school and the age when formal reading instruction begins, review of these practices puts this controversy in a broader perspective.

In Scandinavian countries children traditionally began school and formal reading instruction relatively late—as late as age eight or nine in Finland, for example *(14)*. However, prior to school entrance children often acquire the rudiments of reading at home from grandparents or other adults. Reading in Finland has been a highly valued skill in spite of the late age for school entrance. In past centuries, reading skill, as determined by the minister, was required for all civil participation including marriage and property ownership *(38)*. The late school entrance age was not because of lack of concern about acquisition of literacy; instead, late entrance was due to reluctance to send young children out of the home during the long dark days of winter. Malmquist *(33)* reported that children now go to school at a younger age in Sweden than in the past (at seven). Formal instruction also begins earlier than it used to, but, Malmquist reports, teachers are more concerned with the child's successful experiences with beginning reading than with the age at which reading begins. Children are not hurried into reading.

In contrast to the Scandinavian countries, school entrance at age five is characteristic of Great Britain, Israel, and Hong Kong *(14)*. In England children come to school at age five but, as in the United States, not all five-year-olds begin to study reading. In Scotland, the five-year-olds are more apt to be exposed to early reading. In Japan, entrance into school at kindergarten (five) traditionally did not mean early formal reading. Yet even twenty years ago most of the Japanese children had learned some of the orthographic system used in first grade; in spite of that knowledge, the schools (perhaps under the influence of the United States) did not teach reading in kindergarten. Now, however, teachers tend to teach initial reading since even more children come prepared to read *(41)*. Downing *(14)* observed a trend toward lowering the age for school entrance and for formal reading instruction in many of the nations surveyed. Because it is extremely difficult to conduct valid research across countries with differing languages and cultures, these trends and facts do not tell us as much about the advantages of early reading as does research conducted in the United States.

Under the influence of the theorists who hold that one should wait for natural development for reading readiness, for many years some educators have advised against a structured reading program in kindergarten or even encouragement of young children's reading interests *(34)*. A number of reasons for this advice have been given, one of which was that the visual immaturity of young children might prevent adequate learning. Furthermore, parents were advised against teaching their children because they might unknowingly use confusing methods of instruction. In addition, it was feared that children who learned to read before first grade might become bored when placed in the regular first-grade program. Finally, the most often cited reason for delaying instruction until first grade was that formal instruction in reading during kindergarten would hinder the major kindergarten goals of social, motor, and cognitive development. Durkin's study *(16)* shows that mothers of young children during the 1950s were conscious of these reasons for delaying reading. Although some of these mothers ignored the advice they heard, others discouraged their children's growing curiosity about spelling and reading. New evidence and the demands of changing times have altered this picture somewhat. For example, newer study has shown that children's visual growth is sufficient for them to read at age five *(20)*. Furthermore, study of methods of teaching reading indicates that there is no *correct* method for beginners *(7)*. That is, no method is universally successful or unsuccessful. Children learn to read from a vast array of approaches, so to tell parents that they might use the wrong method is incorrect.

Longitudinal studies of early readers provide insight into one of the questions raised in this section: Are there long-term advantages in early reading? If children benefit from early reading, we will want to include an early reading component in the language-reading program. Otherwise, the argument over reading before first grade is pointless.

Durkin *(15, 16)* explored the long-term effects of early reading. Her early readers were children who had learned to read without school training before the first grade; they could successfully read 18 out of 37 common, easy words, and they could obtain a raw score on the Gates Primary Reading Test. In the first of two studies she reported, early readers were compared through the sixth grade with children who were not early readers. Since some of the early readers had been double-promoted (and had benefitted from double promotion), adjustments in the comparison of the groups were made. The results clearly indicated that children who had learned to read before first grade maintained a reading advantage through elementary school. "The average achievement of early readers who had had either five or six years of school instruction in reading was significantly higher than the average achievement of equally bright classmates who had had six years of school instruction but were not early readers."[1]

In the second study, early readers were matched by IQ with subjects who were not early readers and studied through the third grade. Again, the early readers indicated significantly higher reading achievement than did the others. Parent interviews revealed a greater tendency for the early readers to prefer quiet activities and solitary play. Apparently, a favorable environment for early reading was provided by the interest of the mothers because, in general, the mothers of the readers responded favorably to their children's questions about spelling, letters, and words; on the other hand, the other mothers tended to put off such questions. In another report on the same studies, Durkin *(15)* showed that early readers were superior to their matched classmates in mathematics and social studies as well as in reading achievement. The advantage in reading, which continued through elementary school, meant that children who read early could assimilate more information more quickly than did the nonreaders. While it is true that early readers had very high IQs (in the first study, the range was from 91 to 161 with a mean of 121; in the second, there was a range from 82 to 170 with a mean of 133), some of the early readers had low-average IQs. Generally, interested bright children learn to read with very little instruction, but a few children with low-average ability are able to read early, too. The implications of these studies are far-reaching.

Durkin later initiated an early reading program for four- and five-year-olds *(17)* which indicated that sensitive instruction results in early reading development. The 40 children were in a special program she designed to replicate the environment provided in the homes of the early readers. Her school program began at age four, an age when most of the subjects of the previous studies had begun asking questions about letters, spellings, and words. Initial instruction emphasized writing since that was a common entry into literacy for the early readers. Because the other children had not learned from commercially produced materials in the past studies, few such materials were used in the training program. Furthermore, more emphasis was placed on recognition of whole words from memory rather than on the use of phonetic principles. Oral language activities, reading stories to children, and learning to name the words and numbers used in play activities were emphasized. The goals were to teach children to print, name letters and numerals, and to recog-

---

1. D. Durkin, *Children Who Read Early* (New York: Teachers College Press, Columbia University, 1966), p. 41.

nize a number of words. No standardized testing was done, but criterion-based tests revealed that by the end of the first year, children could identify an average of 14 numerals, 38 letters (lower and upper case), and 29 words. At the end of the next year, the average child could identify 47 numerals, 50 letters (out of 52), and 124 words. At no time were more than twenty minutes a day spent on academic work. This child-oriented beginning reading program, which Durkin *(18)* described in detail in her book, appeared to be successful in achieving program goals.

When the achievement of these children was compared with that of control children who did not have the two-year program before first grade, the results were generally encouraging for early reading instruction *(19)*. The study was complicated by the fact that the regular kindergarten year for the controls included some reading exposure, contrary to the usual curriculum practiced in that school system. When the parents of the control children who were enrolled in the regular kindergarten realized that other children were getting reading training their children were not receiving, they persuaded school administration to start reading instruction in the public program. Thus, the difference between the control and experimental groups was essentially one year of training for four-year-olds and not two years of reading training as initially planned. Nevertheless, the experimental children were significantly superior in achievement to the control group through grade two. Through grade four, although the experimental group was higher, the difference between their scores and the controls was not significant—not greater than chance.

Hall, Moretz, and Statom *(27)* explored the backgrounds of children who were early *writers,* thus extending the finding from Durkin's work that writing was a stimulant for reading in young children. These researchers found that the homes of early writers contained many books and that the parents were well-educated. Parents helped children communicate through writing by taking dictations and by spelling words. Writing interest preceded reading interest in nearly every child studied. Briggs and Elkind *(8)* found that the fathers of another set of early readers read more to their children than did fathers of non-early readers. Also, early readers were more successful on measures of cognitive maturity drawn from Piaget's work.

To discover that early readers have familial advantage is not too surprising. If school training provided the same long-term benefits Durkin's self-initiated early readers had, familial disadvantage might be overcome. While Durkin's early training program showed an advantage in reading for two school years, other studies show shorter benefit from school instruction in early reading.

The Denver Early Reading project *(9)* also made a longitudinal examination of children who read early. After participating either in an experimental kindergarten where reading activities were provided for twenty minutes a day, or in a conventional kindergarten, children were placed either in an "adjusted first grade program" which continued the approaches used in the experimental kindergarten rooms or in a conventional first grade. This type of mixing continued through the fifth grade when comparisons were made. At the end of kindergarten, the children in the 61 experimental classrooms were better at naming letters and recalling words than were the controls. By the end of first grade, the original children were still making better achievement scores in spite of the mixed classroom assignments. By the end of the fifth grade, there was no difference between the two groups except in the case of the experimental subjects who had continued in "adjusted" programs; these children were significantly better readers. The advantages of special early reading training in kindergarten were maintained only if the program in reading after first grade continued innovative instruction may have contributed to reading advantage even without early reading.

In another school-based study of early teaching of reading *(32),* experimental kindergarten children were taught to read with the Distar Reading Program *(G)*.[2] This program is based on an instructional model similar to that of Distar Language, described in chapter 4. It is a behaviorally based program emphasizing individual letter and sound relationships children learn to blend together to form words. Experimental children did achieve higher scores on a test of letters and sounds but not on a test of oral comprehension. The researcher did not report later achievement.

In summary, study of early reading indicates that self-initiated reading has long-term benefits to later achievement in reading and other content areas. Additionally, school-based training in reading prior to first grade has at least short-term benefits; such instruction appears to give children a start on the beginning part of reading instruction. Thus, this writer recommends early reading for children who have skill in important readiness areas and who are interested in learning to read. On the other hand, I would not recommend reading for children who have no interest or whose readiness is not indicative of possible success. These children need *readiness* and motivation. It is important that children who receive training in reading be carefully monitored so that teachers are assured of continual growth. We should remember what Swedish teachers and many others know: early success is critical to later success for each pupil.

There are a variety of commercial materials for early reading used in kindergarten and prekindergartens today. Distar Reading is one. *Alpha*

---

2. Reading programs are listed separately by letter at the end of the chapter.

(0) is another, and stresses auditory and visual readiness prior to the reading of words. Another specially designed program is SWRL (*S*), composed of a series of books with many repeated words and emphasis, as in the two above, on sound/symbol correspondence. Another early reading set is CSS by Crane (*F*), a program with a unique sequence of instruction on sound/symbol correspondence. All four share a high degree of instructional structure; in fact, they have been called "teacher-proof" because the lessons are prescribed as to content and/or methodology. The teacher using these materials simply follows the precise directions given in the teacher guide.

A directly opposite approach to early reading is taken when the readiness and reading activities are integrated into the on-going activities of the class and when instruction is carefully individualized (as in Durkin's early reading training program). Although such a procedure requires teacher planning time and much teacher skill, I prefer it to the highly structured sets of materials because (1) it duplicates the method by which self-initiated children begin to read; (2) it allows for flexible differentiation of those ready to read and those not ready so that there is less social stigma attached to slow progress; and (3) it fits in with the class activities and thus supports a developmental approach to early learning. Specific instructions about adapting reading in preschools are found in chapter 8 after the following discussion on beginning reading.

Beginning Reading

The subsections described below refer to major categories of beginning reading instruction. Because there is often some confusion associated with the terms *program* and *system,* we begin with some explanation of these terms. A *reading system* is a design for the total reading curriculum including the curriculum for children developing normally and for children who are disabled in reading. As such, it requires the attention of many of the school personnel as well as outside resource persons such as psychologists. A *reading program* is a subset of the reading system. The term here refers to the instructional methods and materials used in a classroom or classrooms. A developmental reading program for primary grades in a specific school, for example, includes the materials and teaching approaches used with the children whose reading progress is at expected levels during the beginning reading phase—through grade three level. Thus, we refer to a reading program not simply as a description of prepared materials but as it is intended to be used in the classroom with real teachers. Too often the term *reading program* means just the published materials. Since classroom use of the same published materials varies considerably, the materials by themselves do not compose a program.

Before approaching the first category of reading programs, it is helpful to describe two theoretical differences in early reading around which the categories differ. First, categories of reading programs differ on the kind of vocabulary chosen for the first words learned; some programs select for initial vocabulary those words most frequent in the language while others choose words that have predictable sound/symbol correspondences (such as bat, fat, sat, mat, etc.). The high frequency words enable the writers of beginning materials to emphasize meaningful language, and these programs are apt to emphasize meaning as an important discussion in beginning reading. The authors of materials with a sound/symbol-based vocabulary, on the other hand, sometimes, but not always, emphasize the decoding of words into oral language over the meaning of stories *(10)*.

A second related controversy between approaches to beginning reading stems from the way the reading process is perceived. Those theoreticians and practitioners who view reading as holistic activity tend to structure instruction to resemble natural language learning environments. For example, Goodman *(25)* calls for stress on the language context in initial reading rather than on individual words or sounds and letters. In one program influenced by this approach to reading *(A)*, awareness of sentence intonation after listening to sentences read aloud encourages youngsters to relate their syntactic understanding of sentences (sentence context) to identify words.

Differing from the holistic position are those theoreticians and practitioners who view reading instruction as the acquisition of separate, identifiable skills. In this framework, reading occurs after learning sequentially presented skills [see Samuels and Schachter *(42)* for an excellent presentation of this view of reading]. When materials are developed from this framework, decoding is often emphasized. These differing viewpoints are observable in the programs discussed below.

Reading Programs Based on High Frequency Vocabulary

Although more than one kind of vocabulary control exists, this first group of programs introduces new words in terms of the frequency of use. Vocabulary studies dating back to the 1920s resulted in compiled lists of words grouped by difficulty and frequency of use *(34, 55, 12)*. The authors of programs based on vocabulary control have long believed that the gradual increase of the set words that are most common to the language provides the beginner with core words upon which to base later learning. (The basis of this belief is discussed below.) A major goal of these programs is to establish a basic list of words that can be recognized on sight. Another major goal is comprehension of a passage, even at the beginning of the instruction. The beginning reader's task is to recall words already introduced and repeated often and to understand these words when they are combined in the context of a story. After pupils have achieved a small sight vocabulary, they must learn a number of word recognition techniques. An important word recognition skill is phonics, which helps pupils relate the sound of oral words to the written symbols. Thus, early memorization of a stock of basic sight words, meaning attainment, and later introduction of a variety of word recognition skills are the characteristics of this intructional system.

Among the programs using high frequency vocabulary in the first texts children read are basal series from major publishing companies, such as *Scott, Foresman Unlimited (B), Holt Basic Reading System (H)*. There are more variations in current published basal series than previously, as when Chall reviewed two popular programs of the sixties (10). However, the basic components are approximately as described here. They all consist of readiness workbooks, two or three paperback books called preprimers for the beginner, and at least one hardcover text for the first-grade program. Accompanying the pupils' texts are extensive teachers' guidebooks with instructional guidelines. For each reading selection, the guidebooks describe techniques for introducing new words and practicing old ones, suggestions for preparing pupils for reading, a guide to the reading with questions, and, of great importance, a system for introducing and teaching necessary word recognition and comprehension skills. There are also pupil workbooks for skill reinforcement. In addition, there are other helpful teaching aids, such as word cards, charts, etc. Some teachers find the guides and other paraphernalia very helpful, while others find them confining. The latter group usually adapts the texts to their own classroom needs.

The story content in the first books of the basal series of the early 1960s usually centered on the activities of the family members of one white, middle-class suburban family. During the early 1960s, these books were criticized for being irrelevant to the lives of many American children, especially urban, minority-group children. As a result, the publishing companies included black families in revised editions published in the mid-1960s. In the primer, *The Little White House (Q)*, one finds two families—one white and one black—whose life patterns are indistinguishable. Macmillan Company's *Bank Street Readers (D)* and Follett Publishing Company's *City Schools' Reading Program (U)*, on the other hand, were written to appeal to inner-city children while maintaining the characteristics of the other vocabulary controlled programs. Many people continue to feel that the multi-ethnic character of our society is absent in reading materials. However, the most recent basal series have responded to continuing criticism by including fantasy stories with urban, rural, and foreign settings as well as some nonfiction material. Publishers and authors are not yet free of criticism from minority groups about the representation of people in basal series. Further, researchers have taken interest in the roles of girls and women compared with boys and men and find a recent increase, not decrease, in sex-role stereotyping *(45)*.

There have been some interesting changes in the beginning reading materials published since 1970. Partly in response to Chall's *(10)* criticism of too restrictive vocabulary control practiced in the basals a decade ago, the newer programs have generally increased the vocabulary load required in their first year materials. The history of vocabulary control *(57)* shows that the tight control of new words to be introduced in first grade was based on an early study by Gates and Russell *(24)*. Recent research by Barr *(5)* reinforced Chall's call for reduction in vocabulary control by finding that average and above average learners can profit from increase in the pace of new word introduction. Today, the number of new words introduced in first grade materials varies from 440 to 811 with an average of 551 *(4)*. The average vocabulary load in 1965 was 324 *(36)*.

Another change is in the language used in some newer programs. For example, in the Scott, Foresman program *(A)*, sentences are longer than in earlier programs, and more clearly represent oral speech. Criticism that basals contain stilted and unrepresentative language, true of earlier programs with highly controlled vocabulary, is no longer completely valid. Thus, beginners can probably use context clues more effectively when the language of the reader is like their own *(40)*.

A third change has to do with the word recognition component of the newer basal series. As Popp *(37)* observed, newer programs introduce children to phonics instruction earlier, and they emphasize it as the main word recognition technique. This change is due to two important studies of the mid-sixties.

Bond and Dykstra *(7)* found that the basal programs with control by high frequency vocabulary were simply not as effective as instruction which also included a strong sound/symbol component. This conclusion is supported by Chall's *(10)* study which indicates that early training to decode printed words into oral equivalents is important in the first grade. Specifically, Chall has found that early inclusion of heavy phonics in the first year of reading instruction results in higher word recognition than when phonics instruction comes later in the year and is not strongly emphasized.

Phonics is a method of associating *sounds with symbols* in order to unlock unfamiliar words. Of the different approaches to teaching phonics, one is synthetic in that pupils sound out words by blending letter/sound by letter/sound. The *Phonovisual Method* (*R*) is one example of this approach. Other programs using an analytical approach teach pupils to substitute a sound associated with an initial letter or letters in a word context. For example, a pupil who does not recognize "brat" but knows "cat," "fat," etc. as well as the consonant cluster /br/ in "broke" learns to place /br/ in the context __at. In addition, generalized rules are used when appropriate. A well-known example is the rule that in words of the consonant-vowel-consonant final *e* pattern, the first vowel has a long sound and the *e* is silent. Sometimes these rules are taught deductively; sometimes pupils are encouraged to state the rule in their own words. There are many phonics generalizations; some are more productive than others. Chapter 8 lists phonic elements useful for the beginning reader.

A caution about phonics instruction: phonics, or any system which relates sound to symbol, is only beneficial in so far as it helps the beginning reader to increase his ability to unlock words. The reader's own language must be the oral base for application of phonics principles. The teacher must take care that phonics instruction helps rather than confuses the beginning reader. For example, if the words "told," "old," "mole," and "toll" are all rhyming words in a child's dialect, expectations that he will hear and isolate "told" and "old" from "toll" and "mole" without supportive instruction are unrealistic *(11)*. Whatever the dialect, the sound/symbol program must be a sensible, workable aid in the acquisition of reading.

The phonics program needs to be adapted for speakers of Black English. Since initial consonants vary little by dialect, they are useful beginning sound/symbol skills and are the features most used by mature readers. Increasing awareness of initial consonant letters as cues to words is useful to speakers of all dialects; however, work with final consonants, and especially consonant clusters, can result in confusion if the teacher does not relate the phonics principles with children's speech. Another area of difficulty is with short vowel sounds (*a* in "rat," *o* in "hop," *i* in "pin," *e* in "bed," *u* in "up"). The teacher must ascertain whether pupils articulate these sounds, whether they fail to discriminate them ("des" and "desk"), or whether both situations are true. If children fail to discriminate the sounds, it is best to develop auditory discrimination before initiating instruction of clusters as word clues. Because the effort required to develop discrimination prior to instruction is extensive, because these sounds vary considerably by dialect, because they are often placed in the medial position in the word, and because they are, therefore, less useful clues to words than letters in initial position, it may be best to delay introduction of short vowel sounds until after there has been considerable development of relationships between written consonants and their oral counterparts.

has been considerable development of relationships between written consonants and their oral counterparts.

This excursion into phonics instruction for speakers of Black English indicates just one adaptation for teaching phonics to beginning readers. Other adaptations require more sensitivity to other nonstandard dialects. Nearly all children need continual assessment of their use of the principles of phonics in real reading. Teachers need to determine whether children are applying phonics principles to the new words they meet in reading. In many cases, teachers should deliberately plan lessons on how to apply phonics principles; ability to transfer can be tested using nonsense words.

Most of the programs based on high frequency vocabulary present phonics as an important word recognition skill. The recent heavier inclusion of phonics at the beginning stages of reading minimizes differences between these programs and those in the next category—programs with vocabulary selected primarily on how much regularity exists between the written and spoken forms of words.

Reading Programs Based on Sound/Symbol Vocabulary

Some have stated that the initial task in reading is to decode print into words *(21)*. Some theoreticians and educators maintain that it is more important in the beginning stages of reading to decode words than to gain meaning from the prose [see Aukerman *(3)*, chapters 2, 3, 4, 5]. One method to ensure decoding success is to teach children methods of using decoding principles and to provide them with words that have regular sound/symbol correspondences. Thus, programs based on this principle include words with spellings predictable from their sounds. For example, "to" does not have a predictable spelling because it does not follow the pattern "go," "so," "no," but "mat," "cat," and "fat" all follow a predictable pattern.

In one program, *Basic Reading* (*K*), the vocabulary is controlled in terms of how closely the spelling parallels the sounds heard, although a few necessary function words that do not have a close sound/symbol correspondence are introduced separately from the other words. Because most of the words for the beginning program are selected according to the similarity of spellings with sounds, many more words are introduced than in high frequency vocabulary controlled programs. There is also less repetition of vocabulary. Thus, the *Basic Reading* series introduces about 2000 words by the end of the first year.

There is another way in which beginning reading is presented in programs with sound/symbol vocabulary choice. Beginning in 1963 with *Let's Read: A Linguistic Approach,* the Bloomfield and Barnhart program (*E*), a new word analysis approach emerged on the reading scene. In response to earlier work by Bloomfield *(6),* during the early 1960s the linguistic programs for beginning reading began to stress earlier and more extensive efforts to help pupils "break the written code." In linguistic programs, the major thrust of the first stages of reading is to teach pupils to decode words. Word decoding is achieved by structuring the vocabulary so that pupils *induce* a system of sound/symbol correspondences for themselves. That is, words are presented in groups so that individual words vary only by one phoneme/grapheme ("fat," "sat," "mat," "pat"); later, words are presented in more varied patterns. The stories in the first texts are based on these words and are somewhat limited in their content and style. Not all these linguistic programs are alike, but they share an emphasis on early decoding, control of vocabulary by sound/symbol correspondence, and learning by induction; there is little emphasis on comprehension of the material. Two examples of linguistic systems are *Merrill Linguistic Readers* by Fries, Fries, Wilson, and Rudolf *(I); BASIC Reading Series* by Rasmussen and Goldberg *(P).* According to the Bond and Dykstra study *(7),* use of the linguistic programs results in a slight advantage over conventional basal programs in word recognition but a disadvantage in rate and accuracy of reading. Otherwise, there are no differences.

There are fewer linguistic-based programs in use today than during the 1960s, according to my observations. However, some of the principles of the so-called linguistic approach are used in the new eclectic programs that have a high frequency vocabulary. For example, extended vocabulary load is due to the expansion of words with regular spelling. Many of the basals teach decoding skills using patterns of spelling such as the "fat," "sat," "mat," "pat" pattern presented above.

Reading Programs Based on Alphabet Reform

Under the assumption that the traditional orthography (t.o.) of written English consisting of twenty-six letters with lower and upper case forms is inadequate for representing the varied sounds of the English language (which contains approximately forty-four phonemes), educators have made use of Sir James Pitman's augmented alphabet as an instructional tool in initial reading. This alphabet, called i.t.a., *initial teaching alphabet,* has forty-four characters, each of which corresponds to a phoneme. Upper case letters in t.o. are eliminated in i.t.a. in favor of enlarged lower case forms. With this instructional system, children are introduced to the augmented alphabet and continue to read in i.t.a. for a period of about one year to eighteen months. At the end of this period, they go through a transition period. During transition to t.o., the i.t.a. characters are gradually replaced by traditional letter forms. The major argument for use of i.t.a. is that when each phoneme has an equivalent grapheme, the written language corresponds closely to the oral forms. In other words, i.t.a. orthography is a reliable representation of oral language during the decoding stage.

The i.t.a. instructional system was first introduced in England. These programs did not recommend a change in teaching methods, although there was generally a heavier phonics emphasis than in other British programs. Downing *(13)* has reported that i.t.a. children performed better than t.o. children when each group was tested with the orthography with which they had learned. It should be noted, though, that some i.t.a. children did suffer during transition to t.o.

Mazurkiewicz and Tanyzer have adapted i.t.a. to American standard dialect. Their *Early-to-Read: i.t.a. Program (N)* encourages changes in method in the direction of consciously increased training in sound/symbol relationships. Five of the "Cooperative Research Studies of First Grade Reading," which examined comparative use of i.t.a., showed that it did not result in significantly improved reading achievement except in word recognition. In this case, according to Fry *(22)*, the i.t.a. pupils were better than pupils taught with conventional basals. A more recent study by Robertson and Trepper *(39)* showed that bilingual Mexican-American fourth graders initially benefited from an i.t.a. program. However, a year later there were no differences between the treatment group and others *(56)*.

The high cost of buying story books and content materials in i.t.a. and possible confusion for children who move from one school to another during the program are practical disadvantages of i.t.a. In addition, since i.t.a. is written to represent standard dialect, speakers of nonstandard dialects are at a disadvantage. These children will not receive the possible benefits from the close sound/symbol correspondence inherent in i.t.a.

A less drastic adaptation of the traditional alphabet to oral language is the Diacritical Marking System. The traditional letters are maintained in this system but are marked to indicate pronunciation. This alphabetical change does not require the period of transition which i.t.a. demands. Nonetheless, a three-year comparison of i.t.a., Diacritical Marking, and t.o. has indicated no differences in the three systems *(23)*.

Other programs which alter the orthography for beginning readers are UNIFON *(L)* and *Words in Color (J)*. In the latter program, color is used as a cue to sounds of letters and letter combination. These programs are usually found in schools where one or more administrators or teachers are enthusiastic supporters. Generally, they are not widely used. Research is scanty, although supporters claim undoubted successes in teaching children to read. Aukerman *(3)* states that written English will ultimately reflect slight changes to modern pronunciation of English; perhaps that is the benefit of these pioneering reading programs.

The Language Experience Program

A far more popular program for teaching beginning reading is the language experience approach. One reason for its popularity is due to its flexibility which allows it to be combined with other programs. It is most often combined with high frequency vocabulary basal programs.

For years, teachers of primary grade pupils have on occasion helped their pupils produce experience charts. The teacher recorded children's dictated comments on a specified topic; then, the teacher, the teacher and pupils, or the pupils themselves (depending on the reading level) read the dictated story. The teacher often used key words from the story later in a vocabulary lesson. This procedure was used to record special events such as a new animal in the class, a class trip, or an important school happening. In recent years, this use of group experience charts has been extended as an instructional system for beginning reading.

With the language experience system, children dictate many stories to the teacher even before they are ready to read. Some are individual stories; some represent an effort by the whole class. Teachers use the printed story as a focus for training in prereading skills. Thus, pupils learn to recognize letters within the context of words; they learn to recognize their own names, etc. Words which begin with the same initial letter are isolated and become the material for auditory-visual discrimination. Children learn that spoken words have written equivalents and that the spaces mark off printed words. When each sentence occupies a separate line, they become conscious of how punctuation parallels intonation. Once readiness skills are underway, children who have dictated many stories, have heard those stories read, have identified words which begin with the same letter, have learned to name letters within words, and have learned to distinguish different words which have similar form usually begin to recall words which they have used often or which are critical to a story. (For example, *elephant* may be recalled two days after a story about a trip to the zoo.) Once children begin to recognize such previously used words, Stauffer *(51)* recommends that the teacher initiate a *word bank*. A pupil's word bank is a collection of words which he can recognize on sight. This collection is used as the material for skills development. Children also are encouraged very early to write stories themselves. Dictated and self-written stories on an individual and group basis are continued, but, once reading is underway, group reading experiences from tradebooks or basal texts become important components of the reading program *(51)*.

Advocates of the language-experience system, such as Stauffer *(51)*, Lee and Allen *(31)*, Hall *(26)*, believe that children's learning is enhanced by inductively and independently using language knowledge as a crucial aid in reading acquisition. Because these educators think requirements for accurate spelling are inhibiting to beginning writing, they contend that learning the idiosyncracies of the English spelling system can be postponed until children have had a good start at literacy. When we read the samples below of children's self-written stories, it is obvious that communicability is seldom lost because of the unconventional spellings.[3] Because the writer and reader share the phonological structure of English, there is no difficulty in deciphering these uniquely spelled words. Furthermore, as children listen to word sounds and translate them into printed code, they acquire awareness of sound/symbol relationships which will serve them in decoding unfamiliar printed words.

My dog's name is Furry. I like my dog. I love my dog to peasis.

My Mother and Father won't let me and my sister have a dog. Becose if I had a dog I wood haff to take caer of it and evry day I wood haff to take if for a walk and I wont have time to take it for a walk. Becose I have two cats.

My dog's name was peper. My dog was playful. He likes to be peted n' played with n' pated on the head.

My dog awos jumps on my bed and he awos wake me up.

From a theoretical viewpoint, this instructional system has a good deal of linguistic support. When learning to read with printed forms of his own oral language, the beginning reader finds no mismatch between his syntactic knowledge and the written structures. Furthermore, there is no lack of conceptual background, as the material consists of the reader's unique experience with the world. In addition, each pupil can learn to read with material which represents his language. From a human point of view, this instructional system encourages and requires—when properly applied—one-to-one contact between teacher and pupil as the pupil shares his important ideas and experiences. Not only will the teacher closely share communication, he can use the dictated story to gauge the pupil's conceptual level and oral language skill. Sylvia Ashton-Warner's vivid and compelling book *Teacher (2)* demonstrates clearly the social and human interaction which occurs when a sensitive teacher begins to communicate with his pupils' real level of thinking and experience.

---

3. These stories were written in September 1972, by second graders at the Dogwood School, Park Forest, Illinois.

Research support on the use of language experience is far from conclusive. One major difficulty with study of this method is that, by its instructional nature, use of language experience in classroom differs from teacher to teacher more than with any other program. Duplication of method, required for research, is nearly impossible. However, Allen, one of the early modern proponents of the method, found in his early study *(1)* that language experience-trained children showed achievement gains at least equal to use of those learning with basal readers. Further, children beginning with language experience were apt to write earlier than other children. Data from Bond and Dykstra's first grade studies *(7)* on language experience, on the other hand, indicate its use offered no clear benefits. On the other hand, a long-term study by Stauffer and Hammond *(52)* demonstrated some positive benefits from language experience three years after program inception. Stauffer and Hammond's subjects were better than controls in content area subjects, in rate and accuracy of reading, on an individually administered word recognition test, and on a measure of creative writing.

In a study by Smith *(46)* children dictated personal stories into a tape recorder in addition to their participation in a phonics program and gained a second grade achievement level in comprehension by the end of the first grade, but there was no control group to compare with. In a similar program by Smith and Morgan *(47)* positive results for the experimental children over the control children were not replicated.

Serwer's analysis *(44)* of data from a longitudinal examination of reading achievement of New York City inner-city children is of particular interest. When the achievements of pupils from a basal plus phonics program were compared with language experience-trained pupils, the basal plus phonics pupils did better during the first and second year *(28);* however, by the end of the third grade, the language experience students were significantly better in comprehension than were the other students. Apparently, positive effects from this system become evident only after two or three years of instruction.

Some writers in the field of reading, such as Heilman *(29)* and Spache and Spache *(49),* point out that facilitation of the language experience system is difficult. There are classroom management problems, and there are difficulties associated with initiating and extending decoding training. There is also a need to constantly stimulate pupils' inventions and creative expression. Stauffer *(51),* Lee and Allen *(31),* and Hall *(26)* have described instructional techniques for managing the system; further remarks are found in chapter 8.

Although the instructional system used depends on pupil output, there are commercial materials available. The Encyclopedia Britannica Press produces the *Language Experience Program (B)* by Allen with study guides. Martin's Sounds of Language series *(M)* is an excellent adjunct to the language experience system. Oral reading of poems, songs, folk tales, and fantasies beautifully illustrates rhythm, rhyme, and repetition of language forms. The author presents no prescribed instructional program. Group experiences with these texts can enhance the beginning reader's oral language store and stimulate his own dictated and written stories.

Individualized Reading Programs

There are two ways to individualize a reading program. One is to develop a system for the management of pupil training in specific reading skills; the other is an open approach in which pupils read a wide variety of materials independently with instruction occurring during private interviews with the teacher.

The first type of individualized instruction in reading reflects the adaptation of a general individualized system used in all content areas to reading instruction. In this program, reading skills are specified and placed in sequence. Instructional objectives help to determine the assessment of preinstructional achievement and post-instructional growth. In some programs, the instructional techniques are predetermined; in others, teachers plan their own instruction. An example of the former type of program, in which the teacher is primarily a facilitator of a total program, is the Individually Prescribed Instruction; an example of the latter is the *Wisconsin Design for Reading Skill Development (S)*. The Wisconsin plan is designed to identify clearly skill development needs and to provide a system to meet these needs. Pupils are engaged in a skill program as well as in developmental reading activities.

The other approach to individualization is based on the assumption that learning rates and styles are so varied that grouping children obscures these critical differences. It holds that the best way to approach learning is to encourage each pupil to develop his potential in his own unique way. Some teachers view their role in an individualized system as that of a facilitator and are reluctant to limit their pupils' choice of books and reading levels. Others carefully guide their students' choices of books so that they read different kinds of books at their instructional reading level. This second group of teachers is apt to have a separate word recognition skills program, while the first group may include word recognition training as needed during the individual conferences.

Although Sartain *(43)* reported no significantly positive effects of use of an individualized reading system over use of basals, Johnson's *(30)* study of three years of individualized instruction showed strong positive effects. Spencer's *(50)* study demonstrated higher scores for individually taught pupils who also had experienced a heavy phonics program. It appears that when combined with phonics and when done well, an individualized system is of benefit to students. Teachers report observation of increased interest and independence among pupils taught with this system.

Supplements to both types of individualized programs, and indeed to almost any program grouping described in these pages, are the popular teacher-made games and activities used to extend learnings about reading skills in many classrooms today *(48)*. These games are usually developed to extend practice in a skill: they are motivating, they encourage team learning, they are self-instructional. Pupils report that they learn well with games and that they are fun; however, they would not buy games for learning if they could buy other nonlearning games *(35)*.

In this section of the chapter on beginning reading, we have discussed very briefly some of the widely disparate approaches to reading instruction. There are other approaches and many other programs commercially available; over 100 are described in Aukerman *(3)*. This chapter has attempted to describe some of the differences among programs. Variation in the type of vocabulary chosen for beginning materials, extent of sound/symbol emphasis in word recognition, extent of structure in lessons, and organization of pupils for learning are viewed differently in different program categories. What is most impressive about beginning reading given the vast array of programs and approaches is the likelihood that most youngsters will learn to read in spite of the adult-inspired variation.

Summary and Recommendations

Because some programs emphasize certain skills, we can compare and contrast the programs from the previous section within the context of the model of the beginning reader developed in chapter 5. By so doing, some conclusions about programs can be drawn. Recommendations for beginning reading are presented here based on the applicability of the approaches to the model and on study of achievement in early stages of reading. These recommendations are not necessarily universally accepted, a fact the reader should bear in mind. The figure from chapter 5 is repeated here with the addition of numbers 1 through 8 for reference in the discussion below.

Programs based on high frequency vocabulary are eclectic in nature. That is, they are apt to present a variety of methods for children to use in figuring out unknown words. In reference to the chart and discrimination of features (1), children taught by this method are encouraged to

Figure 3.
Beginning readers

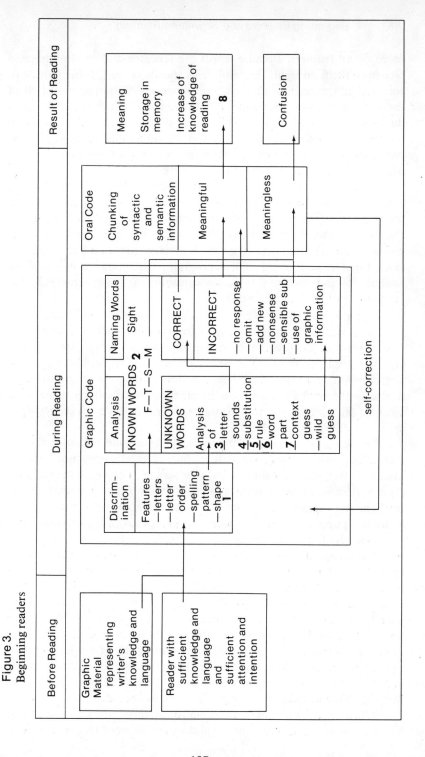

focus on all features. Because words are repeated and children have to recognize them on sight, the result is as shown above (2). In contrast to some other approaches, these eclectic programs encourage use of all of the word recognition techniques listed here from (3) through (7). Individual sounds for mainly initial letters, substitution of initial consonant in a recognizable pattern, use of rules to indicate sounds, analysis of word parts, and extensive use of context to name unknown words are taught. Meaning (8), of course, is very important from the beginning.

Programs that select highly regular sound/symbol correspondence words for beginning reading encourage children to focus mainly on spelling patterns (1). Acquisition of sight words (2) is important but reached through analysis of words rather than through memory. The word recognition techniques used depend on the individual program but usually include (3), (4), and/or (5). These programs de-emphasize use of word analysis (6) and context (7). Finally, meaning (8) is not stressed in the early stages of reading acquisition.

Alphabet modification programs usually stress discrimination of all aspects of words (1). Additionally, sight word recognition comes from word repetition (2). Techniques for figuring out new words stress (3) and (4). The need for rules (5) is nearly eliminated by the change in the alphabet. Context (7) is used. Because authors of these programs often duplicate the reading instruction in other more traditional programs, meaning (8) is important, too. However, *Words in Color (J)* delays reading for meaning for some time.

The language experience program, being a collection of activities that unite children's language with reading, is usually even more eclectic than high frequency vocabulary basal programs. Feature discrimination (1) is varied; word recognition training is dependent on context (7), but teachers can include other sound/symbol oriented instruction as they desire and pupils need. Finally, meaning (8) is of major importance.

Individualized reading programs differ as to the focus of emphasis on word recognition instruction. If schools use one of the management systems to teach reading skills, there is apt to be discrimination training on all aspects of words (1). Sight word recognition is expected at certain milestones of progress (2). Word recognition includes analysis of letter sounds (3) for initial letters, substitution (4), acquisition of rules for phonics (5), word analysis (6), and context (7). When used appropriately, pupils apply these skills in reading for meaning (8). If the independent reading of books is the method for individualizing, the skills program is apt to be less structured, sight word acquisition (2) is stressed, as is meaning (8), and skills (3) through (7) taught as needed.

When selecting a reading program for a school, the decision should be partly based on the presentation and variety of word recognition skills as well as the stress on meaning among the choices. The following recommendations are developed with the author's preferences for meaning-based learning with eclectic and systematic word recognition instruction in mind.

1. Reading is a meaningful process. Communication between reader and writer is necessary for reading to occur.
2. To be able to achieve comprehension, beginning readers have to process the individual words they name through their language knowledge systems.
3. Beginning reading materials should reflect the language structures commonly used by children so that the children can use their language facility in learning to read.
4. Children learn a number of methods for decoding words in their oral but not their reading vocabulary.
5. Beginning readers appear to benefit from training in sound/symbol correspondences during the first two years of reading instruction.
6. Children also use context to figure out unknown words. Explicit instruction in use of context with associated sound/symbol awareness may hasten the development of skilled reading behavior.
7. There are a number of systems for beginning reading instruction. Successful beginning reading is dependent more on teaching effectiveness than on the characteristics of different instructional systems.
8. The most common system controls vocabulary in terms of the frequency of word usage. Many basal reading programs published since 1968 show increased vocabulary, a stronger phonics program, and a greater variety of subject matter than did earlier basals. It should be noted that when using this system, teachers must take care that individual needs are met.
9. Another system for reading instruction is control of vocabulary in terms of sound/symbol correspondence. Sometimes, children in programs based on this system are explicitly taught how to *sound out words;* in other programs, children are encouraged to induce their own methods for relating symbol to sound. Since the first stories in programs of this nature are likely to have little meaning, teachers must take care that children develop the idea that reading is a meaningful process.
10. Another system, the language experience approach, promotes use of children's dictated and written stories as reading material. Teachers need to include sound/symbol correspondence instruction and early reading of published materials to expand reading ability if they use this system.

11. Another system is individualized instruction either by use of pro-
grammed materials or by student choice of reading material. Attention to individual learning styles is required on the part of the
teacher with this system.

12. Another system adapts the printed symbols to provide one-to-one
correspondence between sound and print. Use of such a system
requires a gradual adjustment to conventional orthography.

13. There are combinations of these systems, notably DISTAR,[4] which
is a highly structured decoding approach to reading.

---

4. S. Engelmann, E. C. Brunner, S. Stearns, *DISTAR Instructional System* (Chicago:
Science Research Associates, 1972).

Selected Activities

1. It was recommended in this chapter that preschool children who show interest and ability to begin to read should be taught to read as long as the situation
provides for success and that instruction integrates reading with other, more
common preschool activities. Which of the major approaches to beginning
reading would be the most suitable for following these principles? Why?

2. Why would advocates of sequential skill development disagree with those
who believe reading is a holistic activity on the question of the importance of
phonics in the beginning reading program?

3. Would the following group of words most likely be found in a program
with vocabulary based on high frequency or in a program with words based on
regular sound/symbol correspondence?

top	mop	use	us
same	tame	feed	me

4. For each of the situations below name the major reading program the
student is participating in.

a. Mary is talking alone with the teacher about one book. The teacher is asking questions, and then Mary reads aloud from the book. Finally, Mary
selects a new book to read.

b. Jane is talking alone with the teacher who writes down what Jane says. Then
Jane and the teacher read the written material together.

c. Thomas is sitting with six other children who have the same book, all opened
to page 86. The teacher is asking questions. Then Thomas reads aloud when
his turn comes.

d. Michael is reading aloud. The rest of his small group of peers have the same
book. There are funny marks for letters in the book.

e. Jerry has just finished a worksheet. He takes it to the teacher who checks it; then he moves on to a group learning lesson; then he takes a test. Finally, having passed the test, Jerry gets a check in a space on a large sheet.

References

1. Allen, R. V. and San Diego Public Schools. "Three Approaches to Teaching Reading." In *Challenge and Experiment in Reading: Proceedings of the International Reading Association* (1962): 153–54.
2. Ashton-Warner, S. *Teacher*. New York: Simon and Schuster, 1963.
3. Aukerman, R. C. *Approaches to Beginning Reading*. New York: John Wiley, 1971.
4. Barnard, D. and DeGracie, J. "Vocabulary Analysis of New Primary Reading Series." *The Reading Teacher* 30 (1976): 177–80.
5. Barr, R. C. "Instructional Pace Differences and Their Effect on Reading Acquisition." *Reading Research Quarterly* 9 (1973-74): 526–54.
6. Bloomfield, L. "Linguistics and Reading." *Elementary English Review* 19 (1942): 125–30; 183–86.
7. Bond, J. L., and Dykstra, R. "The Cooperative Research Program in First-Grade Reading Instruction." *Reading Research Quarterly* 3 (1967): 9–142.
8. Briggs, C. and Elkind, D. "Cognitive Development in Early Readers." *Development Psychology* 9 (September 1973): 279–80.
9. Brzeinsky, J. E. "Beginning Reading in Denver." *The Reading Teacher* 17 (1964): 16–21.
10. Chall, J. *Learning to Read: The Great Debate*. New York: McGraw-Hill, 1967.
11. Channon, G. "Bulljive-Language Teaching in a Harlem School." *The Urban Review* 2 (1968): 5–12.
12. Dolch, E. W. "A Basic Sight Vocabulary." *Elementary School Journal* 36 (1936): 456–460; "A Basic Sight Vocabulary." *Elementary School Journal* 37 (1936): 268–72.
13. Downing, J. A. "Initial Teaching Alphabet: Results after Six Years." *Elementary School Journal* 69 (1969): 242–49.
14. _____. *Comparative Reading*. New York: Macmillan, 1973.
15. Durkin, D. "The Achievement of Preschool Readers: Two Longitudinal Studies." *Reading Research Quarterly* 1 (1966): 5–36.
16. _____. *Children Who Read Early*. New York: Teachers College Press, Columbia University, 1966.
17. _____. "A Language Arts Program for Prefirst-Grade Children: Two-Year Achievement Report." *Reading Research Quarterly* 6 (1970): 534–65.
18. _____. *Teaching Young Children to Read*. Boston: Allyn & Bacon, 1972.
19. _____. "A Six Year Study of Children Who Learned To Read Early in School at the Age of Four." *Reading Research Quarterly* 10 (1974-75): 9–61.

20. Eames, T. H. "Physical Factors in Reading." *Reading Teacher* 15 (1962): 427–32.

21. Fries, C. C. *Linguistics and Reading.* New York: Holt, Rinehart and Winston, 1962.

22. Fry, E. "I.T.A.: A Look at the Research Data." *Education* 88 (1967): 549–53.

23. _____. "Comparison of Beginning Reading with i.t.a., D.M.S., and T.O. after Three Years." *The Reading Teacher* 22 (1969): 357–62.

24. Gates, A. I. and Russell, D. "Types of Material, Vocabulary Builder, Word Analysis, and Other Factors in Beginning Reading." *Elementary School Journal* 39 (1938): 119–28.

25. Goodman, K. S. "Miscues: Windows on the Reading Process." In *Miscue Analysis: Applications to Reading Instruction,* edited by K. S. Goodman. ERIC, Urbana, Ill.: National Council of Teachers of English, 1973.

26. Hall, M. *Teaching Reading As a Language Experience,* 2d ed. Columbus: Charles E. Merrill, 1976.

27. Hall, M.; Moretz, S. A.; and Statom, J. "Writing before Grade One—A Study of Early Writers." *Language Arts* 53 (May, 1976): 582–85.

28. Harris, A. J., and Serwer, B. L. "Comparing Reading Approaches in First-Grade Teaching with Disadvantaged Children." *The Reading Teacher* 19 (1966): 631–42.

29. Heilman, A. W. *Principles and Practices of Teaching Reading,* 4th ed. Columbus, Ohio: Charles E. Merrill Publishing Co., 1977.

30. Johnson, R. H. "Individualized and Basal Primary Reading Programs." *Elementary English* 42 (1965): 902–4; 915.

31. Lee, D. M., and Allen, R. V. *Learning to Read through Experience.* New York: Appleton-Century-Crofts, 1963.

32. Luna, E. "DISTAR Language and Reading Programs: Effects upon SESAT Scores." *Colorado Journal of Educational Research* 14 (1974): 2–5.

33. Malmquist, E. "Sweden." In *Comparative Reading,* edited by J. Downing. New York: Macmillan, 1973.

34. Micucci, P. "Let's *Not* Teach Reading in Kindergarten!" *Elementary English* 64 (1964): 246–51.

35. Moustakis, Y. "A Comparative Study of the Effects of Two Methods of Teaching Roots and Affixes." Unpublished paper, University of Illinois at Chicago Circle, 1977.

36. Olson, A. V. "An Analysis of the Vocabulary of Seven Primary Reading Series." *Elementary English* 43 (1965): 261–64.

37. Popp, H. M. "Current Practices in the Teaching of Beginning Reading." In *Toward a Literate Society: The Report of the Committee on Reading of the National Academy of Education,* edited by J. B. Carroll and J. S. Chall. New York: McGraw-Hill, 1975.

38. Ranta, T. "Reading in Finland." Paper at College Instructors of Reading Professionals. Springfield, Ill., October 1975.

39. Robertson, D. J. and Trepper, T. S. "The Effects of i.t.a. on the Reading Achievement of Mexican-American Children." *Reading World* 5 (1974): 132–38.

40. Ruddell, R. B. "The Effect of the Similarity of Oral and Written Patterns of Language Structure on Written Composition." *Elementary English* 42 (1965): 403–10.

41. Sakamoto, T. and Makita, K. "Japan." In *Comparative Reading,* edited by J. Downing. New York: Macmillan, 1973.

42. Samuels, S. V. and Schachter, S. W. "Controversial Issues in Beginning Reading Instruction: Meaning Versus Subskill Emphasis." In *Aspects of Reading Education,* edited by S. Pflaum-Connor. Issues in Contemporary Education, National Society for the Study of Education. Berkeley: McCutchan, 1978.

43. Sartain, H. W. "The Roseville Experiment with Individualized Reading." *The Reading Teacher* 13 (1960): 277–81.

44. Serwer, B. L. "Linguistic Support for a Method of Teaching Beginning Reading to Black Children." *Reading Research Quarterly* 5 (1969): 449–67.

45. Schnell, T. R. and Sweeney, J. "Sex Role Bias in Basal Readers." *Elementary English* 52 (May 1975): 737–42.

46. Smith, L. B. "They Found a Golden Ladder . . . Stories by Children." *The Reading Teacher* 29 (1976): 541–45.

47. Smith, L. B. and Morgan, G. D. "Cassette Tape Recording As a Primary Method in the Development of Early Reading Material." *Elementary English* 52 (1975): 534–38.

48. Spache, E. *Reading Activities for Child Involvement,* 2d ed. Boston: Allyn and Bacon, 1976.

49. Spache, G. D., and Spache, E. B. *Reading in the Elementary School,* 2d ed. Boston: Allyn & Bacon, 1969.

50. Spencer, D. U. "Individualized versus a Basal Reader Program in Rural Communities—Grades One and Two." *The Reading Teacher* 21 (1967): 11–17.

51. Stauffer, R. G. *The Language Experience Approach to the Teaching of Reading.* New York: Harper and Row, 1970.

52. Stauffer, R. G., and Hammond, W. D. "The Effectiveness of Language Arts and Basic Reader Approaches to First-Grade Reading Instruction—Extended into Third Grade." *Reading Research Quarterly* 5 (1969): 468–99.

53. Talmage, H. and Walberg, H. J. "Naturalistic Decision-Oriented Evaluation of a District Reading Program." *Journal of Reading Behavior* 10 (1978): in press.

54. Thorndike, E. L. "The Vocabulary of Books for Children in Grades Three to Eight: I," *Teachers College Record* 38 (1936-37): 196–205.

55. Thorndike, E. L., and Lorge, I. *The Teachers Word Book of 30,000 Words.* New York: Teachers College, Columbia University, 1944.

56. Trepper, T. S. and Robertson, D. J. "The Effects of i.t.a. on the Reading Achievement of Mexican-American Children: A Follow-up." *Reading Improvement* 12 (1975): 177–83.

57. Williams, C. "Vocabulary Control in Primary Readers." Unpublished paper, University of Illinois at Chicago Circle, 1977.

Reading Programs

A. Aaron, J. E., et al. *Scott Foresman Reading Systems.* Glenview, Ill.: Scott, Foresman, 1971.

B. _____. *Reading Unlimited,* Scott Foresman Systems, Revised. Glenview, Ill.: Scott, Foresman, 1976.

C. Allen, R. Van. *Language Experience in Reading.* Chicago: Encyclopedia Britannica Press, 1974.

D. Bank Street College of Education. *The Bank Street Basal Reading Program.* N. Y.: Macmillan, 1966.

E. Bloomfield, L., and Barnhart, C. L. *Let's Read: A Linguistic Approach.* Bronxville, N. Y.: Clarence L. Barnhart, 1963.

F. Crane, B. J. *CSS.* Trenton, N. J.: Motivational Learning Programs, 1968.

G. Englemann, S. and Bruner, E. *DISTAR.* Chicago: Science Research Associates, 1968.

H. Evertts, E. L.; Weiss, B. J.; and Cruikshank, S. B. *The Holt Basic Reading System.* New York: Holt, Rinehart and Winston, 1977.

I. Fries, C. C. et al. *Merrill Linguistic Readers.* Columbus, Ohio: Charles E. Merrill, 1966.

J. Gattegno, C. *Words in Color.* New York: Schools for the Future, 1962.

K. McCracken, G., and Walcutt, C. C. *Basic Reading.* Philadelphia: J. B. Lippincott, 1963.

L. Malone, J. *UNIFON.* Racine, Wis.: Western Publishing Educational Services, undated.

M. Martin, Bill. *Sounds of Language.* New York: Holt, Rinehart, & Winston, 1970.

N. Mazurkiewicz, A. J., and Tanyzer, H. J. *Early-to-Read: i.t.a. Program.* New York: Initial Teaching Alphabet Publications, 1963.

O. New Dimensions in Education. *Alpha One: Breaking the Code.* N. Y.: New Dimensions in Education, 1969.

P. Rasmussen, D., and Goldberg. L. *Basic Reading Series.* Chicago: Science Research Associates, 1964.

Q. Russell, D. H., et al. *The Ginn Basic Readers.* Boston: Ginn, 1966.

R. Schoolfield, L. D., and Timberlake, J. B. *Phonovisual Method.* Washington, D.C.: Phonovisual Products, 1961.

S. *SWRL.* Lexington, Mass.: Ginn, 1972.

T. Wisconsin Research and Development Center for Cognitive Learning. *The Wisconsin Design for Reading Skill Development.* Madison: The University of Wisconsin, 1970.

U. Writers' Committee of the Great Cities School Improvement Program of the Detroit Public Schools. *City Schools Reading Program.* Chicago: Follett, 1962.

Instructional
Procedures for
Beginning Reading

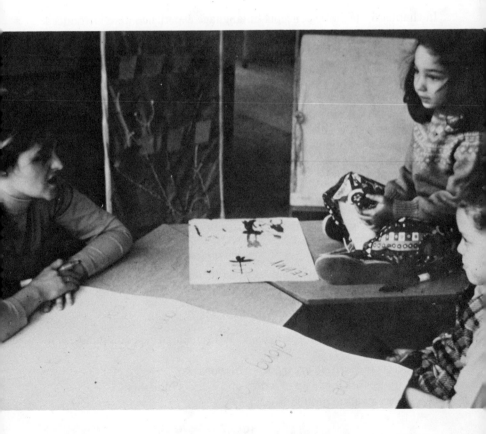

In the three sections that follow, the emphasis is on teacher decision making for instructional needs, planning, and the development of materials. While some commercial programs are good, teacher devised programs are also often effective. This chapter is intended to help teachers develop a total beginning reading program appropriate to their classes.

Based on the analysis and discussion in previous chapters, the recommendations for reading instruction include use of the language experience approach, word recognition techniques, and extension of reading into basal texts and trade books. The prereading period initiates language experience activities and word recognition readiness; the transition from readiness to actual reading instruction should be gradual.

Language Experience

In chapter 6, the basic concepts of language experience were introduced. In chapter 7, we examined the language experience approach as a beginning reading system and found its most salient features included:

1. Use of children's oral language for reading material; the child's written language therefore parallels his spoken language.
2. Built-in provision for dialect and experiential variation.
3. A personalized instructional approach; the teacher and child share important thoughts, experiences, and observations.
4. A natural means for an integrated language arts program; reading, writing, listening (to others' stories), and speaking (dictating) are all involved in the production of language-experience stories.
5. An open system to encourage creativity in children and in teaching.
6. Ease in combining the system with other methods of teaching reading.

Before children actually begin to learn to read, they have acquired the following prereading understandings from their readiness work with dictated stories:

1. Writing preserves oral language. Written language communicates to readers.
2. Speech and writing are made up of words.
3. Sentences are made up of words and express thoughts.
4. Spaces separate printed words.

196

Instructional Sequence

Once children are ready to learn to read, the language experience activities should follow a regular sequence so that maximum use is made of children's stories. The following sequence is slightly amended from one by Stauffer *(29)*.

Day 1: On the first day of the sequence, the child dictates a story to the teacher who reads it back immediately to see if it is *correct.* The child is then asked to identify any words he knows in the story, and those words are underlined. Then, the teacher and child reread the story; the teacher reads and hesitates before each underlined word so that the child can respond.

When taking children's dictation, the teacher should observe a number of conditions. He should encourage free-flowing language as much as possible. That is, the teacher should not interrupt or slow down the story dictation process unless this is necessary. For the unresponsive child, some prodding may be needed, but even in these circumstances, the child's words only are recorded—even if these words are not in complete sentences. For a long-winded child, the teacher may need to suggest alternatives because of time constraints. At a good stopping point, he might suggest that they discontinue dictation and continue the following day. He also might suggest that the child's parents complete the story that night. Under no circumstances should the exuberant child be discouraged.

If the teacher has a primary typewriter available, the dictation process is facilitated. The typed words and spacing are more consistent than in hand-printed stories and are, therefore, perceptually clearer. If there is no primary typewriter, the teacher should be very sure to have a *very neat, consistent* manuscript form and use a black pen for clarity.

Whether a typewriter or pen is used, a carbon should be made of each story and filed in the child's folder. The files then are used for informal progress assessment. The file of dictated stories contains data about the size of a child's reading vocabulary (underlined words), the span of his interests (the variation of story content), his ability to observe the world around him, the complexity of his sentence structures, the development of his conceptual understanding, and the extent of his oral vocabulary.

Teachers are often perplexed about taking dictation from nonstandard-speaking children; however, since the goal of this technique is to preserve each child's language and unique experiences for reading acquisition, I think the solution is clear. The child's sentence structure should be preserved as the teacher writes the story but conventional spelling should be used. I would not hesitate to write double negatives, insert a subject pronoun after a topic name, use nonstandard pronouns or immature or nonstandard past tense verbs, but I would spell each word in the traditional manner. Just as children will learn later new ideas and new ways of expressing ideas from reading other's writings, so too will they learn to understand alternative sentence structures.

Day 2: The previous day's story is reread and, again, the teacher hesitates before each underlined word. If the words underlined previously are identified again, they are underlined again. The reading activity is followed by more sight practice with these words. Twice-underlined words are listed in random order or isolated from the story context by a window card so that clues are minimized and the newly underlined words are practiced.

Day 3: On rereading, those words still recognized in and out of context are printed on small cards by the teacher (so as to maintain model print) and are placed in the child's word bank. A new story can be produced on the second or third day for the active, excited learner, and the sequence begins again.

Development of Sight Vocabulary

The *word bank* can be made from a child's shoe box which has been decorated and labeled by the child (e.g., *Jim's Word Bank*). When there are only a few words in the bank, the cards can be arranged haphazardly. A block can be used to hold the cards upright. There should be ample room for continual growth—a highly motivating factor for beginners. Since all known words are deposited in the word bank, the word bank is the store of the child's sight vocabulary for the first weeks and months of reading acquisition. Therefore, the word bank is very important; it is the source for sight word practice and for other word recognition learning. In addition, the word bank has an emotional appeal to the child; each child saves his *known important* words just as adults save money in the bank. By contrast, a common classroom procedure is to give children cards with words they do *not* know. With the word bank, positive learning is reinforced.

At first, the word bank words will be the words of heavy critical content in the dictated stories, but because the child's stories will include the most frequent words of the language, prepositions, articles, conjunctions, and auxiliaries will soon be acquired as well. The teacher should make certain that the frequently used words are being learned so that the transition to reading in basals and easy-to-read trade books is eased. Words listed on the Dolch Basic Sight Word List *(4)* or in a recent modernized version by Johnson *(19)* should be the source for frequent words. Individual assessment of the growing vocabulary comes from the child's file or word bank; the teacher matches the child's acquired vocabulary with the word list. When there is a dearth of high-frequency function words, the teacher should point out one or two of these words in each story, explain that they are very important to learn, and then underline them *with a wavy line*. When the child recognizes the words on rereading, the wavy line is erased and replaced by a straight line. Since these words are so common, children will use them again and again in their own stories where their contextual meanings—the only meanings these function words have—are clear and learn them with relative ease.

In order to provide sufficient practice and additional skill work with the word bank words, the following independent activities are recommended:

1. Children enjoy finding their first word bank words in newspapers and magazines. They can cut these words out and paste them on the back of their cards.
2. Two children can share their words to see how many similar words they have. New acquisitions are often made this way.
3. Once a child has acquired ten or more words, he probably can make a new sentence by arranging the words in order. Then, when he copies his "new" sentence, he has practice in manuscript writing and early creative writing.
4. Two or three children can combine their words (after initialing their own words) to devise a whole story by placing the word cards and sentences on the floor. Again, the copying procedure reinforces handwriting skill as well as the concept of preservation by writing.
5. After illustrating a story or observation, children should look through their word banks for appropriate words for a title, arrange the word cards in order, and copy the title onto their illustration.
6. In some British schools, teachers teach manuscript writing by having the children trace over the words printed by the teacher. When the child's pencil moves far from the model, he immediately knows his form is inaccurate. After he has developed skill in tracing, the child learns to copy the story words. Later, he copies the story on a new sheet of paper.
7. Once children have learned to look through their word banks for words to use in their titles or for sentence words, they will learn that if the words are in some kind of consistent order, it is easier to find them. This is a natural moment to introduce the idea of *alphabetizing*. A sample chart can be devised as a model for alphabetizing word banks once the children know the sequence of letters in the alphabet. As the teacher explains the chart illustrated below, the

children sort their own cards. (Note that the words are alphabetized at first only by initial letter.)

8. Once the words of the bank have been alphabetized, picture dictionaries are introduced in such a way that the children understand that the same alphabetizing principle is used and that the dictionary serves as a source for even more words. With alphabetized word banks and picture dictionaries in use, beginning readers are well on their way to becoming independent readers and learners.

9. If the teacher provides many opportunities to practice and use word bank words, most children will recognize these words on sight with ease, but informal testing is needed, too. The words should be listed in random order on a sheet of paper and the child directed to name each word quickly. Words not named should be studied again in story context and further practice with word games provided.

10. Practice games with sight words are simple to devise. For example, Bingo is easily adapted to sight word practice. Teachers also can make a long ladder on a sheet of paper with a prize at the top. When each word written between the ladder steps is named quickly, the prize is won. Or a cut-out train engine can reach the station when each word written on the tracks is quickly named.

11. The work with word bank words will not be sight recognition practice alone. These words provide the basis for much of the development of the other word recognition learning which will be described in a later section of this chapter.

When the size of the word bank has increased so that children are able to read nearly every word of their dictated stories, the teacher should underline only the *unknown* words. These words, once learned, are added to the word bank. At this time, children will be reading in texts and trade books (see the last section of the chapter) and will be writing many of their own stories.

Beginning Writing

In the section on early reading in chapter 7, it was noted that children who read early often showed interest in *writing* before *reading (5, 13)*. These early writings are usually children's messages to members of their families about their own objects, their experiences, their desires (e.g., for others to stay out of their room). Early writers occasionally ask adults for spelling; more often they use the phoneme/grapheme correspondences they induce for themselves from minimal information learned from parents *(24)*. These children get much personal satisfaction from their writing. Of course, they also like encouragement from others.

There are basic differences between the products and attitudes of early writers compared with those of children who learn to write in school. Early writers gain intrinsic satisfaction from their writing, especially if their messages in print are acknowledged by their families. By contrast, in school, children learn too early that writing can be criticized—that it can be right or wrong. School-learned writing often carries a heavy responsibility for correct spelling. Early writers also learn something about writing that school-learned writing seldom emphasizes. Early writers naturally write for different audiences and for different purposes. They write for their families, for themselves, for the presentation of direct messages, and for the pleasure of expressing ideas. School-learned writing often is done for one audience and for one purpose; the audience is typically the teacher, and the purpose is to win approval. Finally, early writers feel considerable freedom to write about whatever they want with few constraints about spelling, punctuation, or even content. (The author is reminded of a five-year-old niece who wrote a story about her cat's activities in the yard that communicated clearly but contained elements that are certainly not repeatable here). We might consider a story Read quoted from another five-year-old to note the freedom, expressability, and charm of these early stories:

HOO LICS HANE! WAS OV PONA TIM THER WAS OV BER HOO LOVE HANE THE EAD. (Translated) Who likes honey! Once upon a time there was a bear who loved honey. The end.[1]

Writings such as this often include some words that have been spelled by adults ("loved"), some words with clever spellings consistent with adult expectation about representation of sounds in print, if unconventional ("hoo"), and some nearly uninterpretable spellings ("ead" for "end"). The child writer had not yet learned all word boundaries ("ov pona" = "upon a") but more words are conventionally bounded by spaces than are not. In studying early writings, Read *(24)* found that children develop abstract systems for spelling that are later abandoned as they learn about conventional spellings in school. Meanwhile early writers learn a lot about the language and principles of writing, about audience and purpose for writing.

---

1. C. Read. *Children's Categorization of Speech Sounds in English.* Research Report No. 17, Urbana, Ill.: National Council of Teachers of English, 1975, pp. 15–16.

The language experience method of reading offers some of the advantages of early writing. While many of the first "stories" are dictated ones, children should be encouraged to begin to write their own stories as soon as possible. These stories should replicate the audience and purpose variety of messages written by early writers.

Stauffer *(29),* Hall *(12),* and Lee and Allen *(22)* offer a number of specific suggestions about how to stimulate and extend writing experiences. Basically, children need the following to begin their own writing: mechanical skills for formation of letters, essential concepts of grapheme/phoneme correspondence, internal resources for using concepts of correspondence, and external supports for finding words such as the word bank and simple dictionaries.

The teacher should respect the child's every attempt at early writing. It is crucial that children feel successful when they are applying their vocabulary directly, exploring their own thoughts, and expressing them in writing. Some children will be more creative than others; some will be better at the mechanics; some will have a wider vocabulary upon which to draw. These differences should not be used to differentiate the children, however, since critical comparisons will inhibit development. Nonetheless, differential reinforcement can be used to extend these beginning experiences. This reinforcement is directed to individuals in such a way that the children are praised and shown which aspects of their work are strong and which need attention. For example, with a child whose ideas are good but whose mechanical skills are not consistent, the teacher might say, "What wonderful ideas you have in your stories, John, and look at how well you are beginning to write with big, clear letters. The words on the top line here are especially clear." With a child who has difficulty getting her ideas across clearly, the teacher might say, "Yesterday's story about your family, Clare, was so well done. You told us first who is in your family and then what your apartment is like. Today try to tell us first one idea and then another in a new sentence."

Conventional spelling should not be one of the initial goals of early writing, for emphasis on it will interfere with the more important goal of communicating ideas. A teacher of language can encourage early independent writing by acting as a facilitator of spelling rather than as a supplier of words. Children should learn to use their banks, picture dictionaries, and displayed word charts (color words, weather words, clothing words) to find words they need and cannot figure out themselves. Often, however, a child will ask, "How do you write . . .?" The teacher ought to respond, "Well, say it again to yourself. What sound do you hear first? What letter do you think you should write? Good. Now, what do you hear next?" Children are encouraged to relate their growing sense of the relatedness between sound and writing to their efforts. By so doing, they are developing an actively induced system of sound and symbol which will reinforce both reading and writing success.

Many teachers and parents have expressed fear that early writing which encourages children to write words as they hear them rather than with memorized, correct spellings will result in the acquisition of bad spelling habits. However, with experience, the transition to conventional spelling does occur independently. Many unconventionally spelled words are changed to the conventional form after the children have realized for themselves that their word "luv" is written "love" in books. The teacher can juxtapose the child's word and the conventionally spelled word to hasten this change. Formal spelling usually begins in the second grade and ought to complement the growing sense of spelling accuracy by emphasizing the difficult words which have little sound/symbol correspondence.

Although many of the first self-written stories are brought home by the young author, it is a good idea to collect stories and illustrations on a theme into a book once the newness of the school experience has worn off a bit. Some techniques for bookmaking are:

1. A three-hole punch is used on each sheet, the holes are reinforced, and brass fasteners (or wide yarn) are used to hold the book together.
2. For more permanent books, each sheet is glued on oaktag, laminated, attached to others by strong masking tape, and bound with oaktag. Cardboard covered with bright material makes an attractive book cover.
3. Two or three stories can be glued to a single large chart, a paper cover made and attached to thick yarn in order to make a *huge* book.

Many cities have teacher stores where inexpensive materials for bookmaking and game production can be purchased. Furthermore, many stores have directions for making different kinds of books and sample copies of books.

Of course, some books should contain dictated stories that will continue to provide opportunity for full expression of ideas. Other books of self-written stories indicate clearly that the children's efforts are valued. These books should become part of the classroom library. Children delight in finding their stories and reading them to friends. On occasion, a child's self-written story should be dated and filed with his dictated stories to provide a source for evaluating growth of writing skill.

Classroom Organization

Language experience can be initiated with group experience stories. Groups of children who have observed the same event or have shared any experience can participate in dictating sentences for the group story. The teacher uses the group story as a medium for teaching reading much as described earlier in the chapter. The advantage of the group story is that it increases participation while still teaching a variety of words and structures. Stauffer *(29)* describes how group dictations can be used for assessment of reading readiness and for beginning reading instruction. Children can work with others who are at their approximate level of learning. While members of two groups are engaged at their seats in independent work, one group can be seated around a table. The same story stimulant can be introduced to the whole group by having the other members of the group practice with their underlined words, match their words with those in newspapers spread out before them, illustrate their intended or just completed stories, create sentences with their word bank words, and match each other's word bank words while the teacher takes individual dictation. After each child has dictated and reread his story, the group can listen to each other's stories.

If the teacher is able to develop interest centers that serve as the content of dictated and/or self-written stories, grouping is done by interest rather than achievement. When the teacher is working with each group, he takes dictation, reads with each child, and provides direction for further word practice or supplementary activity associated with the topic. Group organization is facilitated by stimulating activity. When children are excited by a proposed experience, it is much easier to organize them for on-task involvement than when a monotonous routine is followed. When beginning teachers complain about discipline difficulties and disorganization, an additional planned motivating experience is needed.

Suggestions for Language Experience Activities

Teachers using language experience need to be creative in stimulating both the dictated and the self-written stories and observations. The more the teacher relates the language experiences with on-going classroom units and other activities, the more relevant the program will become. The general categories of stimulants discussed here are personal experiences, scientific observations and learning, nature, picture storytelling, role-playing through words, and folk and family stories. Stauffer *(29)*, Lee and Allen *(22)*, Herrick and Nerbourg *(18)*, Hall *(12)*, and Allen and Allen *(1)* offer many more such possible stimulants.

Personal Experiences.   Sharing personal experience should be handled with care. The teacher should never expose a child's personal difficulties, but he and the others in the class should delight in a child's joy. The following are some suggestions for sharing personal experiences in the context of the language experience approach:

1. Introduction of the word "me" on the first day of first grade. The teacher, from that beginning, can carry out introductions in dictated stories that can be collected later into a book of self-portraits [see *A Day Dream I Had at Night (20)* for ideas on how to make books].
2. Illustrated and accompanying stories about the family.
3. Personal lists of "Things to Do."
4. Stories beginning with the following titles: "My Favorite Animal," "What I Hate to Do at Home," "My Favorite Relative," "The Most Beautiful Place I've Seen," "My Favorite TV Program," "My New Baby Sister," "What I Look Like," "My Mother," and "Our Trip."

Scientific Observations and Learnings.   Any simple experiment performed by the children can be translated into an experience story. Ongoing notes of observations are a good idea. Some suggestions in this area are:

1. Descriptions of how an electrical circuit is made.
2. Asking, "Which objects floated and which did not?"
3. Keeping a weather chart to record seasonal change.
4. Asking, "Which objects are attracted by magnets and which are not?"
5. Asking, "Which of these foods have seeds inside and which do not?"
6. Asking, "What would have happened to our plants without water . . without sun . . . with water . . . with sun, etc.?"
7. Developing the concept of measurement of size determined by strings, of weight determined by a simple frame, of temperature, and of measurement of liquids.
8. Descriptions of what happens when oil and water, sugar and water, and detergent and water are mixed.
9. Descriptions of the effect of freezing and boiling water.

Nature.   The world around the school environment is available to stimulate language experience no matter where the school is located. A few activities that can be related to language experience follow.

1. Descriptions of the difference between how people move around outside on a snowy day and on a warm day. The teacher can ask how grown-ups and children differ in how they move.

2. Descriptions of the construction (or demolition) of a nearby building.
3. Comparison of the school neighborhood with a contrasting one.
4. Listing all of the foods eaten by the class gerbil or guinea pig.
5. Descriptions of how the class animal cares for her young.

Picture Storytelling.   This activity is an almost too common way of eliciting stories from the children. Therefore, the teacher must take care in selecting the pictures. As a criterion for choice, he might think of what story he could tell from any given picture. A few suggestions to develop this activity follow.

1. Asking, "How would the children in the picture live differently from the children in the class?"
2. Telling what tools each worker uses by looking at pictures.
3. Beginning to develop a sense of people's diversity by looking at pictures of people from different cultures.
4. Drawing pictures of a classmate, describing him in writing without naming him, and participating in a classroom guessing game to name him.
5. Dictating a story to accompany picture books without words.

Role-Playing Through Words.   In order to maximize the development of abstract language, the teacher should encourage the children to imagine themselves in a new situation. Much motivational introduction is needed before asking the following questions:

1. What would it be like to be an inchworm on the stem of a plant?
2. What would it be like to be a pencil?
3. What would it be like to be the school secretary?
4. What would it be like to be a mother?
5. What would it be like to be a Christmas tree?
6. What would it be like to be a worm in an apple?

Folk and Family Stories.   In *A Day Dream I Had at Night (20),* Landrum describes how older children of diverse backgrounds collected family stories to use as reading materials. Some suggestions for similar activities follow.

1. Each child asks for a special story about his family to be retold and written at school. In a class of children of immigrant parents, the move to America would be a productive source of story material. Each family's celebration of Christmas also might provide material, as might the family's move to a new area.

2. Thinking up a folk tale after hearing the teacher read a number of folk tales and discussing with the teacher their common characteristics.
3. Planning fables to be written by the children after listening to *Aesop's Fables.*

Whatever techniques are used to stimulate language experiences, the teacher should be sure to allow interests to develop naturally from the stimulation that children bring to these programs. Although language experience is important to beginning reading, other components are also needed.

Texts and Tradebooks

It was stated earlier that language experience is flexible enough to be combined easily with basal reading materials. Once children have acquired a basic stock of words in their word banks (50 to 75 words), they can profit from continued language experience lessons plus reading in basal texts. Language experience can also be combined in an individualized program that uses tradebooks (nontext publications) for reading instruction. This section suggests ways of using basal and individualized tradebooks.

Expansion of concepts, exposure to new vicarious experiences, and learning a variety of expressions all occur as children read material written by others. Just as children gain language understandings and reading comprehension ability from stories read to them *(23),* the opportunity for cognitive and language growth is just as limitless when they read alone. Children who have experienced the joy of learning and the pleasure associated with listening to a good story—and all should have—look forward to independent reading with positive anticipation. For example, one six-year-old said enthusiastically as she was acquiring a store of sight words and techniques for unlocking new ones, "Now I don't have to wait for you, my mother, or my father to read me a new story; I can read it myself as many times as I want!"

Children who have learned the basic concepts which are acquired with language experience and have acquired 50 to 75 sight words are ready for a planned program of reading in texts and/or tradebooks. The children will continue *writing* and *dictating* stories on occasion, but a major portion of the structured reading program will come now from this component. We will discuss practical suggestions for use of basal texts and then describe possible activities for use with tradebooks.

Use of Basal Texts in Beginning Reading

Basal texts have improved in a number of ways in recent years making them more suitable for combined instruction with language experience. Basal reading series offer teachers of beginning readers improved and interesting stories about animals, people in different cultural and community settings, fantasies, etc.; structured introduction and development of word recognition skills; group learning experiences; and vocabulary control. This last advantage needs explanation. As discussed in chapter 7, the control of vocabulary had been overemphasized in basal texts until recently. However, slow learning children need considerable repetition of new words, so purchase of basals with strict vocabulary control is recommended for them. Average and above average learning children, on the other hand, will profit from materials with increased rates of new word introduction (see chapter 7).

Generally, in classroom group reading situations, the instructional sequence includes the following components: discussion of story setting, introduction of vocabulary, development of purposes for reading, silent or oral reading, discussion of story meaning, rereading, and enrichment activities. In keeping with the declared goal of promoting independent, self-evaluating readers who comprehend the material and the author's message and who are developing skill in making and verifying predictions, we will make some adaptations to the conventional procedures for group reading.

Focus of Story.   Teacher's guides to basal series include a number of lesson objectives. However, in the author's experience children understand stories better when the reading lesson focuses on one or two basic ideas rather than on many. To plan lessons, teachers should first read the child's story and try to think of the major concepts in it that relate with their pupils' lives. These ideas should be written as objectives for learning with the other parts of the lesson also emphasizing these foci. For example, a focus objective for "Little Red Ridinghood" might be: Pupils will discuss Little Red Ridinghood's basic error. This focus will permeate the structure of the remainder of the lesson.

Story Setting.   It is important that children become acquainted with the setting and important concepts of a story before reading. Pictures and related stories and experiences are used to establish an understanding of the concepts and setting of stories. In the case of "Little Red Ridinghood" pupils might be shown pictures of deep woods.

Vocabulary Introduction.   Some teacher's guides suggest that every new word in a story be introduced carefully. However, if children are to *use* their word recognition techniques effectively, not all words should be identified before story reading. Those words which have unfamiliar *meaning* should be clarified by use of context and concrete reference whenever possible. Words the teacher feels the children will not be able to decode should be identified and after the children's attention has been drawn to the new words through matching activities, the words should be placed in context.

Development of Purpose for Reading. Children should learn that reading is done for a variety of purposes, and we should help them to develop these purposes. When the teacher directs children to read a story only for specific details, they will not learn to diversify their reading; however, when the purposes for reading have been set to attain higher understandings, comprehension will be improved *(17)*. Teachers can suggest that the children read to solve a mystery, to find needed information, to get to know a really weird adult, etc. If children are asked to predict the content or plot of a story from the information contained in the story title, interest is peaked. With "Little Red Ridinghood," a purpose question at the start of the reading might be: As you read the story, try to figure out what Little Red Ridinghood did that got her in trouble.

Oral Reading. When children first learn to read, they usually read orally. But soon after they move into the text reading component of the reading program, they should begin to learn to read silently. Early silent reading is recommended by a number of reading authorities, among them Spache and Spache *(27)* and Heilman *(15)*. There are a number of reasons for early acquisition of silent reading habits:

1. Swift, skilled reading is done silently. When reading orally, children cannot learn the behaviors associated with skilled reading.
2. When children read silently, all must read! By contrast, in typical oral round robin reading, individual children lose interest unless they are the ones reading orally.
3. Oral reading may overemphasize word calling to the detriment of comprehension, which is the real goal of reading.
4. Audience-pleasing behaviors, such as speechlike intonation, are needed for successful oral reading and are very difficult to acquire.

Silent Reading. To introduce children to silent reading, the teacher should first point out that older children and adults cannot be heard as they read. This "grown-up" reading behavior then motivates the children. The teacher then suggests that children try to whisper (and many will need to be shown what this means) their story. After this whispering has been practiced, the children are asked to read without making a sound. After a time, the teacher tells the children to read without moving their lips at all. While these behaviors are being acquired, the children should occasionally read material which is very easy for them. It is important to remember that it takes considerable time for children to acquire silent reading behaviors.

During silent reading (or oral if children have not yet reached the first reader level), teachers often expect children to read just a page or two at a time. This is called *guided reading* and is included in the lesson plans in teachers' guides. It is a good idea to provide a simple purpose for each section to be followed at each stopping point only by answers to the purpose question. One goal of the beginning reading program is to expand children's ability to attend to reading at longer and longer intervals, so teachers should try to lengthen portions of the story at each interval. The questions asked during reading concentrate on the story focus.

Follow-up Discussion.   The follow-up discussion should expand children's literal, interpretive, and evaluative understanding of the story. Good questions ask children which person in the story they liked best, why an event occurred, whether the story was true, what someone meant when they said _____, what the child would have done in a similar circumstance, and what _____ meant in the sentence _____. Follow-up questions develop the idea in the story focus. A few good questions for our example story might be: First, just what did Little Red Ridinghood do that was wrong? Why did she get into trouble? Would she have gotten into trouble if she had talked with someone else in the woods who stopped her?

Guszak *(10)* has shown that teachers tend to ask questions dealing with details contained in the content of the stories far more often than they ask the kinds of questions which elicit reasoning and analysis of the structures of the story. In his study, primary grade teachers were more inclined to ask detail questions than were intermediate grade teachers. Guszak believes that primary teachers are responding to the simple content of the stories found in primary-level readers. Spache and Spache *(27)* have pointed out that children read to fulfill the kinds of questions they have come to expect their teachers to ask. Yet it is possible for teachers to learn to ask questions which encourage interpretive, critical, and creative thinking *(21)*. Since reading comprehension ability requires more than recall of story details, teachers must learn to ask children questions which promote important comphehension skills. These skills include the ability to draw inferences from the content, to recognize the writer's purpose, to understand the organization of the material read, and to understand word meaning *(28)*. Sanders *(25)* is one source for learning to ask good questions.

Rereading of a Story.   This activity is not always necessary, but it provides an opportunity to practice *oral* reading if the story is first read silently. Rereading is good practice if done with a purpose. Oral rereading is effective when children read a story again to prove a point raised during a discussion, when they practice to prepare for reading aloud to parents, and when they read to younger children. However, it is not necessary for the teacher to listen to children read orally every day. An appropriate purpose for oral rereading of "Little Red Ridinghood" might be to read the part that shows the first wrong thing she did, then the next, etc.

Enrichment Activities.   Extension of the content or topics of stories should often accompany reading experiences. Further reading on the same topic, reading other stories by the same author, play reading, dramatic improvisation, oral poetry reading, illustrating the story setting, and writing or dictating an alternate ending are just a few possible follow-up activities. With the example story, children might be asked to draw an illustration of something they could do wrong while doing an errand that could get them into trouble. Thus, in each component of the reading lesson, the story focus is emphasized and ultimately related with the children's real experience.

Alternative Group Reading Structure.   The Directed Reading-Thinking Activity (DRTA) described by Stauffer *(30)* encourages active positive reading experiences. With the DRTA, children constantly make predictions about story content—first, from the title and pictures alone; then, from the information of the first paragraph; then, from the first page; and so on. As the reading progresses, predictions are tested and verified and further predictions are refined. As children disagree about predictions and discuss the reasons for their predictions, they attend to the author's organization, the development of the characters, significance of the setting, and the details described in the setting. With this method, the teacher acts only as a guide to the strategies of prediction and verification used by the children.

Use of Tradebooks in Beginning Reading

In recent years, a number of books have been published which have a low vocabulary load but also have a varied content and are appealing to beginners [see *(9, 26, 8)*, and Groff for lists of easy-to-read books]. While some of these books are available in paperback and can be bought in quantity for group reading experiences like those described, some reading should be individualized to provide for personalized interests and growth.

When children choose a book, read it, and enjoy it, they should share their reactions with their classmates. Some activities to promote sharing include:

1. *Book Salesman:* In order to win a ticket that allows him to receive another book from the class library, each child must "sell" his book to a classmate.
2. *Book Recommendation Period:* Children display their books and suggest why a classmate would or would not enjoy them.
3. *Book Tree:* Children write the titles of their books on green paper leaves. After reading the title to the class, each child says one thing about his book and attaches the leaf to an upright leafless branch.
4. One child prepares to read the first page of his favorite book aloud to the others but refuses to tell what happens in the rest of the book.
5. *New Words:* Children add new and interesting words to a large chart entitled *Words from Good Books.*
6. *Book Categorization:* The children display their library books. In discussion, the children decide into what groups they could put the books. For example, one might have "Real" and "Not Real" as categories. Another might find "Animals," "People," and "Earth Books" an adequate system for grouping.
7. *Favorite Books:* In this activity, both self-read and teacher-read books are displayed. The children write the title of their first, second, and third preference.
8. *Jackets:* Covers of popular books are placed on a bulletin board. The authors' names are masked, but an envelope holds cards with each author's name. The children attach all the cards to the books and then check to see if they have named the authors correctly by lifting the masks.
9. *Dictated Stories:* When children are very familiar with one author, the teacher suggests a topic similar to the content of the author's books. As a group, the children dictate a story like the author's.
10. *Illustrating Books.* There are, of course, a number of ways for children to demonstrate their pleasure in books through art; for example, they can make new book jackets, design a diorama, illustrate a previously unillustrated scene, etc.

As children share their books in a variety of ways, they continue to add new words to their word banks. By this time in the beginning reading program, the word bank does not represent all the words the children can identify, but when the new words are written on cards (by the children now), they still are reinforced and practiced. The word bank becomes an effective source for follow-up activities.

Word Recognition

Throughout the chapters on reading there have been references to word recognition but little explanation about teaching recognition skills. The teaching of these skills is the content of this section. Usually by word recognition we mean major cue systems for figuring and naming words as beginners read. These systems include sight word recognition of known words and analysis of unknown words with phonics, structural analysis of word parts, and context. Since the first section of this chapter suggests techniques for helping children practice words to be recognized on sight, we discuss here only those skills that unlock unknown words: phonics, structural analysis, and context. It should be remembered that the goal of the analysis skills is to help beginners pronounce aurally known words and provide practice with them until these words become sight words.

Generally speaking, educators interested in beginning reading agree on the need to teach children ways to figure out unknown words. However, they disagree on which are the most helpful skills, how much study of skills is required for success, and the best method for teaching recognition skills. What is presented here is a suitable word recognition program for the first year of reading instruction; the program represents both research findings and the author's experience. Sample instructional sequences are included to serve as models for teaching skills.

Phonics

A first requirement for phonics instruction is that teachers have sufficient knowledge of phonics themselves. While we explain some terms and concepts in this section, readers may want to study more completely materials that teach phonics to teachers such as Durkin *(6)* or Burmeister *(3)*.

A second important issue in teaching phonics is the inclusion of every needed step in learning a new phonic element. Too often teachers fail to provide instruction in all the steps needed for use of a phonic principle in reading. The steps are: review of auditory discrimination of elements to make sure pupils perceive the sound(s) to be taught; review of the visual aspects of the phonic element in some cases; use of known words to establish the pattern or principle; statement of principle by pupils and teacher; application of principle to other words; transfer of principle to the reading of new words. This last step is often forgotten despite the fact that children may not naturally understand how to use a new phonic principle *(11)*.

A third critical issue is to decide which of the multitude of phonic elements should be presented. Recommended for the first year are these: single initial consonant sound/symbol relationships; simple consonant clusters or blends (two consonant graphemes that represent two phonemes as in "steam," "cloud," "bring"); simple phonograms (patterns of predictable spellings at ends of words as the *an* in "ran," or the *ing* in "ring"); consonant digraphs (two consonant graphemes that represent one phoneme as the *sh* in "shut" or the *th* in "that"); and basic vowel patterns.

The lessons below are models to be adapted in classroom teaching. The lessons can be part of the basal program. It is also possible to purchase separate phonics materials since such materials abound.

The *Phonics We Use (16)* workbooks and accompanying games are an old favorite in a new edition. Durrell and Murphy's *Speech-to Print Phonics (7)* is also excellent. Garrard Press supplies many inexpensive games to reinforce skills taught in class. Still other old favorites are the Levels A and B *Using Sounds* books *(2)* since these combine phonics skills with contextual analysis. In these few pages, it is not possible to describe fully the materials available to the teacher; however, in judging the merit of phonics materials, identification of the approach used and its relevance to the classroom program, clarity of the presentation, the amount of reinforcement and practice provided, and the motivational quality of the material should be considered.

In contrast to the instructional procedures used in the language experience part of the reading program to teach word recognition skills, we are interested in specific achievement of these skills; consequently, the instruction we advocate is more structured.

Initial Single Consonants.   Readiness training will provide information for initial assessment since the prerequisite understandings are perception of sounds and identification of letters. Once these have been acquired, children are ready to associate single consonant letters with sounds. It is important to note that in the instructional steps below, use is made of known word bank words.

Instructional Steps	*Lesson for p-/p/*
1. Review of sound of initial position.	1. Teacher asks children to listen to "pat," "pick,"

2. Recognition of letter in initial position.

"Peter," "Patty"; he then asks how these words are alike.

2. Teacher writes "pat," "pick," "Peter," and "Patty" on chart; he then asks if the words are alike and, if so, where and how.

3. Supplying of new examples by children.

3. Teacher asks children to look in their word banks for words that begin like "pat."

4. Differentiating which words belong and which do not.

4. Children write *P* on a worksheet for each picture that has the phoneme /p/ in initial position.

5. Application of new concept to new words. Nonsense words can be used to test application if children understand that the words are *not real ones.*

5. The teacher writes sentences on a chart with new words beginning with *p* (e.g., "Bobby *put* the toy away").

These instructional steps form a framework which should be amplified in creative ways. Planning may include a new single consonant sound/symbol correspondence each day for three days. The fourth day can be used for review. Common practice materials are workbooks, or children can create their own. On each page of the child-made book is the target letter on which children paste pictures representing the sound; these pictures are then labeled accordingly.

The sequence of letters introduced needs to be attended to since confusion may arise. For example, since /p/ and /b/, /t/ and /d/, /g/ and /k/, and /f/ and /v/ differ only by the presence or absence of *voicing* (caused by vibrations of the vocal cords), these elements should not be presented next to each other. Furthermore, the instances when two graphemes make one sound should follow the single grapheme/phoneme correspondences. A recommended order is: *p*/p/, *s*/s/, *m*/m/, *t*/t/, *f*/f/, *g*/g/, *b*/b/, *l*/l/, *n*/n/, *d*/d/, *j*/j/, *c*/c/, and *k*/k/, *v*/v/, *r*/r/, *w*/w/, *h*/h/, *z*/z/.

Consonant Clusters.   This area includes situations in which *two consonant graphemes* are heard as *two consonant phonemes:* for example, *st* in "stop" and *cl* in "cluster." (The word "cluster" also has the *st* cluster in the middle). Study of phonograms will include final consonant clusters, but we are concerned first only with initial clusters. The instructional steps are similar to those already presented, but they also include review of each single consonant.

Instructional Steps	*Lesson for cl - /cl/*
1. Review of initial sound.	1. Teacher asks children to identify the initial sound in "can," "cup."
2. Review of other phoneme.	2. Teacher asks children to identify the initial sound in "loud," "lap."
3. Auditory experiences with combined consonant phonemes.	3. Teacher asks children to listen to the combined sound in "cloud," "clam," "close," etc.
4. Visual identification.	4. Teacher presents children with written words "cloud," "clam," "close," etc., and they identify graphic similarities.
5. Children find *cl* words in their word banks.	5. Children supply new examples.
6. Teacher presents new *cl* words in sentence context.	6. Applying new concepts to new words.

Some early important consonant clusters to present are: *st, bl, sp, sn, sk, sl, pl, fl* (*r* clusters in *gr, br, dr, tr, fr,* and *str* are more difficult). Instruction should involve a number of review lessons. Achievement is examined on the auditory level and, more importantly, in use in new words presented in sentence context.

Simple Phonograms. As soon as the children are relatively familiar with the initial single consonants, they can be exposed to some familiar phonograms. At first, teachers help children substitute a single consonant in a phonogram to make a new word; later, the children are encouraged to make their own substitutions with these phonograms so that many new words can be formed (e.g., *-an, -et, -og, -ig, -ed, -ag, -ay, -in, -at, -op, -ell, -all*).

The following list contains some word families with single consonants:

pan	bed	big	pay	cat
man	Ted	dig	may	bat
tan	fed	fig	day	mat
fan	red	jig	bay	sat
can	Ned	pig	say	fat
ran		wig	hay	hat

Once initial consonant clusters have been learned, the following
words (and others) can be added:

span	bled	stay	flat	stop
plan	sled	play	skat	flop
	Fred			

And when the phonograms themselves include final consonants clusters,
these are some more additions to the list:

pest	past	hand	sold	sent	melt
test	fast	sand	told	tent	felt
best	last	land	fold	bent	belt
nest	vast	band	gold	dent	
vest		stand	bold		
			cold		
			hold		

Prerequisite to any inductive use of phonograms is an understanding of
rhyme; this concept should be thoroughly developed during the readiness
period. An instructional procedure for developing independent substitutions of consonants in phonograms follows.

Instructional Steps	*Lesson for -ay*
1. Presentation of known words in a pattern.	1. Teacher reminds children that they know the words "say" and "day."
2. Recognition of rhyme and and graphic similarity.	2. Teacher encourages children to identify two common elements of -*ay:* rhyme and letters.

3. Making a new word.

3. Teacher writes "pay"; children identify graphic similarity; they use rhyming and pronounce word.

4. Supplying new and additional words.

4. Children suggest "may" and "hay" and then search for more examples from their word banks.

5. Making application to new words.

5. Each child pronounces new words: for example, "bay" and "way."

Consonant Digraphs. Digraphs contain two letters but have only one consonant sound. They are few in number (*sh, ch, th,* and *-ng*) but are used extensively; as a result, digraphs are often found early in reading instruction. A possible procedure for instruction of *sh* is:

Instruction Steps	*Lesson for sh*
1. Presentation of oral known words.	1. Teacher asks children to listen to beginning sounds of "shoe," "shut" and supply another word.
2. Assessment of auditory discrimination.	2. Teacher asks children to raise hands only if they hear words beginning like "shoe": "slip," "sham," "church," "shore."
3. Search for pattern in known words.	3. Teacher asks how many letters make one sound in "shoe," "shut."
4. Statement of pattern.	4. Teacher asks children to state number of letters and number of sounds *sh* make and what sound *sh* has.
5. Application to other words.	5. Children read words with *sh*.
6. Transfer.	6. Children presented with nonsense words "shum" and "shob" to pronounce after explanation that they are made-up words.

Basic Vowel Patterns.   Some rules for vowel patterns are useful in that they work with most of the cases; others are not useful. Among the useful ones *(14)* is the short vowel pattern (the vowel sounds heard in "hat," "bed," "hit," "hot," "cup"). In this pattern the short vowel is heard when the vowel is in the middle of a one-syllable word. A less useful rule, but one common to beginning reading programs, is that in words with a vowel, consonant, *e* ending, the *e* is silent and the preceding vowel is long. (A long vowel is the vowel in "day," "me," "ice," "hope," "use.") Although some programs teach the rule that two vowels together result in the first vowel being long and the second silent, the productive vowel pairs are *oa, ai,* and *ee.* Another common vowel pattern taught young children states if there is only one vowel and that vowel is at the end of a word, the vowel sound is long—true of "me," "go," and "so," but not of "to." Not all these principles need to be taught the first year, but it is common for the short vowel pattern to precede study of long vowel patterns and for most to be taught early in reading instruction. Teachers need to concentrate only on the productive principles. Furthermore, it is important to remember that many Black English speakers and many children whose first language is Spanish will have difficulty discriminating the vowel sounds, particularly short vowel sounds.

A lesson, in shortened form, for teaching the long vowel pattern in the vowel pair *oa* might include: first, assessment to find if children can discriminate the long vowel sounds; second, presentation and discussion of the pattern *oa* in the familiar words "boat," "coat," "goal"; next, statement of the principle; and finally, application to other words to be read.

To conclude the section on phonics, the thorough teaching of a few productive principles of sound/symbol relationships is viewed as more important than learning of many principles that may include unproductive ones. Of great importance to the phonics program is the development of children's ability to combine word study with context.

Structural Analysis

Inflections.   Because children use inflections in their oral speech and can understand the meanings associated with inflections when decoding speech, it is a relatively simple matter to teach understanding of these forms when they are met in print. Most language experience stories and beginning basal stories will have these inflections: *noun plurals* (-s, -es); *verb endings* (-s, -ed, -d, -ing) (spelling changes on verbs may include doubled consonants as in "stopping" and "stopped" or deletion of *y* in such words as "carries" and "tries"). When a child has used a plural noun "pots," for example, the root word is presented separately ("pot"), and the child pronounces it. The teacher then asks the child to say the word he uses "when there are two of them." The child can then be directed to listen for the last sound heard when he says "pots." The identified *letter for sound* is added to the printed singular form, and he is told that when more than one is meant, people usually write an *s* at the end of the word. The same procedure can be used for the other inflections. When inflections have resulted in doubled consonants or a deleted *y,* children usually have little difficulty *reading* the words; confusion arises in *spelling,* a matter for more advanced training.

Compound Words.   Early in their reading children come upon words made up of two separate words: "into," "outside," "grandfather." While it produces confusion to teach children to "look for the little words" because of such anomalies as "fat her" in "father," it is a good idea to show pupils how a true compound word contains the meaning elements of the two shorter words while word division of "father" does not.

Other Areas.   During the first year of reading, children come across contractions, possessive markers, and abbreviations. Simple explanations are usually enough to help children use their language understanding to decode the meanings of these conventions. It is far easier to understand the meaning signified by apostrophes than it is to use them in writing; for reading instruction only receptive understanding is necessary.

Use of Context

In Chapter 5, we observed that children naturally use context to figure out words. Explicit instruction in use of context plus sound/symbol awareness will increase the efficiency of contextual use and will also provide experiences which may promote the development of skilled reading behavior. Instruction begins with oral activities. The teacher asks for all possible words which could fit into these sentences:

> The boy jumped over the _____.
> The man walked into the _____.
> The _____ cat ate his supper.

When language-experience reading is underway, the teacher can extract sentences from the children's dictations, write them on the chalkboard leaving a blank, and proceed as in the above cases. Once the children have become accustomed to this procedure, they can make sentences from the word cards in their word banks leaving a space on the table for a word. Another child tries to find a card in his bank to complete the sentence sensibly. Activities to promote use of context proceed to those which more closely resemble the behavior which occurs in reading. Again, using sentences dictated by the children, the teacher can offer two words from which to choose to better complete a sentence. At first, the correct responses will be obvious as in:

We looked under the _____ (tree, run).

After practicing with sentences like these and emphasizing what makes sense, the children should realize that the choices should be words which have more graphic similarity.

Once children understand the concept of choosing words that are grammatically sound, the instruction should proceed to incorporate sound/symbol correspondences with context. A way of showing children how use of initial single consonants will help them figure out an unknown word is to first present a sentence with no graphic clues:

My sister likes to wash the _____.

All the possible nouns should be elicited from the child. Then, the teacher should say that he will give a hint and add the grapheme *d* at the left of the blank. The children should choose which of their possibilities now fits. They would be encouraged to describe the help given by the initial consonant. After a number of these experiences, initial consonant clusters can become the clues. Finally, the teacher might want to devise situations in which initial letters would not be sufficient clues. Thus, in the sentence, "I put on my c_____," "clothes," "cape," or "coat" might fit in the blank. The teacher could then add "ape" to complete the experience, and the children would learn to use the graphic content at the *end* of the word. The children will eventually learn to ask the following questions when meeting an unknown word in their reading: What word do I know that would make sense here? What word do I know that makes sense and begins (ends) with an_____? The children then learn to read the sentence with the chosen word in order to evaluate their hypotheses themselves. If the sentence still does not make sense, use is made of the sound relatedness of the letters at the end of the word.

In conclusion, the beginning reading program ideally allows for both pupil and teacher creativity. Children approach and learn important reading concepts and initial vocabulary through language experience. The more structured word recognition program provides them with techniques for becoming independent readers, while in the group and individual reading of texts and tradebooks, they apply their ability to read independently as they grow in vocabulary, language, and experiential knowledge.

Selected Activities

1. Try to list all the advantages of the language experience approach to the teaching of reading. Include some that are not mentioned here. Then make a list of the difficulties you imagine you might encounter trying to teach with it.

2. Select a good stimulation for a language experience story and try to get a five- or six-year-old to dictate his/her responses to the stimulation. Immediately read the story back with the child. Do the same activity several days later to see if the child's output has increased.

3. Find a good story from a basal pre-primer, primer, or first reader. State a focus you think beginners would be interested in.

4. Compare your focus (3 above) with the objectives in the teachers' guide.

5. Find a good, easy-to-read tradebook, write a focus, plan to teach important words, and present the book as a reading lesson to a beginning reader, following the recommended procedure.

6. Write a lesson plan for teaching the *ch* digraph.

7. Identify the phonic element underlined in each of the following words:

broke_____   fit_____

through_____   street_____

week_____   amaze_____

begin_____

References

1. Allen, R. V., and Allen, C. *Language Experience in Reading.* Chicago: Encyclopedia Britannica Educational Corporation, 1968.
2. Boning, R. A. *Using Sounds.* Rockville Center, N. Y.: Barnell Loft, 1962.
3. Burmeister, L. E. *WORDS—From Print to Meaning.* Reading, Mass.: Addison-Wesley, 1975.
4. Dolch, E. W. *Problems in Reading.* Champaign, Ill.: Garrard, 1948.
5. Durkin, D. "The Achievement of Preschool Readers: Two Longitudinal Studies." *Reading Research Quarterly* 1 (1966): 5–36.
6. Durkin, D. "A Six Year Study of Children Who Learned to Read in School at the Age of Four." *Reading Research Quarterly* 10 (1974-75): 9–61.
7. Durrell, D., and Murphy, H. *Speech-to-Print Phonics,* 2d ed. New York: Harcourt, Brace, Jovanovich, 1972.

8. Groff, P. "Recent Easy Books for First-Grade Readers." *Elementary English* 37 (1960): 521-27.
9. Guilfoyle, E. *Books for Beginning Readers.* Champaign, Ill.: National Council of Teachers of English, 1972.
10. Guszak, F. "Teacher Questioning and Reading." *The Reading Teacher* 21 (1967): 227-34.
11. Gibson, E. and Levin, H. *Psychology of Reading.* Cambridge, Mass.: The M.I.T. Press, 1975.
12. Hall, M. *Teaching Reading As A Language Experience,* 2d ed. Columbus, Ohio: Charles E. Merrill, 1976.
13. Hall, M.; Moretz, S. A.; and Staton, J. "Writing before Grade One—A Study of Early Writers." *Language Arts* 53 (1976): 582-85.
14. Harris, L. A. and Smith, C. B. *Reading Instruction Through Diagnostic Teaching.* New York: Holt, Rinehart and Winston, 1972.
15. Heilman, A. W. *Principles and Practices of Teaching Reading,* 4th ed. Columbus, Ohio: Charles E. Merrill, 1977.
16. Heilman, A. W.; Helmkamp, R.; Thomas, A. S.; Carselle, C. J., consultants. *Phonics We Use.* Chicago: Lyons and Carnahan, 1968.
17. Henderson, E. H. "A Study of Individually Formulated Purposes for Reading." *Journal of Educational Research* 59 (1965): 438-41.
18. Herrick, V. E., and Nerbourg, M. *Using Experience Charts with Children.* Columbus, Ohio: Charles E. Merrill, 1964.
19. Johnson, D. P. "The Dolch List Reexamined." *The Reading Teacher* 24 (1971): 449-57.
20. Landrum, R., and Children. *A Day Dream I Had at Night and Other Stories: Teaching Children How to Make Their Own Readers.* New York: Teachers and Writers Collaborative, 1971. (Available from NCTE.)
21. Lanier, R. J., and Davis, A. P. "Developing Comprehension through Teacher-Made Questions." *The Reading Teacher* 25 (1972): 153-57.
22. Lee, D. M., and Allen, R. V. *Learning to Read through Experience.* New York: Appleton-Century-Crofts, 1963.
23. Porter, J. "Research Report." *Elementary English* 49 (1972): 1028-37.
24. Read, C. *Children's Categorization of Speech Sounds in English.* Research Report No. 17. Urbana, Ill.: The Council of Teachers of English, 1975.
25. Sanders, N. M. *Classroom Questions: What Kinds?* New York: Harper and Row, 1966.
26. Spache, E. B., and Spache, G. A. *Good Reading for Poor Readers.* Champaign, Ill.: Garrard, 1968.
27. Spache, G. D., and Spache, E. B. *Reading in the Elementary School,* 2d ed. Boston: Allyn & Bacon, 1969.
28. Spearrit, D. "Identification of Subskills of Reading Comprehension by Maximum Likelihood Factor Analysis." *Reading Research Quarterly* 8 (1972): 92-111.
29. Stauffer, R. C. *The Language Experience Approach to the Teaching of Reading.* New York: Harper and Row, 1970.
30. _____. *Directing the Reading-Thinking Process.* New York: Harper and Row, 1975.

Index